T0036935

PRAISE FOR
FAT OFF, FAT ON:
A BIG BITCH MANIFESTO

"In her inspiring, no-holds-barred memoir, Clarkisha Kent puts her story out there for all to witness. Her writing is hilarious and intimate, like you're talking to your best friend over drinks at the bar. Kent's debut is a celebration of intersectional identity, heralding a bright, essential new voice."

—**GABRIELLE UNION**, actress and author of
You Got Anything Stronger?: Stories

"Clarkisha Kent has long proven herself to be one of the funniest and sharpest voices in new media. But with her debut memoir, she establishes herself as an absolute force of nature. *Fat Off, Fat On* is full of honesty, wit, and stunning vulnerability that encourages us to reexamine our relationships with our own bodies and how we show up for ourselves."

—**FRANCHESCA RAMSEY**, author of *Well, That Escalated Quickly: Memoirs and Mistakes of an Accidental Activist*

"*Fat Off, Fat On* is funny and smart as hell. Kent's personal story is steeped in an incisive analysis of fatphobia, misogynoir, colorism, racism, sexism, and ableism. As always, listen to Black women, especially Clarkisha Kent."

—**ALICE WONG**, author of *Year of the Tiger: An Activist's Life*

"Heartbreaking, honest, and still somehow wryly hilarious, Clarkisha Kent challenges readers in *Fat Off, Fat On* to not only read about her life but to think about their own. Whether you relate to the pop culture references, the family dynamics, or the awkwardness of sex and dating, Kent reaches deep into herself to show her audience a mirror and in many ways a lifeline to find the words for their own stories. This is a book you will read and reread as you come to terms with your history and your future."

—**MIKKI KENDALL**, author of *Hood Feminism: Notes from the Women That a Movement Forgot*

"*Fat Off, Fat On* feels like a revelation in honesty, humor, heart, and craft. I have long been a fan of Clarkisha's, and this book solidifies that I will continue to be for many years to come. A must-read!"
—**KEAH BROWN**, author of *The Pretty One:*
On Life, Pop Culture, Disability,
and Other Reasons to Fall in Love with Me

"Clarkisha Kent lays it all on the line to bring her moving, emotional, and complicated journey toward self-love to life. Kent's ability to frame high-level concepts like fatphobia, colorism, anti-Blackness, and family-induced trauma around her personal stories make for a simultaneously entertaining and educational read. *Fat Off, Fat On* will help us all confront the negative thoughts we have about ourselves, interrogate how those thoughts manifested in the first place, and give us hope that confronting our personal demons is way better than allowing them to run our lives."
—**LESLIE MAC**, digital strategist and movement auntie

"*Fat Off, Fat On* is one of the most captivating books I've read in a long time. Clarkisha Kent tells her story in such an unapologetic light, and as a reader, I hung on to every word. Clarkisha is a dear friend, and I'm blessed to not just read her truth but to fervently support such a work that I feel everyone should read."
—**VILISSA THOMPSON**, LMSW, founder of Ramp Your Voice!

"In her stunning debut memoir, Clarkisha Kent explores the impact of colorism, fatphobia, church trauma, familial abuse, disability, and queerphobia on her journey toward being at home in her body and with herself. Raw, comical, and thoughtful, *Fat Off, Fat On* is a survival story with a heroine you can't help but root for."
—**BROOKE OBIE**, award-winning author of
Book of Addis: Cradled Embers

"Screaming, crying, and cackling are just a few of the words I can use to describe what reading *Fat Off, Fat On* was like. Clarkisha Kent artfully weaves together years of love, loss, joy, and sorrow into a tear-jerking, smile-inducing memoir that perfectly chronicles all the things that make life worth living and leaves you wanting more even as you reach the last page."
—**KESHAV KANT**, executive director of Off Colour

"Clarkisha Kent's searing humor, intelligence, and vulnerability are imbued within every single page of *Fat Off, Fat On*."
—**PAULA AKPAN**, journalist and historian

"Clarkisha Kent's *Fat Off, Fat On* is a scintillating work of humor and intellect. A masterful storyteller, Clarkisha crafts chapters with precision, where pop cultural references live alongside difficult memories of trauma, both apt and optimistic. Her manifesto allows for multiple truths, but from her rare, informed, and personable perspective."

—**TRISH BENDIX**, writer and contributor to the *New York Times*

"Clarkisha Kent is a writer whose work you can hear in your heart. She continues to absolutely raise the bar on what it means to write with courage and authenticity. I laughed, I cried, and I felt enraged. I sat a bit more comfortably in my own fatness and identity. Truly a transformative work, and I couldn't be prouder to add *Fat Off, Fat On* to my bookshelf."

—**MARS SEBASTIAN**, author, producer, and essayist

"*Fat Off, Fat On* gives vulnerable and honest insight into the coming of age(s) of Clarkisha Kent, never missing a slice of humor in its discussion of difficult topics. Kent's writing challenges us to hold the complexities of our experiences without shame, regret, or the burden of respectability."

—**SYDNEYSKY G**, writer and fat liberation advocate

"Filled with pain and humor, *Fat Off, Fat On* is an explosive read. By read, I mean drag. Clarkisha Kent reflects on her past and, in turn, delivers a story that holds a mirror to many parts of our own lives existing at intersections of oppression. This is a book you need two copies of: one to share with friends and another to keep in reserve when your friend 'loses it.'"

—**DARKSKYLADY**, writer and Rotten Tomatoes–approved film critic

"Clarkisha Kent's distinctive, powerful voice flourishes on the page in *Fat Off, Fat On*. She's candid and sharp in recounting some of the most vulnerable moments in her life as a young millennial—specifically as a fat, disabled, queer Black woman existing in America. *Fat Off, Fat On* is incisive in its critique of systemic oppression, and Kent's warmth, wit, and humor evoke a feeling of being in the room with her as she traces her journey back home to her Self and her body. Readers can expect to cackle, scoff, gasp, and cry their way through this book, and will get to the last page wanting more. Kent's debut memoir is a healing balm in these chaotic times and a testament to the restorative power of introspection and storytelling."

—**ROSLYN TALUSAN**, culture writer

CLARKISHA KENT

FAT OFF FAT ON

A BIG BITCH MANIFESTO

THE FEMINIST PRESS
AT THE CITY UNIVERSITY OF NEW YORK
NEW YORK CITY

Published in 2023 by the Feminist Press
at the City University of New York
The Graduate Center
365 Fifth Avenue, Suite 5406
New York, NY 10016

feministpress.org

First Feminist Press edition 2023

Copyright © 2023 by Clarkisha Kent

All rights reserved.

 This book is supported in part by an award from the
National Endowment for the Arts.

 This book was made possible thanks to a grant from the
New York State Council on the Arts with the support of
Governor Kathy Hochul and the New York State Legislature.

No part of this book may be reproduced, used, or stored in any information
retrieval system or transmitted in any form or by any means, electronic,
mechanical, photocopying, recording, or otherwise, without prior written
permission from the Feminist Press at the City University of New York, except
in the case of brief quotations embodied in critical articles and reviews.

First printing March 2023

Cover and text design by Drew Stevens
Cover photograph by Monica Escamilla

Library of Congress Cataloging-in-Publication Data is available for this title.
ISBN 978-1-952177-74-3

PRINTED IN THE UNITED STATES OF AMERICA

To my teacher, Machel Mills-Miles.
To my teacher, Elaine Plummer.
To my teacher, Jane Fetters.
To my teacher, bell hooks.
To my teacher, Alice Walker.
To my teacher, Toni Morrison.

Thank you for taping my wings
back together so I could fly.

CONTENTS

MY GRAND OPENING

My favorite show in all of existence is *Scrubs* (as proven by the titles of each chapter). Well . . . let's run that back. My *second*-favorite show of all time is *Scrubs*. It used to be my first, but since I am now aware that *BoJack Horseman* exists, an addendum was needed.

Barring the horse show, I love *Scrubs* more than life itself. More than air. Perhaps even more than food—with which I have a sordid relationship that borders on the absurdity of the "will they, won't they" relationship between one John Dorian and Elliot Reid. As you will soon find out.

Still. Part of the eternal appeal of *Scrubs*—even as its age is beginning to show—to me is its central protagonist, Dr. John "J.D." Dorian. J.D. starts his journey in the famed medical dramedy as a hapless young adult who teeters on the precarious and metaphorical seesaw of being excessively and narcissistically confident in his abilities as a young doctor (throughout the series) and being pathetic yet highly relatable in his failed attempts at trying to navigate adulthood, life, religion, health, sex, and love. It's this tense relationship that he has with self-confidence and deep insecurity that kept me coming back. That kept me wanting more. That made him exceedingly relatable to me.

Particularly because he is shown as being highly similar to, if not a bit sappier than, his mentor and reluctant father figure, Dr. Percival "Perry" Cox. The best and quickest way to describe

Dr. Cox would be to dial up the narcissistic confidence to 1.2 billion, mute the nagging and internal insecurity, throw in a clear substance abuse problem, mix in an aversion to interpersonal relationships, and add a weird Superman-meets-Wolverine complex on top like it's a cherry on a sundae. The caustic, brilliant, and deeply flawed and traumatized Dr. Cox is both ally and adversary to J.D., simultaneously pushing him to be great, tearing him down when he seemingly can't reach that greatness, and recoiling at how often the young doctor reminds him of himself.

It's a fictional relationship that I've come to appreciate a lot, particularly because my thoughts on both characters have evolved from viewing one as a dickhead and the other as a nincompoop to viewing them as two sides of the same coin.

I share J.D.'s occasionally misplaced optimism and doe-eyed terror at life while maintaining that I can *totally* get through it all with my astounding brain and stupendous ability to put pen to paper. I also share Dr. Cox's unstoppable pessimism and "it is what it is" philosophy that life is the shittiest thing there is and that as a human being who was inadvertently placed on this Earth after your asshole father declined to skeet into a dirty sock or balled-up Kleenex, it is your job to get through it the best way you know how—and with the hope that you minimize any damage you could possibly do to anyone else.

Of course, this admission that I readily relate to both characters presents a couple of problems, but the chief among them is the fact that these are two grown-ass white men that I'm admitting I identify with. To be clear, there's nothing wrong with identifying with fictional characters who look absolutely nothing like yourself. But as a dark-skinned, fat Black woman who is bisexual and disabled, I could not be more *different* than the two of them. This begs the question:

Where's the Black female version of J.D. and Dr. Cox? The dark-skinned one? The bisexual version? The disabled one? Or even the fat one? I have no answer. But it would have been nice to have those versions of these characters as people to look to while I was growing up.

I know, I know. Blah, blah, blah, the whole "representation matters" slogan doesn't really hold up because it *usually* results in surface-level "diversity and inclusion" that doesn't translate into any type of social or material change. Not to mention, politicians of the 2010s and 2020s have beaten that sentiment to death, nominating people to power that might look like my Black ass but endorse policies that would most certainly *kill* my Black ass.

However.

A fat, dark-skinned little Black girl with 4C hair is not gonna wanna hear all that bullshit about the politics behind the aforementioned slogan. On the contrary, they're going to go by what they see, read, or hear—particularly on TV. Or in movies. Or in their favorite books.

In *Salvation: Black People and Love*, bell hooks (RIP) recalls gleaning life lessons as regards race from (segregated) mass media. TV in particular. She mentions that such media was a "constant reminder" of her "subordinated status" as a Black child. bell reinforces the intentions behind such media when she talks about how three-dimensional images of Blackness were nearly erased by white-dominated media as backlash to any gains garnered by civil rights struggles.

This is of particular note because whether we like it or not, under a capitalist system where parents barely have enough time or energy to invest in *properly* parenting the children that were dragged into this realm of existence, TV shows and movies do a lot of heavy lifting in terms of "raising" kids, or at the very least serve as the origin behind viewpoints that have a fifty-fifty chance of getting carried to adulthood.

Most of these viewpoints will be bigoted and biased against a marginalized group or class. Prompted by whatever social radioactive waste that said child-turned-adult observed while coming up on such media. Hell, not even *Scrubs* is immune to this, considering its diet homophobia, the . . . *interesting* way Turk's Blackness is discussed, its constant and unchallenged (medical) fatphobia, the ceaseless misgendering that occurs between Dr. Cox and J.D., and the bizarre, anti-Black "running joke" that was killing Laverne off just to bring actress Aloma Wright back as another Black nurse that *coincidentally* looked like dearly departed Laverne. And, you know, much, *much* more. Because of this, it's up to newly minted adults to figure out which viewpoints are truly worth keeping and which viewpoints need to be unceremoniously yeeted into the sun.

Part of my own grand journey has revolved around me sifting through positive and toxic viewpoints. Both about my own body and about the world around me. Many of said "viewpoints" and the messaging I received while growing up (from parents to peers to media and general society) greatly affected my capacity to see myself as human. Or rather, it colored what "humanity" looked like to a fat, Black, dark-skinned little girl. And whether it was my destiny to be simultaneously invisible, hypervisible, and reviled in perpetuity.

And most of this journey and examination of this "destiny" is documented in this book.

I'm not claiming that this book is going to be a magical healing balm to anyone who happens to relate to the issues raised in it. Nor am I claiming that it holds the secret answers of the universe in terms of eradicating fatphobia (and every -ic OR -ia and -ism that decides to latch on to it) on both a personal and societal level.

What I *can* say is that I hope *Fat Off, Fat On* offers insight into the type of messaging that Black girls are perennially bombarded with as they attempt to navigate a world that would rather they not exist. And I hope it reassures them that they, too, have the right to be here.

That, yes, life is *also* the Black girl's birthright.

MY SHITTY FAMILY

You know the saying that goes "Charity begins at home"? You do? Good.

Because it's bullshit.

Well, I shouldn't go that far. The sentiment isn't *entirely* fictitious, but I will say that this idea of love and charity being common things that one comes across in "the home" just isn't as true as society would have you believe. If I *were* to rewrite the quote into something more seemingly relevant to not only myself but some of my immediate peers, I'd probably rewrite it as "*Insecurity* Starts at Home: Electric Boogaloo," or perhaps a more stinging one, like "Trauma begins at home."

Yes, dear loves, life is *not The Cosby Show*. Or *Family Matters*. Or *That's So Raven*. Or even *The Proud Family*. And as fate would have it, both of these quotes about life apply to me. I feel I came out pretty okay, all things considered; but there's no denying the fact that my family did quite the number on me where my self-respect and self-esteem are concerned.

In essence? I cut off my family. And I do not know those niggas.

When I tell people that my entire family is cut off, I usually get one of the following reactions:

— For real???
— Damn.
— Really? *Why?* (In a sad, annoying tone)

— Oh.
— That *really* sucks. Do you think y'all will ever work it out?
— Something, something, something . . . those are still your parents though. I hope y'all fix it.
— Awkward silence and mild embarrassment at having asked me whatever stupid-ass question that required background on my toxic family to begin with.

All of these answers are vexatious in their own way. But they are also very telling of the fact that, even today, people still cling to the idea that growing up with a warm and loving family is the norm, rather than an experience that is actually not all that common (in my experience). They couldn't bear to consider the fact that some childhood experiences are so ungodly that one would never, ever want to lay eyes on that randomized group of Sims one refers to as "family" ever again.

You've probably guessed by this point that I'm not overly fond of the concept of family. Truly. My base definition of such is "niggas who had the (mis)fortune of being born together and now have to decide if they actually like each other or if they just pretend to based on the proximity and responsibilities of birth."

My own take aside, "family" isn't appealing to me in other general iterations or definitions either. Particularly with how the concept is regarded in an American and/or Western context (in that it's more so regarded as an economic feature than anything else). But also with how, in its expanded form, it's touted as the thing to do or have. In the name of "tradition." Or else you are bankrupt in whatever way people deem fit to define you as bankrupt. It's all a bunch of nonsensical bullshit to me, but even I, as an impassioned detractor of "traditional" families, cannot begin to downplay their importance.

Or rather, the impact—disastrous or otherwise—they tend to leave on you as a being who exists.

I mean, think about it. "Traditional" families are typically the first "structure" you are introduced to upon birth. A mini-society even. And like most "structures," there is indeed a hierarchy, even in the most progressive of families. In this society where patriarchy is a thing, fathers are *usually* at the top, with everyone else on the bottom, organized according to varying degrees of importance. And even so, this structure will bring forth the very first social interactions that you are subject to and will determine how you interact with people for the rest of your life. Or until you figure it's time to learn new ways to interact with people. Many don't get to that latter point.

I'm trying to.

But to try to understand the inner trappings of "traditional family," and develop the right tools to properly put to rest— rather than bury—the trauma wrought by this particular unit, is usually a one-way ticket to understanding how shitty your family indeed was.

This leads me back to the subject of *my* shitty family.

Whenever I feel like engaging niggas on this level, I usually just say, "They're not good people."

Sometimes, the questioning persists instead of ceasing. And rather than immediately saying "mind your fucking business" (which, to be clear, is *extremely* effective), I settle by using this rather diplomatic zinger:

"Your familial experience is not my familial experience." And then it gets quiet.

Because it's all projection, right?

Of course, since I'm currently writing this book that is taking a deep dive into my life like an episode of *Forensic Files*, I don't have the luxury of telling you, dear reader, to mind your fucking business. Because you see, I have invited you straight into my business. Given you a front-row seat, even. And (some of) my business is exactly what I will be spelling out in as great detail as my bipolar II disorder will allow.

So, shall we start from the beginning? And by the beginning, I mean I'm gonna give you the typical origin-story spiel before I get to the, how do you say, "good stuff."

MY FATHER, Sunny Eduwa—to be clear, this is not his *actual* name, but because he's a *narcissist* and because I would *never* give him the satisfaction of being *recognized* in a public forum like a published *book*, this is going to be his name—immigrated to America from Nigeria (by himself) in the eighties, probably searching for the "American Dream" or whatever the fuck. The naive among you may assume that he went ahead to prepare a clear path for immigration and citizenship for my mother and sister, but no.

And at this point, part of a twenty-four-year-old Sunny's version of the "American Dream" included being able to properly sow his wild (American) oats solo-dolo. So, he left the twenty-three-year-old version of my mother, Caroline Eduwa, and the infant version of my sister, Kalindi Eduwa, behind in Nigeria.

For *twelve* years.

Don't even get me started on that time frame.

My father dove headfirst into fucking his way across fifty states while getting his nursing license. Because fuckbois need money and status too. He made pit stops in states like New York, Louisiana, and Tennessee, and eventually just settled on Tennessee because it was, in his own words, "dirt cheap." At least that's what I think he wanted us to believe. If you ask me, while Nigerians quite frankly sprout up everywhere across the globe like *weeds*, the likelihood of my father bumping into a Nigerian from his larger community (i.e., village especially) was incredibly high in places like New York or Michigan (where my mother had family). So, Tennessee, in his mind, was the least messy option.

But since fuckbois are messy by design and notorious for not knowing how to wrap shit up (I mean this quite literally), he created his own toxic situation in Tennessee by siring a second child, Rupert Eduwa, with a Black American woman by the name of Phyllis Johnson (which is *also* not her *actual* name— as I'm sure she has no desire to be mentioned anywhere near my father). And suddenly, his whoring days came to an abrupt halt with the arrival of his first child-support order.

It was then, and only then, that my father realized that he was truly not in *Nigeria* anymore.

Which, as you can probably guess, bred an incredible amount of resentment in him, which he thus directed at my brother, Rupert, and his mother, Phyllis. The latter who, thank Gaia, was smart enough to peep my father's "well-hidden" unhingedness and opted to keep herself and her baby in Memphis rather than moving to Nashville to be closer to him.

You may be asking, "Okay, but where do you enter the picture?" Excellent question.

After having to quickly get his act together upon the arrival of a second child, a couple of more years passed before he finally decided to bring my mom and sister over in the early nineties, where they briefly stayed together in a housing project in East Nashville. And if there weren't already cracks in my parents' relationship, fissures in their union made themselves known due to poverty and the existence of a love child.

Still. For some reason, they *still* decided to conceive and give birth to me, Alexandria, a year later. Even though it was clear that that was the worst fucking thing to do at the time. Just dense as fuck. And at the risk of sounding like my narcissistic progenitor, my birth was truly the most horrific turning point for my "family." Not because of anything I did in particular (I was a baby, after all) but because my birth set off a chain of unfortunate events.

Those who know narcissists well, particularly narcissists who are *parents,* know that children (especially *their* children) breed a specific type of hatred in them because they perceive said children as "competition" when it comes to garnering the attention of their toys—ahem, I mean *partners.* And for my father, this was also complicated by the fact that he dodged getting medicated for schizophrenia until I entered high school. Anyway, my father was already perpetually annoyed by Kalindi because she was entering her preteen/teen angst phase and required extra care from my mother. But when I arrived? Whew. You could truly see the smoke emerging from his ears if I so much as hiccuped, because guess what? Babies need even *more* care and attention.

My needing care as a baby meant that my mom got distracted from my father's narcissistic outbursts. And this act of "purposeful" neglect, which I'm sure is how my father viewed it, would eventually lead to the event that would hereby be referred to as The Terrible Thing That No One Talked About™.

"Stop ignoring me!" Kalindi screamed at my mother, who was screaming and crying back. Meanwhile, my father kept yelling "I didn't mean to" over and over again. "And stop lying! Fathers aren't supposed to 'touch' their daughters. Not like *that*," she said.

To this day, I cannot tell you what prompted that argument. Or what prompted them to rehash all of that when everyone was much, much older. Because I have no fucking idea. I can only tell you that I was eight at the time. Listening late at night on the stairs—out of sight and confused as fuck. I would then go on to side-eye the fuck out of my father *especially* for the foreseeable future.

Both my mother and father attempted to bury it. Sick, right? Especially on my mom's account. That bird-ass bitch. But secrets have this funny way of leaking out, even when we don't want them to. But no one would go on to expose that shit or talk about it at length until the summer of 2018 when I moved away. From all of them.

AS YOU can imagine, The Terrible Thing That No One Talked About™ had a huge ripple effect across the entire household. To be clear, its effects (since it occurred when I was still an infant) had been in place the entire time. But after overhearing that explosive conversation, I became acutely aware of the Eduwa household's *true* dynamics.

Such effects showed up in how my mom acted toward me as the second and last daughter. It showed up in my father's increasingly wicked and oppressive behavior—a byproduct of my sister being vocal and aware enough to call out the evil that had happened to her. Because how dare she be an outspoken young girl? Gasp!

It also showed up in how my sister quietly simmered and outwardly rebelled against my mother and father: doing things like breaking curfew, going out whenever she wanted, dating much older men, leaving my mom's fugly-ass church (to be discussed), and becoming hypersexual. Which, I'm sure, stemmed from her rightfully resenting my mother for not protecting her before the incident and definitely *failing* to do so in the aftermath.

Like, why was she still with this nigga? Exactly.

Unfortunately for me though, I was not spared from my sister's wrath.

For the longest time, I felt that my sister was mad resentful of me for maybe not being abused in a similar way.

That I *know* of, truth be told. That's how demented that household was.

Hand to God.

Her wrath leaped out of her in the form of angry outbursts directed at my fatness. It didn't matter that I was a *baby* when The Terrible Thing That No One Talked About™ happened. In her eyes, my arrival to this ghetto space rock was always going to be associated with that *thing*. And I also have no doubts that she latched on to tearing me down for being fat because, in her eyes, being fat, and thereby more "unattractive" than her, meant I was able to avoid any future abuse. Which in her view meant that I was able to avoid such situations—even though there's plenty of work out there that shows that being "ugly" will not spare one from abuse (because sexual abuse is never merely about looks anyway).

I'm especially talking to weird pick-me bitches who think

that this could never happen to them if they just do, say, or wear the right things.

One memorable instance of my sister's fat antagonism, besides her and my father taking turns referring to me as "Fatso" as a nickname, included her eating all my Chinese takeout leftovers when I was twelve. This was something my sister did frequently. She'd go out of her way to find something that I had put away in the fridge and gobble it right on up. This time though, I had been looking forward to eating the leftovers all day—because our cafeteria at school decided to serve some mysterious "chicken" patty that none of us trusted whatsoever.

"Has anyone seen my leftovers?" I opened the fridge for the third time as if they were going to suddenly reappear. I looked at my immediate younger brother, Craig, who was sitting at the dining table eating something that didn't look like my leftovers. He shrugged. My second-to-youngest brother, Jeffrey, was still at school. And Tommy?

Well, Tommy was four. Which immediately ruled him out as a suspect.

"Seriously. Where did my leftovers go!" I was getting increasingly irate.

"What the hell are you yelling about?" Kalindi walked into the kitchen. She easily bumped me out of the way, towering over me (remember, she has a good twelve years on me), and reached into the fridge for one of her daily Naked smoothies.

"Someone took my leftovers!" I replied.

"I took your leftovers." She was nonchalant as she closed the fridge.

"I was gonna eat that!" I yelled at her. She blinked at me, probably surprised that I had just yelled at her. Honestly, I was waiting for her to smack me. It was one of her other occasional pastimes. It was no secret in this house that I was everyone's primary and *favorite* punching bag. This isn't to say that my other siblings didn't get beaten or "whooped" either. But if you were to count the instances, you'd see that it happened to me more often. And sometimes quite more viciously—depending on who was doling out the beating. In descending order, the worst violence usually came from my father, Kalindi, and finally my mother.

I stared my sister down and awaited what I was certain was going to be a stinging slap. Instead, my sister got down to my level and smirked at me.

"You shouldn't be eating *anything* at all." She glared at me. "You fucking fatso."

Now that I'm older, I wish I would have just put my own life on the line to fight her. Like, I'm sure I would have died in the process, but I've been suicidal since I became aware of my existence at like four and it would have been so worth it to see the shock on her face after I presumably headbutted her in the face.

But I wasn't twenty-seven-year-old Alex. I was still twelve-year-old Alex.

So I burst into tears. Snotty, nasty-ass tears.

Kalindi stood back up like she was so proud of herself. Meanwhile, Craig, who was absolutely *terrified* of her, decided to speak up.

"You're a meanie!" he croaked. "Why are you so mean!" She looked over in his direction, seemingly insulted that he was even breathing in the same area as her.

"I'm sorry, did Mr. Sissy Boy say something?" She cocked her head to the side. "I'll stop being mean as soon as she stops being fat." She looked back at me before stomping out of the room.

Such were the dynamics of this house. But my father was the primary ringleader.

You see, my sister didn't conjure Craig's "nickname" out of thin air. Nope. My father had come up with it as soon as he determined that doling out excessive abuse was going to be the thing to keep us in line and prevent any of us from speaking to an outsider about The Terrible Thing That No One Talked About™. Or any other terrible things that happened in the house.

He was a despot. A *crazed* one. And he loved being one too.

Without going into the *grisly* details, what made my father's abuse of all his children *potent* was the fact that he tailor-made said abuse for each *individual* child. Yes. He was *very* talented at picking up on a person's potential insecurities, what they shrank back from, and what they wanted to hide in general, and he always used that to his advantage.

With incredible precision.

My sister, the eldest, was his first target, for obvious reasons. He honed in on her even more as a teenager because of her tomboy stage (to be explained later). But that quickly tapered off when she started rebelling against him and my mom. And when she, in a twist that no one expected, started joining hands with him to abuse the rest of us.

Most of his abuse toward me fell into two categories: zeroing in on my fatness ("Fatso" was his idea), or on the fact that I was dark-skinned. His favorite thing, besides screaming at me not to eat so much, was telling me to "stay out of the goddamn sun." You know, since I was dark *enough*. And shouldn't aim to be darkened further, I guess? And Mom didn't help, with her comments about "scrubbing the black" and dirt off whenever I showered.

My three younger brothers weren't spared either. My brother Jeffrey happened to be on the spectrum. Autistic, to be specific. He was a really smart and sweet kid that didn't bother nobody. But as many of you know, being aneurotypical in this world means that you may need a little extra care; mostly because of ableism. But also because it is completely fucking okay for people's needs and wants to vary from person to person.

My father didn't see it that way. Like his irateness at the fact that my mom had to give me extra attention as a baby, he was also irate at the fact that raising Jeffrey was going to require a different or more thoughtful approach. Which meant more of my mom's attention.

Wouldn't you know, he took that personally. Took Jeffrey's neurodivergence as a personal affront! And as a result, he took every opportunity to call Jeffrey "retarded boy." Especially if he did something that he didn't like. For example, breathing. He said it often. Freely. Like some demented superhero name or something. He wouldn't stop until I got older and called him a fat, bald fuck after he berated Jeffrey one day. I got my ass beat across all fifty states, but when I tell you that I would do it again!!

Tommy, who was four, had a brief moment when he didn't have a target on his back. His age was a factor, but my father had also deemed him his "favorite" and was trying to, I'm sure, impart his wicked ways to him. But one thing narcissists are good at doing is sabotaging their own narcissistic efforts. In due time, my father's affinity for abuse, degradation, and animosity toward anyone in the vicinity (just to boost his shitty ego) won out against his "love" for Tommy. And soon after that, he began to harp on Tommy's height (he was supposedly short for "his age") and loved to refer to him as a "stupid midget."

Craig, as you read above, was a prime target because he came off as "fruity" to them. Not manly enough. A touch too "effeminate." Too "sensitive." So my father and my sister would call him "sissy/sissy boy" or a slew of other virulently disrespectful things. You couldn't tell my father shit though. He still counted himself as "progressive" and "enlightened" because he never outright called Craig a faggot. To make matters worse, Craig was often more aggressively targeted by not only my father but also my older sibling and mother with violence. Almost like they were trying to beat it all out of him.

I'm aware that they did it to discourage the potential of him being "a gay"—which makes it all the more ironic that *I'm* the flaming gay one. Truly. They spent so much time making sure "the gay" didn't suddenly leap out of him that they overlooked me and conveniently forgot that you couldn't force anyone's sexuality to merely *go away.*

But just like my father and sister's outright torment of me based on my weight and my shade taught me a lot of shit about fatphobia and colorism, their torment of my brother taught me a couple of things too. The most important thing was that if the people in *this house* so thoroughly despised femininity and were virulently femmephobic in general, the outside world probably looked a lot *worse.* And while femininity is generally despised more when it is "detected" in cis gay men, trans folks, etc., it was very much despised in cis women in my household too. By *cis women,* ironically.

I remember casually observing how my mom shat on other more "feminine" women at her church—of course, because *she* didn't look like that and wasn't motivated to look like that "as a mother of five." She loved saying that silly shit. I also remember Kalindi proudly proclaiming how much of a tomboy she was: flaunting her clothes, her hats, and her shoes. Her Jordans especially. She claimed superiority because of that with the same energy and fervor she would yell at my brother to "man" up with. I had tomboyish tendencies too for a while, but I eventually didn't have enough energy to pretend that I hated things like, say, the color pink.

But, unfortunately, such attitudes—that is, fatphobia, femmephobia, colorism, and homophobia—were poised to be my undoing in that regard. And not just with my clothes (to be discussed) either. But for the rest of my "formative" years in that goddamn house.

A HUGE part of being a "precocious" child is the burden of recognizing, right away, that something is very *off* about your environment. And about the people around you.

I fully remember gaining consciousness at like four years old. And suddenly being hyperaware of my mother and father's screaming as they chased each other around in the kitchen with knives and plates. Hell, I remember running into the kitchen and trying to get between them at one point. I was promptly knocked to the ground, barely missing broken plate pieces that were splayed out across the ugly linoleum tiles that my parents called a floor. Crying as Kalindi resentfully picked me up and walked me out of the kitchen.

Over time, there *continued* to be moments just like that one. And rather than focusing my anger on the unfairness of it all (to be clear, I set aside some anger *just* for that purpose), I focused most of it, from age four to age eighteen, on crafting a sound escape plan.

It wasn't long until writing became that escape plan.

I know self-praise has a reputation in this country (rightfully so), but I don't have a problem with saying that I enjoyed, and was very good at, "the arts." I had picked up several instruments as a child—mastered the recorder, got started on the guitar, and became pretty intermediate where the piano was concerned.

I loved painting, but I loved sketching even more. I would steal the remote to my father's big-screen TV, press the PIP button, freeze a scene shot from shows like *Kim Possible* and *The Proud Family*, and sketch them all. And you couldn't tell me a goddamn thing! I was so good at it. I was so good at it and I loved it so much that I considered, maybe, growing up to be a cartoonist or someone who worked in animation.

I don't know who the hell told me to say that to my father, my *Nigerian* father, who didn't see value in any job that wasn't a doctor, a nurse, or an engineer. But I said it like a dumbass and received the nastiest beating via belt. And it pains me to say it, but that beating ensured that I would never so much as think of looking at a sketchbook again. Or sketch in general.

Safe to say that I can no longer sketch.

A tragedy of epic proportions, to be honest.

Writing *almost* suffered this fate. Almost. I remember an instance when my father expressed disdain for my small paper "books" that I had co-fashioned with one of my church friends, Regina Phillips. He didn't see a point to it, since it had no relevance in terms of medicine in his mind. But he left me alone and left me to it for the most part. The about-face from him came when I got to middle school and wanted to be part of our school newspaper. I was eleven or twelve at the time. He got red in the face, telling me that I was not to be a part of "that stupid shit." I was notoriously stubborn (as I am now), particularly as I got older.

So, I hatched a plan with my mom to leave my dad out of the mix and join the newspaper anyway. Of course, the plan was contingent on my mother picking me up *on time* and *every time,* while she made up some valid excuse about me missing the bus or some shit. My mom stuck to this plan for about a day. But the day after, she conveniently "forgot" because she had opted to go grocery shopping (something she saved for Fridays and weekends). To this day, I'm sure she did this on purpose. As a kid, I had thought the opposite. But writing this book, stringing these words and memories together, has made it clear that my mother was no bystander. And she only rebelled against my father up to a certain point. Only for purposes of appearing like she was the *better* and *kinder* parent. The more *understanding* one.

My mother's supposed brain fart meant that my father ended up having to be the one to pick me up. And boy, did I pay for that shit.

He got creative this time. Instead of going straight for the belt, my father made me kneel in the corner. And raise my arms. As high as they would go. My fellow Nigerian children know this punishment well. Every time it even looked like I was getting too tired and that my hands were gonna sink, my dad would pop me in the back of the head. Or pop me in my legs. Or arms. Or my neck. To add some more torment, like salt on some fries, he'd occasionally get in my face and start taunting me. It was some sick shit. But he didn't care. Hell, I had long believed that my father got off on all the demented shit he did. That was the only thing that made sense to me at that point.

"You think you are a big girl, don't you?" He glared at me, eyes full of hate and lacking any ounce of humanity. "That you know better than me?!"

"No," I said quietly, trying not to cry. He popped me upside the head anyway, like I hadn't given him the right answer or something.

"That will teach you to disobey me again," he barked, backing away.

Kalindi would end up coming home to this scene first. And just when I thought she was going to be a true big sister this time and save me from my father's wrath for once, she simply shrugged. She couldn't be bothered to intercede. She called me a fat, spoiled brat and said that I should have listened to him—despite the fact that it had become her whole identity to buck against him and my mom.

Frankly, I don't think she even believed for a second that I should have been obedient at all. I just think that she liked seeing me hurt and in pain. And that moment became one of the final nails in the coffin of our relationship.

My mom would come back much later and end up in a fight with my dad over the whole thing. Like she was so *incensed* by what had happened. She ended up coming upstairs later and comforting me as I tried to fall asleep covered in bruises. She offered to continue taking me to newspaper staff meetings and apologized profusely for forgetting to pick me up from school.

I tuned her out, mostly because the damage was done with the newspaper situation and I could not risk being subjected to another one of my dad's psych-out sessions. Shit. I'd rather get beat with a belt than do that again.

On the contrary.

Kneeling in that corner had proved to be downright horrendous and traumatizing. Yet my father insinuating that I was too big for my britches did stick with me. Because for once,

I realized that I hadn't *actually* done anything "wrong" like both of my parents liked to scream at me over and over again—especially when it came to little shit. No.

He said that shit because he was *scared*.

Because he knew, like I knew, that if I got really good at this shit, my escape plan would work. And one of his *toys* would be gone.

Forever.

It's been about sixteen years since that incident. Sixteen years that included writing my way to the top of my class. Writing my way into several prestigious schools. Writing my way into an array of respected and highly esteemed digital media outlets.

And writing my way to this *here* book.

So. It's safe to say that my escape plan worked.

MY TERRIBLE, AWFUL RELATIONSHIP WITH CLOTHES

My relationship with clothes has always been fraught at best. Tenuous at worst. But honestly, that's just me being nice about it. If I were to be completely honest, anything involving clothes—but mainly shopping—was (and kinda still is) enough to launch me into a full psychological breakdown.

To start wider, greater society *runs* on fatphobia. Like fuel! And society's fatphobia purposefully makes it impossible for fat people like me to, say, find proper clothes that *fit*. Those airline seats that are *way* too *small*, even for your *average* ass? Fatphobia too. I'm also including those ugly-ass barstools at these bars and clubs that can't even hold a single ass cheek, let alone the rest of your body. Shit, fatphobia can even affect your job prospects. And that's just the beginning.

Clothes were the touchiest thing though. For me anyway. Mainly because facing exclusion in that realm based on size was a very subtle but poignant highlight of the kind of bigotry one faces as a fat person. The idea is that if we can't properly dress ourselves or if there are places that won't even hold *literal* space for us, it will discourage us from coming outside.

Discourage us from being seen or wanting to be seen. To be clear.

Still. While I'd love to blame all my shit about clothes squarely on society, the truth of the matter is that this complex *started* with my family (my mother in particular), as all instances of self-hate do when you are born from dysfunction.

In the last chapter, I talked about the horrific dynamics of abuse that had played out in my family for nearly two decades while I was still there. I mentioned that fatphobia and colorism were the primary weapons of choice when it came to any adult (and soon-to-be adult) deciding that they wanted to torture me with something. And I talked about the Original Sin™ in the household that started it all.

You know, The Terrible Thing That No One Talked About™.

But what I haven't gotten a chance to talk about yet is how fatphobia was *benevolently* brought on to my head by my "well-meaning" mother. And this version of fatphobia manifested in her buying me ill-fitted and ill-sized clothes in perpetuity. She will swear to this day that she did it to help me. Did it as a favor to me. But let me be the first one to tell you that she's full of shit.

Like the previous chapter, this started from my mom's lack of courage and conviction when it came to acting on The Terrible Thing That No One Talked About™ and its subsequent fallout. Meaning that she chose not to act. At all. Wasn't keen on losing her husband. So. Instead of addressing him and his evil directly, that guilty and vengeful eye of hers got turned onto us kids.

Indeed. She took her conflicted feelings out on both Kalindi and me in ways that some of you are familiar with. She would call us "fast" and refer to our bodies as "sinful" and "tempting" (gotta love those purity politics). And as some backward solution in her mind, she would make us cover up at every turn (as if that would do anything), but especially on nights that my father was home from working a twelve-hour shift at the state's special needs facility—that just so happened to be a maximum security *prison* because this is America. Where he happened to be a *psychiatric* nurse.

Yep. Ironic, right?

This country is a joke. And vets no one.

My mom's behavior never made any sense to me growing

up, of course, but because she was my mom, I gave her the bene-
fit of the doubt and honestly assumed she was out to protect us.
It was not until I turned about fourteen—a.k.a., when I started
to develop breasts—that I figured out that this was not the case.

To put it bluntly, puberty brought a particularly sick and
twisted form of jealousy out of my mother. One time, in a left
turn to rule all left turns in the Eduwa household, my father took
my side in an argument. I was in high school by that point. And
I had wanted to go see one of my friends for the evening since I
had finished my homework early *and* made sure the house was
super clean. You know, because I couldn't have either parent
making up excuses as to why I couldn't leave the house.

Anyway, my mom was being a dickhead and told me that I
couldn't go because she "didn't know my friend that well or her
family that well." This friend happened to be Eve Odard, one of
my oldest friends besides Regina. We had met in middle school
and despite my mother's lies, they had met before. No. This
was a shorthand excuse that many Nigerian moms employed.
Usually to express displeasure at the type of family said friend
came from OR to discourage you from making friends that
weren't Nigerian. They were big on that. The mother or father
had to be from one of their shitty churches or shitty social clubs
for them to be even remotely comfortable with you hanging
out with this person.

Eve was a good friend. A real nigga. But she wasn't Nigerian. And my mom took full advantage of that.

"No," she said to me as she calmly chopped onions on the
kitchen counter.

"But Mommy—" I responded.

"I said no!" She cut me off, her chopping getting faster and
more pointed. I looked at her, truly annoyed with her obsti-
nance. And I did what every rebellious teenager did when
one of their parents refused to sign off on certain plans or
shenanigans:

I opted to go talk to the other parent. My father.

Despite how risky that sounds and the even riskier potential consequences, my dad . . . agreed with me. He signed off on allowing me to visit Eve. Mainly because I had in fact done my homework and my chores (some that weren't even mine) and he didn't see any reason why I shouldn't get to go. Particularly because I wasn't one to get in trouble that often, in comparison with, unfortunately, Kalindi.

My mom kirked out.

This, for any parent, is gonna happen when a child tries to play you and the other parent against each other. It *is* pretty underhanded. No arguments about that here. But the unfairness of the situation, to me, superseded any ethics that would have my mom be in the right. I didn't act smug about it or anything, even after I told her. I simply stated that I was gonna pack my things and leave soon. And she took that very personally. Within seconds, she flew across the kitchen with a knife and pointed it at me. She had blocked an important exit from the kitchen and stared me down.

"You wicked gehl." She narrowed her eyes.

"What?" I responded.

"Shut up!" she snapped. "You heard me!" I opened my mouth to say something and then I closed it. Speaking wasn't really a good idea. Because if I did, she would use anything I said against me. She would twist my words in a way that only she was capable of and use them to harm me. On the contrary, my not talking didn't deter her at all. And she then went on to say something so wretched that it pains me even now to recall it. "Are you sleeping with him?"

"*Huh?*" I blinked at her.

"*Are you sleeping with him!*" she repeated, with even more venom, flicking her eyes down to my breasts and then looking back up at me again.

Whoa.

By now, we all know who my mom is referring to. And yet, I could not believe it. I could not believe that my own *mother* had insinuated . . . *that*. But I know where her demented suspicion was coming from. Besides the obvious, my *father* never took my side in anything. Never felt the *paternal* urge to defend me from anything. He delighted in any and all calamity that I happened to experience day in and day out. But that's not what happened here. And my mother noticed right away. To this day, I think my father only agreed to let me go to provoke this reaction in my mom. Or just to sow the seeds of chaos in general. Even if my mom never said this shit.

But she did say this shit. And it was vile. Such a vile thing, and such a vile thing to have heard and witnessed in real time. The insinuation that my father was only taking my side in these arguments because we probably had some sort of sexual relationship was so sick to me. So disgusting. And even more disgusting to know that it came out of my mother's mouth. The one parent that claimed to be the *normal* one in this shithouse.

It did not matter that he was my *father* and it did not matter that someone my age at the time (fourteen) couldn't even consent to something like that—if, God forbid, that was a thing that was happening. Made no sense. But she said it anyway. Because in her mind, you guessed it, Kalindi would always be a reminder of what happened. And as for me, who had not experienced such violence from my father (that I know of), my mom would always side-eye me, thinking about if that had happened. Or if it was still going to happen. If some *mini-temptress* like Kalindi or I were going to steal the spotlight from her. And steal the attention away from her sicko husband?

"What the fuck did you just say to me?" I squinted my eyes right back at her. Being fourteen meant that I had already been introduced to cuss words. And I wasn't afraid to use them. Still, cussing out any parent is a death wish. But cussing at a *Nigerian* parent? Well, I certainly should have been drafting up my will right then and there. Truly. But I didn't give a shit because registering the sick shit my mother just said to me meant that I was well within my right to call her an unrepentant bitch who was sick in the head. Her eyes got wide when she realized what she had said. And when she realized that I was about to press her on it. *"What the fuck did you just say to me?!"* I waited for her to answer. Stared into her face like I had heat ray vision. She cleared her throat instead and looked away. "You're fuck-ing *sick*, you know that?"

I'd love it if there were some alternate universe where she apologized and then everything magically got fixed or resolved—with my father finally ending up under a jail. But I do not live in such a universe. My mom would never apolo-gize. Would never even hint that what she said was wrong and twisted. Nope. She just slinked away, clearly embarrassed. And dropped the issue.

THAT WASN'T going to be the end of my issues with my mom though. As I've mentioned, it was clear that my burgeoning womanhood and sexuality were big problems to her. Big, *big* problems. And it wasn't long before she started getting creative about "solving those problems."

One such solution for her was trying to keep me ugly. Frumpy. And in a perpetual state of childhood.

This had actually first manifested two years prior, when I was twelve. And in the seventh grade. I was definitely too old to be wearing jellies and bobos. And I did ask my mom to send me to school with something more age-appropriate like corn-rows. Or microbraids. I wasn't trying to get lit up at school. But I especially wasn't keen on showing up like that because it was *weird*. In general. Whether my school peers said anything about it or not.

My mom refused to listen to my wishes, and my legitimate concerns, and sent me to school in them anyway.

I got a lot of weird looks that day. Rightfully so. And I basi-cally slinked into my homeroom class to hide out. The class itself belonged to my Black math teacher, Mrs. Irving. She was hyperaware of how embarrassed I felt about the whole thing.

And in an act that I shall never forget, she pulled me aside during lunchtime and did what any responsible Black woman would do when you're a good person and you know that a little Black girl is being fucked over: She took down my hair. And she rebraided it herself. Into the cornrows I had asked for from the very beginning.

I ended up getting yelled at by my mother as she had this whole *thing* regarding cornrows (to be discussed). But I really didn't care. My opinion of my mom was morphing by the second. And it made me more eager to leave my house forever.

My mom's weird fatphobia-sponsored mind games didn't cease. In fact, they ramped up from there, the fatter I got and the more developed my body became in terms of my hips and my titties. The next step for her was to target me with clothes.

It's true. My mom opted to do this by often buying me over-sized clothes. Clothes that would hang off me like grocery bags. Or even obscene parachutes, to be more specific. My father would later join in on this, probably because it was fun for him. And another opportunity for him to torture me. My sister didn't want to be left out of the shenanigans either and she engaged in them by giving me the most atrocious hand-me-downs. It would backfire on her later though when I got further into high school. Mainly because there are still a lot of things that a Taurus could do with "ugly" hand-me-downs.

Anyway. My mom called herself being helpful because I was "fat and couldn't help it." But I knew the reasoning behind it. And it would eventually inspire me to get my driver's license ASAPtually. So I could start working and start buying my *own* clothes.

I started working at T.J. Maxx when I was freshly sixteen. It was a "godsend" for me (I remember writing that specific word in my journal in terms of what it offered—like free-dom). But in some ways, it kind of made the situation worse. T.J. Maxx itself had pretty decent clothes. But any fat person growing up between 2000 and 2012 will tell you that the plus-sized pickings at stores like T.J. Maxx were slim. Size-wise. With shit barely going up to a large or an extra-large. This was especially applicable to the dreaded "Juniors" section that I stared at every day at work. The women's section wasn't any better, either, mostly because even if my size was present, the clothes still happened to be . . . very atrocious. Very unsightly.

The "fat fashions" that were available in the women's section made me want to starve myself and do other horrible, terrible shit (like developing a purging disorder), just so I could fit in a large/x-large in the Juniors section.

Peplum skirts and shirts everywhere. Cold-shoulder blouses from here to Africa. Capris that made you want to throw the fuck up and die. Dresses that looked like tents. Dresses that looked like you murdered your grandmother for her floral couch and used the couch to make a dress. Replicas of Mormon skirts that promised to obscure any fat person's legs. Hell, there were even remnants of the low-rise jeans trend of the late nineties and early 2000s in the section. But they completely ruined it by making the pants flare out in the ugliest way at the bottom. And brought the waistline to a higher place—one that proved to be awkward. On purpose. You know, the kind of change that is designed to embarrass you as a fat person by literally cutting your belly in half.

Like I hinted at, this would definitely inspire the series of eating disorders I developed during my skinny summer (to be discussed).

But for me, it was very much worth it because I was tired of having to help restock clothes that I couldn't fit in while working at T.J. Maxx. I was tired of having breakdowns about it in the break room. I didn't have the heart to go into another dressing room at JCPenney or Kmart or Sears or Forever 21 and bawl my fucking eyes out because nothing would fit.

I mean, yes, I had outwitted my mother when it came to trying to sabotage me with large and ugly clothes. But as a teenager? And as a fat Black one? Nah. I wouldn't be outsmarting greater society's fatphobia anytime soon.

And that was by design.

MY SKINNY
SUMMER

The first time I heard the word "yo-yo dieting" as lovingly referred to as "crash dieting," I couldn't have been more than ten.

I won't go on another self-indulgent spiel about how I was a "precocious child" or how I was so "gifted" that I sought out unconventional things to read as if I was the sophisticated-yet-clearly-emotionally-stunted Lorraine "Ray" Schleine (played by Dakota Fanning) in *Uptown Girls*. What I will say is that around that time, my mother had managed to score a subscription to an interesting group of magazines, including *OK!*, *Us Weekly,* and the like. I referred to these subscriptions as her tabloid-lite indulgence, mostly because my mom would never stoop so low as to subscribe to, let's say, the *National Enquirer*. Or any related trash.

But this was acceptable trash.

Still, her preoccupation with these magazines naturally inspired my own, and soon I was taking in images of Brangelina and their globe-trotting philanthropy (to avoid the heat they were getting for Brad Pitt and Jennifer Aniston's divorce), images of a "crazy" Britney Spears (three years before the infamous buzzcut/umbrella incident; I cannot tell you how relieved I am that she is *free* now), and, of course, images of Janet Jackson over the years, with her weight fluctuating and the words "yo-yo dieting" being somewhat bolded next to her name. Mind you, this was around 2004, in a post–Super Bowl XXXVIII world. You could certainly tell by the fact that every magazine alive used to love to take swipes at her appearance and her dating life as an extended punishment (with the initial punishment being blackballed from, like, everything).

In 2004 I was ten, just a fucking kid. And I didn't know the historical context of any of these images besides the fact that these were people I did not know, would probably never meet, but seemed to have interesting lives despite that fact. What I did know was that Janet was someone I had looked up to my entire life (my family, shitty as they were, had good taste at the time, and loved The Jacksons). That she was a Black woman who had shaped music and culture forever. That she was, at her worst moments, a size that was very close to mine or perhaps slightly smaller. And that even if she was the pinnacle of "health" 99.9 percent of the time (which, of course, no one can say for sure except her), any slight weight fluctuation from what the public was used to was still enough for many of these magazines to completely eviscerate her.

Janet's "yo-yo dieting"—as well as that of many other female celebrities—was the object of obsession for many fucked-up people for years and years. I'd damn near say it was even more "compelling" to some than the recurring "who wore it better" segment that many of these magazines dick-rode into the ground. I ain't afraid to name them either. *People. Us Weekly. Star. OK!* The central idea behind it was always supposed to be like "Oh, look who's fat again! Wow!" and would supposedly make whoever was reading or watching feel like maybe despite whatever shortcoming—perceived or otherwise—they had, at least they would never be fat.

Doesn't matter if people deny it. That's how it was.

And of course, being a ten-year-old, I caught on to all of this fairly quickly. And became obsessed with myself. Not in a "haha, let me join in on this shittiness" way but in a way that made me painfully aware of the fact that if Janet Thee God Jackson could be dragged in some tabloid magazine for gaining some weight, someone like myself would always be fair game for being "fat."

This was a terrifying thought and shouldn't have become my truth at such an early age, but unfortunately, my life at that point supported this bleak hypothesis. My home life was an instantaneous confirmation—with my parents and elder sister being eager to dump on me because of my weight and crush my spirit. And as far as life outside the house, at school? While the teasing about weight would eventually subside, thanks in part to me leaning into people associating me with food because of my weight (I kept a large purse so I could occasionally put food in it, just in case you were wondering), it was a journey. To say the least.

My elementary school experience could literally be summed up in an overdramatic and quite explosive Michael Bay montage of me stomping some kid's face in and showing up in the principal's office all innocent-like as if I didn't know what the word *punching* meant. Middle school marked a huge shift from my "hit first, ask questions later" policy because now I was getting to be at an age where all a punitive-happy school administrator would have to do to end my whole school career was to take my greatest (literal) hits reel and plop it into my "permanent file"—which, by the way, I never found out if that shit actually existed, but of course, the threat of it was enough to make me get my shit together.

Anyway, middle school was mad different. And that's because I had to make an abrupt 180 and move from dueling all this gendered and racialized fatphobia away with my fists to dueling with my words. My first go at this was at age twelve when I wrote my bully what I now refer to as my first diss letter and she returned to school sobbing the next day, saying I was so terribly and amazingly awful and in such a dramatic way that I might as well have actually hit her. And come to think of it, I don't even really remember much of anything I wrote in that letter, but I do remember distinctly writing "you're fugly" about three times, so I'm not really sure I want to know what I wrote, to be honest.

While words became my primary weapon moving from elementary to middle school, high school was an entirely different ball game. Fists were out (mostly). And words were only as effective as your reputation was. Who were you to be saying this? Who did you know? Did people like you? Would they jump in if your place in this system was threatened? Or would you be eagerly toppled and thrown to the wolves to make space for someone else new? Sure, at the end of the day, fists could be deployed to get the point across, but that was "ghetto," lowbrow behavior. Meaning that it didn't need to come to that if you played your cards right.

Yes, dear reader, I had quickly entered the political arena known as high school and I was so not fucking prepared. It might as well have been called Game of These Bad Ass Kids™ and I might as well have been mouth-breathing-ass Jon Snow walking in with my equally confused dire wolf (A)Gh(a)st.

It was an interesting change. Unlike, say, my elementary school, this one was majority *Black*. Featuring Black kids from *all* economic backgrounds. White liberals would call it an "inner city" school, but let's be real, this shit was in the *suburbs*. Pre-several waves of white flight.

Additionally, the Metro Nashville Board of Education had *just* instituted their "standard school attire" policy to "improve discipline" across all schools and cut down on bullying that had to do with clothes or the valorization of designer labels. Which resulted in the invasion of tucked shirts and khaki pants as soon as I set foot on campus.

The quiet part, in my opinion, was that the policy was yet another way to get niggas caught up in some school-to-prison bullshit for something as small as an *untucked* shirt. The *other* quiet part was that a couple of teachers my particular class of peers had previously dealt with had been ousted for inappropriate conduct with students and SSA was supposed to cut down on teachers being "tempted" by teenage titties.

"More discipline," my ass.

Thankfully, I wasn't dealing with the high school from *Mean Girls*. There was no Regina George in sight. Still, all high schools have their own politics—including a majority Black one.

A majority Black school meant that several racial dynamics that were *previously* on full display in past schools wouldn't be as readily visible here. But . . . things like colorism and fatphobia still existed, only they showed up as multilevel insults or in the obvious lack of visibility or *desirability*. I say that last part to stress that I'm not really interested in sanitizing any part of this story or even the experiences many of us go through. You wanted to be *hot* in high school. You wanted to be liked. Thirsted after. And desired.

Period.

These are your peers, after all. And if they don't like you, something must be off, right?

That was a question that popped up for me periodically. I wasn't super obsessed with changing my appearance before I started working at T.J. Maxx (hello, you need money for that and I didn't have it). But I was definitely taking very detailed notes about how some of my peers and even friends were treated, based on how they looked. Skinny girls were the wave and you got extra points if your hips and boobs weren't concave. Blackness was desired, yes, but definitely garnered much more attention if it was lightened or if it was "mixed" with something. White was the standard, but as time went on, being "Blasian" got increasingly popular. I almost kinda wanna blame Kimora Lee Simmons for this, but hey. Whatever the case, the more "exotic" the "mixture," the better. Hard-ons for intelligence fluctuated depending on the guy doing the thirsting, but at the end of the day—as is true now—they definitely wanted to be smarter and funnier than you. Whoever you were, but especially if you were a girl.

I went through my freshman and sophomore years and quickly noticed I didn't fall into the desirable part of any of these categories . . . and was thus rendered invisible. If I was visible, I usually was being passive-aggressively insulted by someone who knew better but did it anyway. I got really obsessed with the movie *Matilda* around this time and figured I could start blowing fatphobic fucks up with my thoughts if I just concentrated hard enough and long enough.

But back to more important things at hand, I was objectively fat. I was darker than a good chunk of my friends—indeed, my parents were two very proud and bullheaded Nigerians, nothing "mixed" about them. And I literally had nothing else to fall back on besides my certified smarts and my burgeoning sense of humor. Which, of course, wouldn't help much since I believed I was straight at the time and since I *knew* guys had a complex about that. For a while, I just let it be. I did that thing that ugly people do where we really work on our personality to make sure it's bomb as fuck so that we can grow on people like barnacles even if we don't look the part. I also put a lot of energy into my friendships and made sure I could be *valuable* in that at least—before I knew what "mammies" and "mules" were. And when I wasn't focused on any of that, my grades were the priority—with the promise that if I was super-duper smart, I'd one day escape this hellhole to the faraway lands known as Chicago or Los Angeles.

That was true to an extent, but that was also, like, years away. So, in the meantime, I suffered.

And by "suffered," I mean that since romantic relationships were *prized* in high school (and to be honest, are probably still considered such presently as well), my strong friendships were frequently dashed every time a new crush showed up, and I wasn't really seen as crush material because I was book smart and perhaps "overinvested" in friendship. And while there was an attempt to keep my jealousy at bay, it was almost always overridden by the fact that I was all-too-often read as invisible in favor of someone lighter or skinnier or more "exotic." It was maddening, really, and the penultimate straw was when a crush of mine was oddly forthcoming about not being into me because I wasn't Blasian like the girl he was actually into, even if I was very "nice." I think I stewed on that ill-fated confession for weeks. Actually, I lied, months. I'm pretty sure I stewed on that for like the rest of the school year and definitely didn't look at ol' boy or ol' girl the same. (It wasn't her fault, but as most people who end up on the upside of lopsided privilege, she very much enjoyed it. And occasionally *encouraged* it.) In fact, it was much easier to avoid them rather than to be constantly reminded of my aesthetically challenged features and my other aesthetic shortcomings. So, I tried to focus on building myself up for the rest of the year. You know, maybe change up my look and wardrobe to make myself feel a bit better.

And then I had that goal shattered at age fifteen when my mom took me to our local KMart and I suffered a psychological breakdown because I couldn't find a goddamn thing to wear, and what I *did* find encouraged a *massive* muffin top and put me in the same class as the Pillsbury Doughboy. Which wouldn't be as terrible if I were still a child (read: fatphobia still affects kids, of course), but definitely was not it since I was barreling straight toward raging adolescence as a cis teen girl.

I MARK the infamous breakdown at KMart as a major turning point in my life. Even above seeing the words "yo-yo dieting" next to a photo of the iconic Janet Jackson. That breakdown set into motion another layer of a lifetime of tragic, confusing, and occasionally hilarious body issues that would always be traced back to that singular moment in time. It was like the assassination of Franz Ferdinand but in my head.

And thus began the commencement of my skinny summer. The summer right before junior year.

I get fuzzy about what my order of operations was right after the breakdown. But if I remember correctly, the order went something like:

— Get a job
— Get my driver's license
— Revamp the family dumpster fire car
— WORK, WORK, WORK, WORK, WORK
— ??????????
— Money
— Buy "healthy" groceries with said money
— Invest in exercises like elliptical training and dancing
— Lose 45 pounds
— Profit (?)
— End my skinny summer and commence my skinny junior year

Now obviously, displaying this in list form makes it seem like the whole process of losing weight wasn't that big a deal, but it was. I just wanted to spare you the unnecessary exposition-like bullshit writing that it would have taken to explain all that, so trust me when I say I'm doing you and myself a big, fat solid by skipping straight to the good shit.

As far as the good shit goes, I walked into my junior year of high school forty-five pounds lighter and seemingly more confident—and with a semi-new wardrobe. A.k.a., what I could sneak past the school district's "standard attire code" without getting sent to the principal's office. Unlike in most movies where there's some big makeover sequence that morphs into an even bigger reveal, the shock at my transformation wasn't necessarily instantaneous or even obvious, but the shock did eventually come. Actually, maybe *shock* is the wrong word. It'd probably be more accurate to say *change*.

Yes, as every fat, formerly fat, or fat-adjacent person can attest to, there was a stark change in how I was treated from the moment my classmates caught on to the fact that I was now forty-five pounds lighter. Granted, my friends hit me with the "you look different" and kept it moving. But everyone else? Not so much. Suddenly, I went from Invisible Man status to straight Wolfman. But make it sexy. Or as "sexy" as an attention-starved sixteen-year-old could be. *Hypervisibility* was the word of the year and your girl was it. There were no more passive-aggressive, thinly veiled insults about my weight. I was the (assumed) picture of health.

Every dude who I was mildly attracted to finally registered my existence. My crush of the hour—which I will not get into (for now), because I am still quite embarrassed about it—started "bumping" into me more. And this was surprisingly tame stuff. The really intense stuff came when I was eventually pulled to the side by a handful of female classmates who then asked the following question:

"How'd you do it?"

This seems like a fairly innocuous question ... until you remember that I lost forty-five pounds in only three months.

And every time this was asked, I'd contemplate lamenting about an entire summer of meal-prepping that included endless cases of bottles of water. English muffins. Brown rice. Green grapes. Fiber One bars. Low-fat or calorie-"free" ice cream. Fucking SlimFast drinks. The occasional piece of black or honey ham. *Chicken.* Avocados before they were twenty bucks a pop (thanks white people), with this "diet" stretching into my junior year. This of course all resulted in me shitting my brains out, but that was a mere distraction in terms of where I wanted my body to go.

I also greatly considered revealing how I obsessively committed to *hours* upon *hours* upon *hours* of exercise, with my chosen torture methods being the elliptical and I guess contemporary dance, all powered by a two- to three-hour-long playlist on my Zune (or was it my iPod?). I know you think the "hours upon hours upon hours" quip is an exaggeration, but it wasn't. I would lock myself away in the garage, which was sweltering as shit, and even threw up occasionally (only if my stomach hurt). Doing these things for what seemed like an eternity, and I would only emerge to confirm I had indeed tortured myself for the day in my exercise journal and do my homework. As in . . . exercise literally took up as much—if not more—time as it took to complete the homework for my 928347728483936 AP classes.

It's a wonder I managed to *stay* an A+ student.

There was also the fact that my obsession with what I was putting in my body, how I was exerting my body, and the kind of duress my brain was under trying to hold it all together—GPA included—dictated that I had to take a break somewhere. That I needed slack somewhere. And so, during lunchtime, I'd be sure to gorge myself on every "terrible" and "empty calorie" thing I could find. Mainly pizza. And cheese sticks. And brownies. Fries too. With my chosen Minute Maid drink of the hour. And then turn around and add an extra hour on the elliptical at hyperspeed.

And really, I'm glossing over the exercise thing in a half-assed attempt to not dissociate. Because if I were being 100 percent honest, I'd tell you that the exercise thing got bad. Like, I mean really bad. Like hella bad. When we talk about eating disorders and body dysmorphia presently, there's always a hyperfocus on calorie counting or how these diseases drastically change our relationships with food. But there's not as much (at least in my experience) focus on what people who suffer through these diseases put themselves through where physical exertion is involved. This *hyperfixation* on exercise as a rushed means of weight loss is now referred to as a particular kind of *purging disorder*, but it's not something that was commonly discussed when I was going through all of this shit. And in terms of physical exertion, rather than exercise being the relaxing and stress-relieving activity that it has the potential to be, it becomes a disciplinary thing. A form of punishment. A toxic, knee-jerk response as a result of surpassing your "calorie count" for the day.

Even if it's literally by one fucking calorie.

Because the calorie indicates failure, lack of discipline, and single-handedly could be the difference between you (me) hanging on to your (my) fragile, skinny body and you (me) reverting to your (my) formerly fat (un)glory. Hell, even meeting the calorie count was still a failure. The goal was always to be under said goal. There needed to always be a deficit. And in my mind, that was only achievable by fanatical physical punishment.

Which is to say . . . if anyone reading this is in denial that excessive exercise falls into the disordered eating category, it's time to wake up. Because just because you're not bending over a toilet with a finger in your mouth or inhaling everything in sight after long stretches of no eating does not somehow make you better.

Of course, this is all a shit ton to tell some unassuming sixteen-year-old girl who is staring at you with wide eyes and thinking you're going to recommend some wholesome food and exercise tips. So, I always opted to tell them something simple, like "drink more water" and "cut down on meat if you can." And both things were technically true and didn't require me to divulge what I now know was disordered eating and body dysmorphia. Or divulge the fact that food and exercise had quite literally taken over my life.

You may be tempted to ask me if it was worth it. And of course, the "correct" or "expected" thing would be to say no, especially looking back and reflecting on how it still factors into my body image and body awareness today. Like, I still don't have a very healthy relationship with food and will often try to avoid it entirely to circumvent unnecessary freak-outs. But that would be a lie. Because at the time, it *was* worth it. I technically got everything I had hoped for and wanted. The boy. The respect. The attention. And I had finally escaped the contradictory spotlight that fatphobia casts on its unsuspecting victims—which is the dual punishment of being rendered invisible and thus disqualified from anyone's love, attention, and respect, and of being rendered hypervisible and thus being subjected to constant ridicule, denigration, and, annoyingly, concern-trolling.

That was the interesting thing about this whole ordeal. This whole summer. There was always a nagging feeling that what I was going through wasn't right and wasn't fair. And that I should be able to exist—fat and all—safely without any of the bullshit. But none of that mattered at the end of the day because I wanted to be happy. And happiness at that moment in time didn't mean being healthy, confident, funny, smart, or self-aware.

It meant being skinny.

MY NAPPY HAIR

One thing about me, as some of you know, is that I fucking love *colorful* hair.

Just like I think tattoos are ordained art when it comes to how we use them to adorn our bodies (regardless of their meanings), I feel very similarly about hair. It's one of the things that *crown* you, you know? Even before you open your mouth, your hair is one of your first "representatives." Sometimes it can tell you far more about a person than even the person in question themselves. Hence my preoccupation with hair and the really cool shit you can do with it to express yourself. Color in particular.

However. I wish I could sit here and say that my path to arriving at my affinity for (colorful) hair was a positive one and an affirming one, but if that were the case ... I probably wouldn't be here writing this, now would I? Nope, my hair's origin story goes way back. And most of it was not nice at all.

I should start off by saying that being a Black girl in this anti-Black world and this aggressively anti-Black country meant that I was unfortunately predestined to be saddled with issues about my hair. Even before escaping the womb. Now, being dark-skinned definitely added some additional hostility to it. And its texture (I'm in the 4C family—even though it seems like the collective is moving away from that particular hair texture chart) guaranteed that I'd be catching hell from many a nigga—including members of my own family who had the same fucking hair texture—for not having "good hair." But what I certainly wasn't prepared for was how being fat was primed to make all of this a lot fucking worse.

Let me elaborate.

Back in September 2020, rapper and songstress Lizzo sat down with Jameela Jamil to talk about body image and how she navigated social media as a fat Black woman. My personal feelings about the aforementioned actress aside, the sit-down left an impact on me. Not just because it was a pleasure to watch Lizzo on the rise but because Lizzo was sharing some experiences that I deeply empathized with and still experience. The thing that left the *biggest* impact on me as it pertains to that conversation was when Lizzo opened up about her hair— or rather, the negotiations she had to make with her hair as a fat Black woman.

One thing that stuck with me is when she said, quite frankly, "My cousin once told me, like, big girls shouldn't have short hair." And as she continued to elaborate, it clicked in my head— based on my own experiences—that having short hair wasn't even really something that we were "allowed" to do as fat Black women.

You see, by Lizzo sharing that small anecdote about her cousin, she hinted at an issue that fat Black girls and fat Black women deal with day after day: that sometimes we use the ever-changing state of our versatile hair to absorb the heavier blows of fatphobia fueled by anti-Blackness.

It's so funny. There are a lot of things fat people have to do to survive the everyday violence that we face from a society that finds our existence cumbersome. The same goes for bitch-ass niggas who need someone to punch down on. Much of these survival tools are defense mechanisms, and the first one that usually comes to mind is humor. And humor by way of self-deprecating jokes. And I'm not gonna lie, that's valid. In fact, it's so valid that I'm using that shit right now to get through writing this goddamn book. And yet. Focusing purely on that one defense mechanism against fatphobia starts to expose how ignorant everyone is about *racialized* fatphobia and how it's not possible to survive that through humor alone.

I don't have the luxury of being ignorant of this type of shit. This is precisely the reason I have often oscillated between my hair as a form of self-expression *and* also as a weapon of sorts, or rather a shield, in an attempt to protect me both from fucked-up respectability politics and from fatphobia.

Sometimes I think Solange wrote "Don't Touch My Hair" just for me. Because the song in itself manages to capture all the feelings—love, reverence, and even loathing—I've felt for the bundle of keratin strands coming out of my head. Hair has always been a Big Deal™ to me and for me. It was a battle-ground in my überconservative Nigerian home growing up. And no kid in that house could escape it or opt out of it. Both my mother and father were very strict about how all of their kids were expected to keep up with their hair. They were *aggressive* gender (binary) essentialists. In their mind, masculine = boy = short hair. And feminine = girl = long hair.

My parents absolutely deplored the possibility of any of my brothers walking about with long hair. It was true. And they didn't mind traumatizing them in order to enforce this "concern" of theirs. They made that abundantly clear when they shaved my youngest brother's, Tommy's, hair when he was about to turn three.

Tommy was super young then. Practically still a baby. And though he didn't have the language at the time to *properly* object, I remember my father bringing him back home from the barber-shop one day and he was *sobbing. Boohooing* honestly. And over the course of the next week or so, I'd observe him sitting in front of his toys, not playing with them at all. Instead, he'd be touching his head absently. Staring off into space. Probably wondering where his hair went. And if it might ever grow back.

But my parents clearly didn't care and pressed on with this gendered hair bullshit.

In fact, this weird essentialism of theirs even stretched to styles like, say, cornrows—mainly because of their gender bias, but additionally because of the nasty and anti-Black way American media had completely demonized that hairstyle on Black men. To them, they didn't want their sons walking around looking like "criminals" and "felons." So, cornrows or anything that looked similar was out of the question. The boys were expected to have everything cut very low, in a neat fade. But even that had its own rule. The fade itself wasn't allowed to have any sort of "crazy" design or line cut into it. A simple, clean fade was all that was allowed.

For us girls? Well, the ridiculousness of their essentialism was intensified because of misogynoir, of course. My mother had the most say over this, and she had strict rules about the upkeep that included monthly perms, touch-ups, and required length. And she mostly did all this herself because she had many reservations about anyone else touching our heads (other Nigerian and immigrant children know what I'm talking about). But also because she was very cheap. And she didn't think she should have to pay anyone to do all of this. The only things she outsourced were protective styles like braids and sew-ins. And even then, she still tried to be cheap, and we, the girls, suffered by proxy, as it made it that much more difficult to get our hair done. Word traveled quite quickly about her trying to haggle with assorted hair braiders and stylists.

Nigerian women talk, okay?

Anyway, though my mother took over our hair responsibilities, she would occasionally allow my dad to chime in. And the only time he really chimed in was to reiterate that we needed to keep our hair long and healthy and straight in order to look like properly *feminine* girls, and then grow into properly *feminine* women. This meant that haircuts were completely out of the question for both me and my sister. There would be none of that! No autonomy—but particularly hair autonomy—was allowed.

This bullshit rule about "feminine" hair applied doubly to me because of my dark skin. There are a lot of silent rules when it comes to respectability politics and what is considered "feminine" for someone of my hue. And Father knew them well! Like I already mentioned, he wasn't exactly pleased with my skin tone, despite him being dark himself, and that was made worse by my being the only fat child in the family. Essentially, I already had two strikes. So, basically, my hair was my last way to placate him—especially where my bird-ass mother was concerned—and make sure I could avoid additional physical and verbal abuse. And this was proven time and time again when my father would treat me much, much better when my hair was done in the type of "feminine" way that *he* liked.

I'll let you unpack the gross and borderline incestuous implications of all that while I continue.

Anyway, the anti-Black gender essentialism where hair was concerned didn't stop at my childhood "home" either. Nope. It stretched far beyond those walls.

Case in point, there were a couple of elders (unfortunately, and usually, women) at my mother's church who always had something smart to say about my weight. They'd make snide comments to my mother about what she was feeding me and that I was probably eating very "well." Some even got bold enough to tell me that I would be so pretty if I just lost some weight—while pointing at my round belly with either their eyes or their fingers. This was technically *mild* compared to what I had heard from my own parents. But hurtful nonetheless.

However, on the days when my hair was particularly on point? When my mom had burned my forehead and ears just to give me a silk press, or I was fresh off of a perm, with a head full of perm scabs? Well, there were no snide comments. No side-eyes about how I looked in comparison to skinnier church girls. All of the attention was focused on my hair and how "good" and "respectable" it looked. Suddenly, all the covert and overt hate tossed at me, a child, over my body evaporated if my hair looked "good" enough that day. Suddenly, my hair somehow cloaked the other "ugly" parts of me—like my skin and weight—and turned them into nonfactors.

It was mind-boggling. And really, really fucked up.

And unfortunately, because I was a child, and my higher self and my brain were fighting for their lives, I took the wrong lesson from this. I didn't clock that society hates fat Black girls so much that they require everything about us—especially when it comes to our appearance—to be in *tip-top* shape before we even receive a granule of respect. Nor did I clock that having to use my hair as a fucking defense mechanism was all the way fucked up. Nor did I clock that all of this shit was unacceptable and I should be respected regardless of how fat I was. Nope. Instead, I internalized that I could avoid *potential* abuse concerning my weight if my hair was distracting or "respectable" enough.

Eventually though, as I grew older, *distracting* didn't necessarily have to be *respectable*.

The turning point came during my senior year of high school—mainly, the summer before my first year in college. You see, ever since I started working at sixteen, my mom decided to saddle me with all hair expenses, since I was "grown" enough now. Which, on the surface, sounds completely reasonable to *some*. But understand that with my parents, everything they did always turned out to be some adverse reaction to something I or my siblings did. Both parents hated the fact that I was making a little money of my own from my T.J. Maxx job. So my mom became hands-off with my hair but still required the same kind of upkeep as before, and my dad sometimes would straight-up react with violence, because narcissists who happen to be parents always react violently when their pet children gain a semblance of independence.

I was getting to the point that I could not afford to keep up with my ridiculous hair schedule *and* put aside money so

I wasn't completely destitute as I stepped onto UChicago soil for the first time. I tried asking for help from my parents—even offered to pay them back, which . . . lmao—but they didn't go for it. So, eventually, when the summer rolled around, I had had enough and I decided to commit a cardinal sin in the Eduwa household as a girl.

I opted to go straight for the Big Chop™.

My. Parents. Were. Furious.

I still remember us all standing outside the garage that day because my mom saw me in the window as I exited my car. And by the time I had walked up to the garage, she'd flown out there with my dad. My mother started crying and throwing up and shitting and pissing. You would've thought that I had stabbed her. My father? Well, he took the opportunity to turn it into more verbal abuse.

"Look at yourself!" he barked. "Fat and ugly. Made it worse. You look like a man!" I remember taking a deep breath and staring at both of them.

"You don't pay for my hair anymore. And Mom doesn't pay for my hair anymore," I said. "Therefore, you don't get a say in how my hair looks anymore." I stared him down until he scoffed and stormed past me and into the street. Meanwhile, my mom continued to sob. I finally had enough of the both of them and walked past her and into the house.

It was so interesting. While I had been apprehensive about cutting my hair, I had ultimately felt good about doing it because it was one of the first ways I was able to reclaim autonomy in that household—the first being the day I decided to get a job. And I had let myself be happy for two seconds before I got home . . . and before it was ruined once again by my parents. Like it was their whole life.

I'd like to sit here and tell you that their reactions, particularly my father's, didn't harm me at all and that I immediately rose above it. But that wouldn't be true. These are people who were supposed to protect me and build me up. And send me into the world as the best version of myself. And they were hell-bent on doing the opposite.

The whole situation further damaged my relationship with hair. And myself. So much so that this damaged perception of Black hair found its way into my writing. Into my art. I can't tell you how many character descriptions that included lovers observing other lovers' "long, wavy hair" popped up in my short stories. Descriptions of lovers seamlessly running fingers through each other's hair in my poems. Like, I truly wish Willow Smith's "Wait a Minute!" had existed back then, because the lines where she discusses how her dreads weren't made to have fingers ran through them might have hit differently—and convinced me that my hair was *not* the problem.

Despite what I had been told my whole life.

Going into college with this hair-obsessed mindset proved to be fairly difficult. And additionally damaging. But it didn't start out that way ... at first. After my Big Chop™, I wore my hair naturally for quite a while, in a burgeoning Afro. This went on for about two years. And I'm proud to say that freeing myself from perms and heat damage—a personal choice that unintentionally coincided with the natural hair movement of the early to mid-2000s—meant that my hair practically blossomed. Like a big cloud on my head. It did wonders for my self-esteem, not only because I felt "beautiful" but just for the pure fact that it made me feel like my decision to go natural hadn't been in vain—despite the fallout I had experienced from my parents because of it.

I existed in this space for a while. But as time passed, I started to notice that it didn't quite have the same effect that it did with my "respectable" hair, the hair of my past that had been permed and burned and fried to death. To make matters worse, for obvious reasons, my hair growing *up*, rather than down, did some interesting things to my brain too. Because by growing up, my hair probably wasn't doing the same work to distract from my face and my body as it had done before. I was that fucked up about it. I was pissed that it wasn't *obscuring* me properly as it had before.

So, in my day-to-day, I still found myself overcompensating with humor, being stared at in public while eating (of course, I'm no punk, so I always mean-mugged back), or having my space violated because, by virtue of being fat, people assume that you are already taking up enough space. Plus, there were so many white people—who by definition have no boundaries—that kept trying to stick their unwashed hands into my 'fro. This continued until about my second or third year until: a) I tore my ACL and literally didn't have the ability or the range to do my own hair anymore, and b) I saw someone in one of my film classes with brightly colored pink hair. And resolved that I wanted a similar look for myself.

Enter my current preoccupation with brightly colored hair.

I should note that prior to my decision to begin experimenting with brightly colored hair, I was also experiencing some additional hurdles in trying to make peace with my hair and repair our relationship. Tearing my ACL and losing my ability to walk for a while meant that I was back to putting on more weight. The weight that I had worked to keep at bay throughout the end of high school was slowly creeping its way back. So, the probability of my hair "failing" to obscure the parts of me that I didn't like was made even more intense. And on top of that, my hair unfortunately became a magnet for a certain hue people, and their nasty-ass hands, and their penchant for exoticization and fetishization. I found that it had also, weirdly enough, rendered me invisible. Like seriously. It was almost like people saw the puff . . . and then nothing else.

And I technically should have been "grateful," in a way, for the invisibility. Because at least no one was abusing me because I was fat and, in this case, becoming even fatter. But it wasn't that simple.

There were a few things going on here, but for me, it turned out to be something I'd bookmark, in terms of how it made me feel. I know people like to pretend that they don't want or crave attention, but it's a painful thing to go unseen. And unnoticed. Particularly when you're coming out of an abusive environment, where all you heard all the time was how terrible you were. And quiet and overt disgust about having to coexist with you—based on how you look. It does something to your brain. And if you're not careful, it can send you down a really, really dark and existential path. And have you asking questions about whether you even exist. Or if you're merely an apparition. A Sim in someone else's game.

All of this, of course, is fucked up and literally contingent on combinations of anti-Black racism, fatphobia, colorism, texturism, and respectability politics—all made more potent by way of internalization.

But I didn't care.

Nor is this something I really thought about. I wasn't interested in pondering the forces that were making me feel this way. I was merely concerned with, you know, *no longer* feeling this way. No matter what form that took.

The very next week, I returned with my own electric-blue wig. And as expected, perceptions of me changed in big and small ways. I remember suddenly becoming *visible* in that same film class. It was like I was a new student and I had just transferred to this godforsaken school. The professor made a comment about how cool my hair looked (that was the first time he had spoken to me all year, as we were closing in on *midterm* season), and some cishet boy I had been eyeing the whole time decided that today was the day to notice me and say hi.

Unbelievable. But I ate it up at the time, of course.

Even with my so-called friends, there were compliments about the drastic change in my appearance and how "good" I looked—with me taking silent notes that I had never received said compliments when my hair was natural. What's more is that once my hair had undergone this change, I didn't feel the need to do the same old disarming shticks I did to distract from being fat because there was no need.

My hair was back to *technically* doing all the disarming for me.

But in a way that gave me the "positive" attention I had been feening for since I left my parents' household.

Years later (about two), I would circle back to this moment after having some come-to-Jesus moments with myself about my hair and body, and even ask these same friends some hard questions about why they suddenly felt more comfortable around me with my hair being louder and more "feminine" and less "Black." Some answers, like my brightly colored hair ironically "softening" my appearance, I expected. Such answers were still anti-Black, but they were again expected. Others, like apparently my new hair making my friends suddenly forget to notice the rest of my body (i.e., that I was fat) and focus on other parts of my personality and being (my face, too, for example), took me for a spin—even with my sordid relationship with hair and weight.

After all, I had spent over two years with some of these individuals. Laughed with them. Cried with them. Had mental breakdowns with them as we tried to avoid flunking out or living in a perpetual state of academic probation. Imagine how jarring it was to hear that most of these people never even once thought about the full range of my humanity—past my body—until my hair changed to something less "ethnic," or unless I was cracking some funny joke because I was so damn "hilarious."

See? I told you this was all fucked up.

Miraculously, this mindset didn't last forever. No. Because moving to California (to be discussed at length later) would prove to be even worse than this. It would be the *supreme* breaking point.

After college, my first string of jobs in LA, including the media ones, were very brutal—save for my time at Into(more). This was made worse by me being bombarded daily with fatphobia and colorism. Indeed. The city drove me to be so obsessed with my appearance and how I felt about it in "comparison" to everyone else, and, once again, I ended up snapping and shaving my head. Also known as my second Big Chop™.

Granted, I know that it is probably *very* fucked up that every time I try to free myself of societal bullshit, I end up running clippers through my hair like my name is fucking Samson. But in my mind, freeing myself of the thing that was driving about 50 percent of my anxieties over my appearance (because it's not like I could run clippers over my body and my fat) could help me move past my currently shitty time in LA. And start from scratch. Again. I had to disrupt the obsession. The hyperfixation. I had to rid myself of this shit taking up valuable real estate in my brain.

It was pretty risky business on my part. But it ended up paying off in a big way:

I had to look myself in the face. Bare face. Body too.

Without the bells and whistles that was my hair. And teach myself to fall in love with all of it. Not again, but for the *first* time.

As I am writing this, it's been 1,004 days and counting since I left that fucking city and that fucking state. And my journey of fully accepting myself and my looks continues. After letting my hair do its thing and just *exist* post–the second Big Chop™, I'm back to experimenting with it again. Back to trying different colors and styles. Currently, I'm in an extended loc phase.

I am happy to report that my experimentation with hair has slowly, but surely, moved from being motivated by the self-loathing I had reserved for my whole body. These days, my experimentation stems from another place.

A place that is genuinely curious about who I am. And maybe who I want to be. A place that is committed to meeting every possible iteration of myself. And shaking her goddamn hand for making it this far.

You know, multitudes and all that shit.

MY (LACK OF) RELIGION

I don't have a lot of bad things to say about being a Taurus. Mostly because I'm not a man—yes, whatever you do, please stay away from Taurus men—but mainly because we're pretty glamorous and all about enjoying the pleasures of life. Now, how we go about doing that can potentially have good or bad repercussions, based on how grimy or not grimy we are in our pursuit of pleasure.

However, something Taureans struggle with, as a collective, is how *invested* we get when it comes to certain things—like actual physical "things" or even ideas. Once we get something in our brains, or we form an opinion on something, it's pretty hard to change our minds. Pretty hard to *move* us, so to speak. We go in full throttle and it's gonna take, ironically, an act of God (or several acts, if I'm being honest!) to dissuade us from the particular notion we are trying to desperately hang on to.

This includes belief systems we choose to adopt. And for me, this was the infamous Abrahamic religion known as Christianity.

Whenever I mention to people that I am an ex-Christian (ex-Baptist specifically, or "Full Gospel Baptist" as spoken in my mother's church), the reactions are usually split. There's either complete disbelief because of how critical I am of its doctrine, OR people figure that it tracks . . . again because of how critical I am of its doctrine. Eventually, people always ask what the *thing* was that did it. What the final straw was that caused me to completely walk away from that bullshit. It's not an easy question to answer, and when I say that, I'm not talking about mere trauma, because that's a given. No, I'm talking about how it actually wasn't just *one* thing that set me off. There were several things. In fact? It was practically everything. Like every single thing.

You see, when you are raised under a religion or "faith" that tends to attack all aspects of who you are or even how you think, at separate intervals of your life, at one point, any rational person is going to fucking snap.

This is, perhaps, what I would call my comorbid beef with Christianity. The fact that it attacked me on all fronts. I'd had to square off against its fatphobia-fueled purity culture, not to mention the fact that I was also fighting for my life when it came to my undiscovered bisexuality.

Attending my mother's church, which I shall hereby refer to as Doorway to Heaven Church, was my first introduction to all of the bullshit I mentioned above. And you can imagine the damage it ended up doing over nearly two decades.

On the surface, the church looked harmless enough. It was comprised of a thriving community of Black people—predominantly Nigerian. The presence of various tribes and ethnic groups within that (including Edo, Igbo, and Yoruba) made for interesting demographics as well. This aspect had been very important to my mother since she had left her larger community and family back in Nigeria. And as expected, everyone primarily worked in healthcare, law, education, finance, or something complementary or acceptable enough to group with the other four.

Of course, if you didn't work in any of those sectors, you may as well have been useless or dead. And if you weren't Yoruba, you may as well have been *doubly* dead.

But that's a conversation for another day.

Anyway, the church was predominantly run by the Sowandes, a Yoruba duo with a rack of kids. Or excuse me, *Rev. Dr.*

Phineas Sowande and his wife *Rev.* Mrs. Agnes Sowande—since titles were so important to them and all. We had attended for as far back as I can remember—which would mean that it had been a thing since I was at least four (a.k.a., when I gained consciousness and awareness of my existence, a.k.a., the day my life ended). With "we" being my mother, me, and my other siblings.

My eldest sister would eventually branch off and go do her own thing—mainly because she didn't buy into the whole "no premarital sex" bullshit. And she got the side-eye for it, of course. This was always funny to me because there was a lot of "pot meet kettle" hypocrisy going on with several prominent members and their children . . . and enough babies to show for it, if you know what I mean. I'd wanted to leave with my sister, but because she low-key high-key hated me and because my mom was determined to "hold on," a.k.a., have control over at least one of her daughters, I was forced to stay at my mom's shitty old church and (attempt to) be just as "devout" as my mom was about this iron-fisted religion.

And this devoutness of hers included her being at Doorway to Heaven Church nearly 24/7 . . . and praying just as much in her closet back at home—with my father, the child molester, in the next room. Quite the juxtaposition I would say.

Still. Praying in itself isn't a bad thing, but she did so in a way that was very . . . obsessive. But when you place the frequency of her prayers along with her hyperfixation on church attendance, you'll start to realize something that I didn't clock until years later. I don't believe my mother was actually religious. Nah. My mother *posed* as hyper-religious because she was a sinner who had abjectly failed my sister post-abuse. Rather than taking actions against my father that I cannot legally print here, actions that a mother *should* take in defense of her daughter, my mom conducted herself like many abusers and enablers conduct themselves. Which is to say that many abusers and enablers believe that if they pray hard enough, God may look the other way as they continue to rape, abuse, violate, molest, terrorize, and harm people and the world around them.

But what many don't realize is that there are absolutely things in this world that God should *not* forgive you for.

That said, staying at Doorway to Heaven Church with my faker of a mom proved to be a watershed moment in my origin story. Because you see, while it was in my nature, as a child, to keep to myself and fly under the radar just so I could experience a modicum of peace, that was not possible at Doorway to Heaven Church. Nah. I don't know how, but there was an intense spotlight on everything that happened in that church and everyone who happened to set foot in that church. Honestly, if I'd known what the word *surveillance* meant back then, that's definitely what I would have called it.

I mean, sure: we were all there to listen to the word of God—allegedly—but really, Doorway to Heaven was a glorified social club and cult all wrapped up in a neat bow . . . with a dash of tribalism. With Rev. and Mrs. Sowande at its ugly head.

They ran the church with an iron fist and, as my friend Regina would say, their *bully* pulpit. Case in point, every child of a certain age, I'm talking preteen and teen, was expected—no, required!—to be in the always-off-key church choir. We were also required to sit in the first two rows of congregation seats so we could always be "close to the stage" whenever the pastoral staff wanted to summon us to sing some song. Which . . . I call bullshit to be honest. I know they sat us down there to make sure we were paying attention to their long-winded sermons about nothing. It also didn't help that from the pulpit, the Sowandes' favorite place, you could see everything going on in those first two rows. And they *loved* calling you out in front of the entire congregation if you dozed off, were talking, were reading (something that *wasn't* the Bible, as Regina and I often did), were breathing, were writing (in my case—it's a wonder I didn't have my journal or series of short stories confiscated), or were otherwise distracted in a way they didn't like. And they always called you out by name, to be quickly followed up with some dry, passive-aggressive joke—which you just *knew* you were going to pay for later when you got home and had to hear from your parents how you had "shamed" them that day. And God forbid your parents decided to add to that embarrassment in real time by summoning you to sit beside them like a wounded puppy for the rest of the service.

The choir itself had a dress code. I mean, we technically had robes and all, but none of these so-called church and choir leaders could ever get it together where tailoring was concerned. So a separate and fluctuating uniform was established. It usually consisted of black bottoms—could be slacks or skirts—and some solid-colored top (which was often blue or white, sometimes red). The top typically had to be nice and buttoned. Dresses were allowed only if they fit the above color code and the hem at the bottom passed your fingertips. Skirts had to follow the fingertip rule as well. Or, depending on the day, make it to your knees. It all sounded simple enough, but it was nothing but.

You see, the choir-member-to-proper-and-upstanding-lady-and-wife-in-training pipeline was no joke. And the choir's dress code quickly became a way to reinforce this pipeline. The main goal of the choir itself was to make sure none of us niggas, including the fellas, had any fucking free time to "get into trouble"—so to speak. We seriously were there for almost half the week: Wednesday. Saturday. Sunday. Sometimes Friday too. For Bible study or choir practice. And the choir's dress code meant that all elders—ALL elders—had a free pass to heavily scrutinize and criticize our bodies for everything that appeared to be a flaw or an offense.

Curves, and particularly curves that accompanied *fat*, were considered particularly flawed and offensive.

It's true. And as a girl, even if you met and exceeded the infamous fingertip rule, you weren't safe. Any inkling of having an ass, tits, or hips—even under your appropriate uniform—was met with lecherous stares from grown-ass, decrepit, "godly" men and jaundiced stares from grown-ass, passive-aggressively malicious, and "godly" women. We were constantly chastised and lectured for *tempting* these men and boys and leading them astray—particularly if they decided that one of us had curves that were very offensive that day. Not to mention the fact that fat on top of all that meant that you'd get extra heat. I cannot tell you how many times I or my mother got pulled aside and had to listen to strangers advising me that I should lose some weight and advising me on *how* to lose said weight.

I got so annoyed with it all that I tried to avoid skirts and dresses, and instead wear pants. But that was never quite enough because, again, ass and hips are going to do their own thing regardless, even under your slacks. Titties in particular became a point of contention for me because I was a "late bloomer" (I hate that fucking term), and my titties didn't really *drop* until I was about fourteen. Because my mom was committed to keeping me in a state of perpetual preadolescence and adolescence, she pretty much ignored my changing body. And so, here I was, walking around with moderately large and floppy titties—to the chagrin of older women and the delight of older men. All until Rev. Mrs. Sowande took it upon herself to gift me my first training bra.

Now, I know what you're probably thinking. You're probably thinking that it was really "sweet" that Mrs. Sowande decided to gift me something like that and spare me from further embarrassment and unspoken hostility from the masses, but, again, it wasn't that simple. And she wasn't *really* doing it out of the goodness of her heart.

To explain, the training bra she gave me was several sizes too small. I'm sure by design, just to highlight how inexcusably large my titties were getting. And the way she presented it to me was brilliantly cruel. Like, if you weren't looking closely, you would have missed the cruelty entirely.

"Alexandria! Hi! How are you, my child?" Mrs. Sowande waved me over from where I sat in the second row. She stepped down from the pulpit and began to walk to her seat. Church had ended about ten minutes ago, and everyone had mostly exited. I was dragging a bit because I had to pack up my belongings.

"I am very well, auntie. Thank you for asking." I walked over and curtsied in front of her (at a distance), my bag hanging from my shoulder.

"Good! Good." She added, "Would you come over here please?"

"Yes, auntie." I stepped closer.

"I have noticed you are growing taller. Like a weed. Getting very big too!" She smiled and I smiled back. "Very, very, *very big* in fact." She cut her eyes to my belly and then looked back up at me. Her smile was still intact, but mine had evaporated from my face. "Anyway, I wanted to give you something."

Mrs. Sowande reached into her oversized purse and pulled out an off-white bandeau. She nearly shoved it into my hands before addressing me again.

"You are big on top as well," she continued. "You are a lady. And that is no way for you to be walking around. This will help. Since your mother is too busy to, I'm sure." She smiled again. "Please greet your mother for me, okay? Okay!" She held her disingenuous smile before grabbing her purse and sauntering off.

"Thank you . . . ?" I stood there in stunned silence.

I truly didn't know whether to laugh or to cry. On one hand, she'd made a very valid point about my mom being checked out when it came to me growing up. My mom often ignored shit like this until it was too late. And then she would blame you for not "saying something," as if she wasn't the fucking parent. On the other hand, the Sowandes looked down on everybody in this damned church. Everyone. Absolutely everyone! But this was much, much more pronounced with my family because our dysfunction—thanks to my parents, who often demanded an audience, particularly with any pastor who would listen—was more widely known than others'.

Explaining what had happened to my mother later was ...
well, I'll let you guess.

As predicted, my mom was not very pleased. It was clear
she was horrified that I was growing up and advancing in age,
a fact my new training bra made undeniable. From the look
on her face, you would have thought I'd threatened to kill her
with the damn thing when she first saw it in my hand on our
drive home.

At the house, however, she changed her tune slightly. She
expressed slight gratitude when we were all settled and I had
put the bra away in my underwear drawer. I remember her referring to Mrs. Sowande as wise. And helpful. And so intuitive. She
praised her for taking initiative in a way that she had failed to.
I was relieved at the positive shift in her tone and thought that
would be the last I'd hear of it.

Wrong!

As all Nigerian youth like myself know, elder Nigerian
women tend to be rather—to be frank—phony and shady, while
dressing it up in thinly veiled flattery. Sisterhood between any
random group where they were assembled was strained at best.
It was giving *Real Housewives of Lagos*. Frenemies all around.
This episode featured my mother versus Mrs. Sowande.

By the time 6:00 p.m. rolled around, my mom was warming
leftover rice and beef stew in the kitchen—and loudly fuming
over the bra incident from hours earlier. My father was at work,
working his usual twelve-hour shift. Thankfully.

"Who does Agnes think she is?" my mom hissed. "She thinks
she is better than me, eh? She thinks she knows better than me?
Me, Caroline Eduwa?" She slammed the microwave shut. "It is
not possible. It is not possible!"

I placed the last plate on the table, which officially ended
my current task of setting the table. As *soon* as I set the
plate down, my mom turned to me like I had just smashed
it. I braced myself for one of her impending (and extended)
screaming fits.

"And *you*," she continued her tirade, "why did you take it? Why did you pocket her gift? Is it because you want to shame me? Embarrass me? Is that it?"

"Mom—"

"*Shut up!*" my mom shouted. "Don't you *dare in your life* talk back to me," she hissed again. "You should not have taken it. You could have said 'no thank you' like an obedient child. Instead, you took it. So you can humiliate me."

No surprise that my mom was being melodramatic. But this time, the melodrama was accompanied by straight-up lies. While she was, perhaps, rightfully embarrassed by Mrs. Sowande's actions, depending on how you look at it, there's absolutely no way she would urge me to reject a gift from the pastor's wife (and by extension, the pastor) if she'd been in her right mind.

Like many other people who attended Doorway to Heaven Church, one of my mom's hobbies included kissing the Sowandes' asses. I'm talking full sycophant shit. I guess everyone did that to curry favor with the elitist pair. Or get on the church staff. Or get into advantageous positions that would lead to planning the women's or men's retreats. My mom's main reason consisted of her trying to distract from the reject circus that was my family. Either way, no sane person was going to reject a gift from those two—no matter how insulting the gift turned out to be.

My mom continued yelling at the top of her lungs while I walked away. She got even louder when I exited the room, which tracks. Several minutes later, I returned with the bra that had set her off.

"Mommy, I am sorry for accepting her gift, even though I didn't know that I wasn't supposed to do that." I couldn't help but end with a little snark. "I am going to give it to you so you can give it back to Mrs. Sowande."

"So I can be embarrassed again? I don't think so," she scoffed, piling rice onto the plates on the table. "I don't want to see that rubbish anymore. Take it away from here."

"There's no pleasing you. Shocker," I said under my breath. Her head snapped in my direction. "What did you say?"

I began to weigh my options carefully in my head, running several equations on what the chances were that I would die here today—in this very spot. And as you know, dear reader, the chances were very high. Black parents across the African diaspora aren't fond of backtalk in general. But Nigerian parents? Ha! You'll receive one beating after another after another and then they'll ship you off to their great uncle—or whomever—back in Nigeria so that you can learn "manners and discipline."

"Can you not speak? I said, *what did you say!*" she screamed.

I briefly considered throwing in the towel and apologizing for my insolence. But since I was already wildly suicidal even at this age, I restated my snarky comment.

"There's no pleasing you," I said. "You're mad that I took the gift, but you would have been mad if I said no to Mrs. Sowande. And I would have been 'disrespectful' then too." I shrugged. "So there."

Needless to say, while it was great to get that off my chest, the price I paid was very high. Not only did she smack the shit out of me (like a *string* of slaps till I hit the ground) but she told my dad as soon as he got home and I ended up getting another beating the next morning.

And yet. It was worth it.

Because I never heard about that stupid-ass training bra ever again.

DESPITE ALL the chaos that this so-called church was dragging into my brain and into my parents' house, my stubborn, Taurean mind was still deep in this horseshit and committed to trying to abide by it. And for a while, after the bra fiasco, I managed to fly under the radar.

And then everything changed, AGAIN, when I and my other peers officially became *teenagers*.

I swear to God that every psychopathic church looks forward to this moment. You know, the moment where kids are in the thick of puberty and vulnerable in so many ways because they don't know what the fuck is going on with their minds and their bodies, and are learning about what the fuck hormones are for the first time. Yes. This is the crucial moment that they seize to impart—you guessed it—the infamous rhetoric and doctrine known as purity culture.

What the fuck is purity culture? Great question. Let Linda Kay Klein, purity culture recovery coach and author of *Pure: Inside the Evangelical Movement That Shamed a Generation of Young Women and How I Broke Free*, explain some of it for you:

> In purity culture, gender expectations are based on a strict, stereotype-based binary. Men are expected to be strong, "masculine" leaders of the household, church, and (to a lesser extent) society. Women are expected to support them—to be pretty, "feminine," sweet, supportive wives and mothers.
>
> Sexual expectations vary by gender. Everyone is expected to maintain absolute sexlessness before marriage (that means no sexual thoughts, feelings, or actions). And upon marriage, they are expected to flip their sexuality on like a light switch. However, men are taught their minds are evil, whereas women are taught their bodies are evil. That is to say, men's thoughts and actions are said to be either pure or impure, while women *themselves* are said to be either pure or impure. Sexual metaphors abound: A "pure" woman is compared to a brand new shiny car while an "impure" one is compared to a used car that everyone around town has already driven and that isn't worth much anymore; a "pure" woman is compared to a delicious hamburger just set down on the table while an "impure" woman is compared to the last slobbery bite of that hamburger, etc.[*]

Like I alluded to earlier, the best part of this poppycock is that women and young girls—with our pure and impure

*Linda Kay Klein, "What Is Purity Culture?" on Linda Kay Klein's official website, accessed September 10, 2022, https://lindakayklein.com/what-is-purity-culture/.

bodies—are blamed entirely for influencing the thoughts, feelings, and actions of men when it comes to sex. They're the head of everything, right? And we can't be distracting the "head" with our titties, right? We can't lead these "men of God" astray with our voluptuous and impure bodies, right? Because surely if they even think about one little titty, they won't inherit the kingdom of God, right?

Right.

It was insane. It was crazy. It was fucking *nuts*! But this was the expectation. This was the *gospel*. And the church surely hammered it into us. This was not any type of safe space for a young girl. Fuck a safe space. There would be no sexual liberation here. No sexual empowerment. No impassioned talks about "owning" one's sexuality. Nope.

Sex, here, in this context, was a weapon. A demonic weapon that promised to drag both men and women to hell if abused, a.k.a., performed *out* of wedlock. And the only way to stop this doomsday scenario was for a young girl, like me, to *protect* my "virginity" until my dying breath—or, you know, marriage.

Yup. The only way to avert the apocalypse apparently was to be a good Christian girl by closing my legs and making sure that my pussy remained *untouched* (yes, masturbation included) and *unseen* until some random man of God decided to present himself for marriage. Then, and only then, would my life—and sex life post-wedding night—be "perfect."

Now some people like to split hairs on whether saving the bullshit known as virginity was set in place to honor God or to be presented as the best gift ever to your husband when it's time to consummate your marriage. The latter obviously makes the most sense with this whole "men are the head of everything ever" bullshit, but in my short, two decades of life, I found that the former also plays a substantial role.

You want God to bless your marriage, right? And I'm assuming you want it to last forever and ever and ever and ever? Well, with this line of purity culture logic, God won't be blessing your marriage if you drag your "impure" pussy into it.

I think the most fucked-up part about this is that even if you abide by this fuck-ass shit, it's a lose-lose for you . . . particularly if you're a *Black* girl. Firstly because Blackness and purity culture are technically *incompatible* because of Blackness itself being read as "impure." And because purity culture itself is a white supremacist concept. Secondly, because if women's bodies are already inherently impure according to the gospel of purity culture, then that means that *Black* girls "exist" in *doubly* impure bodies.

And if you have the unmitigated gall to even *think* about "being" gay, God help you again.

Purity culture and its binary gender laws and mandates don't allow any room for homosexuality or anything that strays from 100 percent uncut heterosexuality. All and any sex is only allowed to happen between a singular cis man and cis woman. Any sex "had" outside of that is demonic and not of God.

So I probably don't have to tell you that I was approximately *triply* fucked considering that I was a (fat) Black girl who wasn't yet aware that I was bisexual and demisexual.

The introduction of purity culture launched a complete onslaught against crucial parts of my identity and being. It was endless. I had managed to get most of the Nigerian elders off my back where fatphobia was concerned when my binge eating, my purging, and my yo-yo dieting started to yield results, but I was still no match for the demonization of sex *and* nonstop slander against members of the "Rainbow Mafia."

Everything from Sunday school to standard church sermons emphasized saving sex for marriage. But some of my peers experimented in the shadows anyway, only to be saddled with the guilt of one thousand sinners. Sex was only for marriage, the church said, even as out-of-wedlock babies started popping up sporadically in the congregation. "No marriage, no sex" was all the rage, even as purity culture made future couples who were unlucky enough to buy into the hype completely sex-repulsed.

Chaos and sexual repression existed all around me and were constantly drilled into my brain. Sometimes, it got so bad that I'd completely dissociate whenever my high school friends started talking about sex because I didn't want to be caught slipping. Mind you, I was growing up in a time where the book *I Kissed Dating Goodbye* was experiencing an interesting resurgence and going head-to-head against TV shows like, you guessed it, *The Secret Life of the American Teenager* AND *Pretty Little Liars*. *Pretty Little Liars* was especially a big deal back then, seeing as one of its main characters and secondary characters were both gay *and* nonwhite. And I'm not ashamed to say that watching both characters love on each other got maybe like two synapses firing in my brain, and I briefly entertained the thought that maybe, just maybe, Christianity was full of shit when it came to demonizing homosexuality.

Eventually, my curiosity about sex won over repression, and I started experimenting with masturbation heading into high school. But even my curiosity couldn't survive the constant gay-bashing that Doorway to Heaven Church was so, so fond of.

"How can a man lie with a man and a woman lie with a woman?" Mrs. Sowande, in full reverend mode, sneered from her pulpit during a sermon one Sunday. "It is wicked. It is a wicked thing! And not of God. May God punish those who even *think* about doing such a thing."

I remember thinking, "Well, damn. A nigga can't *think* now?" I was seventeen then, but I quickly pushed the thought away—because following that trail of thought would have surely led me down a rabbit hole where I would have discovered my bisexuality much sooner.

Another Doorway to Heaven fave was invoking the infamous "Adam and Eve, not Adam and Steve" mantra. Luckily, Doorway youth weren't fond of the phrase, seeing as it was downright corny. But another phrase, "Love the sinner, hate the sin," caught on like wildfire. The disgust at gay *anything* still existed. Its presence was still at the core of the phrase. But unlike throwing around words like "faggots" or "fairies" or "sissies" or "demons" or even "eternal damnation," The Gays™ were simply dismissed as confused sinners that would eventually come back from the dark side and step into the light if you, a pious and perfect Christian, were simply *nice* to them. Not genuinely kind. "Nice."

Admittedly, I fell for the latter phrase. The passive, toothless nature of it spoke to me and convinced me that hate in this context didn't need to exist because everyone could be saved. Duh! *Of course,* I was against the virulent hate preachers like the Sowandes spewed from their pulpits day in and day out. But I still was hellbent on operating according to "the Word." And the Word said that The Gays™ had a one-way ticket to hell if they *remained* gay. So I became overly concerned about using niceness (I know, I know) to save my homosexual brethren and sistren.

I told the "nicer" version of The Gospel of Sky Daddy™ to everyone who would hear me. I'd shyly throw it into conversations when the topic came up. I still can't believe that none of my nonbelieving friends and peers at the time told me to shut the fuck up. Because I definitely would have told me to shut the fuck up. But they were patient with me. Exceedingly so. And still, I continued to be on that bullshit.

Ultimately, this was challenged when one of my good high school friends, Alyssa, came out as a lesbian.

The most interesting part is that she came out in *stages.* She didn't know it at the time, and I'm not even sure she knows it now as I'm writing this, but it's the smartest thing she ever could have done. And the way she did it greatly affected what I thought about all those Christian sermons I was taught.

Alyssa was super tactical about coming out. And she started by routinely holding one of her *friend's* hands (occasionally linking arms, too, if only to beat the homosexual allegations). It was my senior year at this point. And I was two seconds from stepping onto a college campus. And because everyone else in our grade was focused on getting into college, too, no one really noticed that. No. No one really started paying attention until Alyssa started walking her "friend" to class. Like every day. Lots of folks dismissed it as the two being really, really, *really* close friends. Which obviously made sense. But I remember briefly weighing the possibility of that girl actually being Alyssa's girlfriend, but then I decided that I was delusional and needed to mind my business.

And then Alyssa confirmed my passing suspicion when I dropped her off at her house one day.

"I asked her to go to prom with me." Alyssa was grinning so hard. "And she said yes!"

". . . I'm confused?" I put the car in park right outside her house. "Why would you ask her to prom? I thought Connor asked you—"

She cut me off. "I'm gay, Alex. I'm gay. Connor never had a chance."

Regrettably, my only response, following a silence that lasted way too long (like unforgivably long) was to say, "Awesome!"

I remember her hitting me with an exasperated sigh before chucking deuces and going into her house. I sat in the car for a couple of seconds longer before I finally drove off.

How could God let this happen? How could God allow this to hit so close to home? Was this a test? Was I supposed to go full Christian dickhead and tell Alyssa, very *nicely*, that while I thought she and her now-confirmed girlfriend were cute, she was going to hell? And hope she received that kindly? How in the shit was I supposed to deploy "love the sinner, hate the sin" logic against her, my *close* friend?

Exactly. It didn't make any sense.

None of this shit made sense to me. And I pondered it all the way home. I had seen how she and her love constantly interacted. And nothing about that shit came off as "demonic." Or "wicked." There was real love there. And the Sowandes and other Christians I knew were always really hyped about referring to God as "love." So if there was *love* present in Alyssa's relationship, how in the fuck could it be considered "ungodly"? What is "ungodly" about two girls—Black girls to be clear— loving and adoring each other?

That one, tiny little question about Black girl love was enough to shake the foundations of nearly two decades of hate that I had been indoctrinated with.

I carried this question with me even as I received acceptance letters from colleges. Even as I ended up committing to UChicago. Even as I sat through Alyssa's valedictorian speech. Even as I walked across the stage to collect my high school diploma in my honors sash. Even as I packed my bags and left for Illinois. And even as I trudged through my first year at the school "where fun goes to die."

Hell, by the time I came back from UChicago for my first holiday break, I had turned the question over in my brain so many times that I wasn't shocked when my apprehensions about the question leaped out of my body and in front of two of my oldest friends, Eve and Harlow Washington.

Both of them had also just returned from college and we were hanging out at Eve's place, shooting the shit and taking one of the 348972304230741 quizzes Eve had come across and forwarded to us right before we all pulled up to her house. The latest one—the quiz of the hour—was basically an abbreviated version of the Kinsey Test. She'd come across it while she was taking a gender studies elective and had discovered that she might be asexual. And she had been curious to see what I and Harlow would discover about ourselves as well.

The two of them went back and forth about their results for like twenty minutes while they were sitting across from each other on an old sectional. And I was on the ground in front of them, legs crossed, quiet as a mouse. After the twenty-first minute, Harlow looked down at me and noticed that I kept staring at my phone and then off into space.

She cleared her throat. "Lex, you good?"

"Yeah, you haven't said anything for like half an hour," Eve said. "You okay?"

I started rubbing the bridge of my nose, specifically the part between both of my brows—a telltale sign of stress when it came to my assorted tics. Eve got even more concerned and sat up.

"Yo, what's going on? Are you pissed about the test? Because if you're pissed about the test—"

I cut her off. "I think I might be bisexual."

MY BISEXUAL AWAKENING

Last time on *Dragon Ball Z* . . .

Kidding! Kidding. Kind of.

And by kind of, I mean that I suppose I should tell you what happened after I let my friends know that there was a strong chance that I was, in fact, a card-carrying bisexual.

Well, before I dive into that, I should probably tell you that a small part of me had suspected that this was the case all along.

So, let us take a journey down the road of the origins of my bisexuality . . . starting with the phrase *girl crush*.

Such an interesting term! Both as a whole and when we look at the two words individually. "Girl" has an obvious definition, but when you deep it, it seems rather redundant to put in front of the word *crush* on its face; since "crush" is merely describing a brief yet intense infatuation with a certain someone and doesn't even particularly hint at the gender of the someone in question. Still. Growing up and then subsequently heading to high school meant that I quickly learned that "girl crush" functioned as shorthand for a couple of things.

The first included giving someone like myself—sometimes girl, sometimes woman—the opportunity to express admiration for another girl. That admiration could include everything from appreciating their brain, appreciating their looks, or straight-up fantasizing about what it would be like to walk in their fabulous shoes for a day. However, "girl crush" quickly took on another meaning the deeper I got into high school and the more people

came out to me (especially in private). Through passive observation, I noticed that many of my "straight" friends (because
I truly believe heterosexuality is a myth, now that I've been
on this planet for almost three decades) used "girl crush" as a
stand-in to illustrate that "I am literally too straight to exist and
probably shouldn't even be admitting that I have an aggressive crush on this girl. Despite this, my crush persists. So, to
cover my ass just so people don't think I'm gay, I'm just going
to put 'girl' in front of 'crush' and everything will be A-okay."
On the flip side, with my closeted friends or friends who were
still questioning everything, "girl crush" meant that "I am still
sorta kinda exploring this whole queer, gay thing and this is
the quickest and cleanest way I can demonstrate that I do,
in fact, have the hots for this girl without any of the baggage
that comes with 'officially' assigning myself a letter from the
LGBTQIA+ umbrella."

The whole idea of a "girl crush," to me, was to take the edge
off of possibly being attracted to someone who shared the same
gender as you, to give yourself a moment to identify where
such feelings were coming from and what that meant, and to
prevent any meddling and bigotry from Bible-thumping rela-
tives or friends.

In other words? The word was safe. Comfortable even. And
something you could bookmark and return to later.

I'm not sure if people really use "girl crush" like that
anymore, mainly because I think that it's hella unnecessary
these days. But prior to high school in 2008, and specifically
in elementary and middle school, I had no knowledge of that
term. Nor did I *truly* know what the fuck "gay" was (besides
bigoted church shit) or what it meant in either school until I
was on the cusp of stepping into high school.

Case in point, I remember constantly spending time with an
old, *old* friend, Henry, in elementary school. He was famously
clandestine as fuck. A young lad who often opted for not saying
too much. And he always chose his words super carefully.

Even as a five-year-old kindergartner, I always found him interesting because he was super fond of hanging out with me and my other girlfriends during breakout play or nap sessions, and even during recess. In fact, it became very clear that he exclusively preferred our company over anyone else's. Other boys in our classroom honed in on that right away. And as little shits like them tend to do, they *attempted* to bully him, but they quickly learned that such behavior was a suicide mission based on the fact that I was notoriously violent—even as a small child.

Seriously. I once squared up with this little white boy who decided to cut in front of me in line on PBJ and chocolate milk day. Needless to say, I ended up in supermax timeout, and he ended up in the nurse's office.

Anyway, Henry wasn't fazed by the bullying, nor was he fazed that other boys thought he was "strange" for always hanging around us. All of which struck me as particularly ballsy. Eventually, my curiosity got the best of me and I asked him why he chose us, this classroom full of girls, as his constant companions.

He shrugged. "I dunno." We were sitting together on some swings and had paused our challenge of who could swing up into the sky the longest and the highest without fucking themselves up. "You guys are more fun, I guess."

I stared at him for a second before replying. "Oh, I like that. That's cool. You're really cool." I smiled. Henry smiled back at me, revealing a missing tooth.

I meant what I said when I called him "cool," but as time went on, I realized that "cool" had been a way for five-year-old me to acknowledge that Henry was definitely *different* in comparison to the other boys in our grade. He wasn't into the whole I'm-a-young-boy-so-I'm-going-to-bully-this-girl-that-I-allegedly-like to full-on-abuse-as-an-adult pipeline. And he didn't like all of the things he was *supposed* to like as a "boy." This was significant because of his dad. Occasionally, I'd see his dad pick him up and drop him off at school. His dad liked to put on a show of being this macho, abrasive-ass *drunk* of a white man who openly showed disdain whenever his son engaged in what he constantly referred to as "fruity" behavior.

Henry being himself despite all that shit spoke to me. So, I called him "cool."

In the absence of my knowledge of the word *gay*.

And before you dismiss all this as a presumptuous assumption on my part, Henry would eventually come out to me and another small group of friends at the beginning of our freshman year in high school. And it was another event in my life that I bookmarked and planned to revisit later, despite being knee-deep in The Gospel of Sky Daddy™.

I just didn't have the terminology to describe my personal journey into the depths of queerness (a word I didn't know existed), and particularly bisexuality (another word I *definitely* didn't know existed). And all I had to lean on was, as I mentioned earlier, the term "girl crush."

This issue intensified when I developed my first girl "official" crush at age eight.

On Rosario Dawson.

The first time I saw Dawson was while watching *Men in Black II* with the rest of my siblings. The year was 2002. My burgeoning obsession with television and film meant that she *immediately* captured my attention as "The Light of Zartha"—a.k.a., the long-lost daughter of Queen Lauranna and the heir to the Zarthan throne. I remember thinking, *Holy shit, this bitch is beautiful*, but, you know, without the cuss words. I noticed the sharp angles of her face, her huge brown eyes, and her immaculate skin. But what I distinctly remember is that godawful haircut she was sporting in that movie and how terrible it would have looked on anyone else.

And yet. And yet. Still smoking hot.

I had a moment, as any gay who doesn't yet know that they're gay, where I dismissed my current line of thinking and tried to focus back in on the movie. But when my sister finally chimed in on how good Rosario looked, my brain registered that maybe what I'd just been thinking wasn't wrong or odd at all.

To be clear, me and my sister *still* had a shitty relationship, which meant she tended to disagree with me by default. But even she concurred, without a hint of irony, that Rosario was indeed "hot." And so my thinly veiled obsession with Rosario Dawson began. This meant that whenever I heard she was starring in a movie, I was *there*, no matter how *inappropriate* the movie turned out to be for someone my age. This included tracking down *Josie and the Pussycats* on DVD, watching *He Got Game*, sneaking into the ultra-violent *Sin City*, suffering through *Death Proof*, and sitting through the immensely melodramatic *Seven Pounds* because I really, *really* liked her and her shared chemistry with Willard Smith (word to *MIB II*).

You think I would've put two and two together: the intensity of my obsession with Rosario plus the fact that I didn't feel as strongly about certain boys my age—which dead-ass should have been the first giveaway that I was *far* from straight. But with the term "girl crush" as my guide, the significance of my feelings eluded me until I was almost eighteen, when I *finally* learned about the term "bisexuality" in its totality after that fated quiz I took with Harlow and Eve.

Put a pin in that. Because it gets even more thorny from there.

Rosario, as a "crush" in my life, was not alone. I had been super "crush-happy" growing up, and now that I reflect on *who* I was crushing on during those times, it definitely skewed toward the wildly problematic side of things of what many of us know about "desire." Pre-full-scale bisexual awakening. Or what niggas dismiss as "preference." "Girl Crush" Rosario remained supreme, of course, but I slowly began to realize that my other crushes, regardless of gender, shared a very similar trait to Rosario: they were either very pale (occasionally white), completely fictional, and/or light-skinned like Rosario.

You want the shortlist? Here's the shortlist, sans Rosario:

This included my elementary school crush Rod—who

ironically and brutally roasted me for my dark skin and Jackson 5 nostrils. Alicia Keys. Tommy from all the superior seasons of *Power Rangers*. Zac Efron—who I only felt super attracted to in *High School Musical 1* and *2*. Corbin Bleu... up until the white side of his genes caught up with him. Night-crawler of the X-Men. The entirety of the R&B group formerly known as B5. Yusuke Urameshi and Yoko Kurama of *YuYu Hakusho*. Brad Pitt (fuck him). Captain Li Shang of *Mulan*. Inuyasha of *Inuyasha*. Left Eye. Even Matt a.k.a. Yamato "Matt" Ishida from *Digimon*.

All of whom were dangerously too close on a color gradi-ent. And most of whom would pass the brown paper bag test with flying colors.

Of course, in my even *younger* youth, I did the thing that all head-ass niggas do and shrugged it off as a preference, but it started to get a little dicey when at fifteen I noticed that none of my crushes really resembled me at all. Not in color or other attributes (besides maybe gender). Preference aside, that had to mean something, right?

Being the head-ass that I *was* (am), I didn't clock the impor-tance or the ramifications of such a realization until my "girl crush" for Tika Sumpter blossomed in 2011.

The minute details of how this crush emerged are still a bit murky to me (thank you, mental illness!), but I recall seeing her on *The Game*, giving Malik a piece of her mind. And I was like, "I'm fucking obsessed"—absolutely glued to the TV screen after I managed to wrestle the remote from one of my brothers.

And like Dawson's, Sumpter's career became something I was interested in following.

I watched her slay hearts and sidewalk runways and eat preppy white people alive in *Gossip Girl*. Despite my allergies when it comes to anything that comes out of Tyler Perry's brain (the exception, to me, only being *Diary of a Mad Black Woman* and *Tyler Perry's Why Did I Get Married?*), I tuned in to her playing messy-ass Candace Young on *The Haves and The Have Nots*. I fawned over her as she lit up my screen in *Bessie*, as she smoldered and sizzled in *Get on Up*, and stole my heart like a goddamn bandit in *Southside with You* as Michelle Obama.

Like all my crushes, her looks and her various talents kept me coming back for more, but I distinctly remember being especially awestruck because she was so unlike what my usual "girl crush" looked like. She further cemented this phenomenon I experienced when she was interviewed about her role on *Gossip Girl* and why it was fairly significant (and rare) to see someone of her complexion step into that world and completely own it. She shared stories she was sent about permitting other younger dark-skinned girls to feel proud about their appearance. It all made me take a step back when she talked about growing up in an environment with parents that celebrated her darkness. I was like, "Wait, that can happen? That's a thing that exists? Positive reinforcement and love from your—gasp—*parents*??"

It was at that point that I deeply reflected on my ongoing "girl crush" on her. And what it meant that my other crushes didn't look anything like her.

Ultimately, I figured that not only was my so-called *preference* a sham (as were "preferences" in general—which I'm gonna talk about later) but it had also heavily been shaped by factors like the hostile "home" environment I had grown up in. Or in my larger community where passive-aggressive commands from elders to "stay out of the sun" were casually thrown around. Honestly, my upbringing had trained me to covet the kind of person, girl in this case, that was the exact opposite of Tika. Which manifested in "preferences," "girl crushes," and regular crushes that inadvertently reflected what I felt about *myself*.

Catching so much shit about being dark and fat—with the additional hell I caught over my nose and my 4C hair—bled into who I considered myself attracted to. It was then that it dawned on me that attraction wasn't a neutral or apolitical thing. Neither was desire. Attraction and desire didn't occur in some vacuum, and both happened to be political as fuck—whether you personally wanted that to be a thing or not.

Either way you spun it, both constructs promised to be either very oppressive or very liberating.

And I was trying to be liberated by this shit, you know? You know.

Now. This is the part where I'm *supposed* to tell you that coming to terms with my bisexuality was smooth sailing from there. But . . . I'd be a fuck-ass liar if I did that.

Truthfully, my journey toward that point in my life was still in its infancy. And while my crushes on both Sumpter and Dawson had put me on a pretty promising path, there was one obstacle that threatened to undo all that progress and put my ascension to bisexual greatness on hold:

White gays.

Particularly, white gays that happened to be girls.

What the fuck do they have to do with this? Excellent question.

As you probably deduced, my friend Alyssa and her girl-friend were the *only* queer Black people I knew personally in high school. And Alyssa's sexuality wouldn't be revealed to me until my senior year of high school. So at this point, which was freshman year, I didn't have any examples of what the marriage between Blackness and queerness was supposed to look like. But what I did observe, in spades, were white girls exploring their sexuality in interesting ways. Sometimes in ways that were . . . *questionable* and potentially would cause issues where consent was concerned.

One of the most infamous incidents was the recurring event of Lyndon and Terri, both white girls who were freshly refer-ring to themselves as "bisexual," engaging in their make-out sessions that threatened to turn into full-blown fucking during every gym period. They were part of a revolving group of white girls who routinely made their journeys into bisexuality every-one's business when they announced whether they were now "bi" or "straight" depending on the week.

I know you're probably thinking that I should have minded my fucking business, and you'd be absolutely right. And

I am proud to say that I was minding my Black-ass business. Only Lyndon and Terri were hellbent on making sure that it was impossible for me, not to mention the other girls that shared the locker room, to mind our collective fucking business.

Every time our gym period was winding down, Lyndon and Terri would find each other in the locker room and commence their ritualistic make-out session while in their underwear. For the most part, everyone in the locker room left them to it, which I'm guessing Lyndon and Terri didn't like. Because the less attention, stares, and hoopla they got, the more they dialed things up.

When the "shock" over their traveling make-out sessions wore off, they started to loudly push up on each other against their respective lockers. Unfortunately, Lyndon and Terri's Black locker-neighbors eventually had to move to prevent violence from occurring after being inconvenienced by their performance. And to be clear, it was *extra* intense because this was a majority Black school and I found it rather interesting that two out of the four white girls in this gym period were pulling this shit.

Still, the locker collective persisted and we eventually went back to ignoring them. The breaking point, however, arrived quickly when they upped the ante by openly "calling" people out for "watching them." They'd point at some random Black girl nearby and say some snide shit about them apparently never seeing two girls kiss before. As if they were the first ones to ever do it? Talk about Main Character™ syndrome.

This new antic of theirs found its way to me. I remember getting dressed in the locker room and trying to get one of my friend's attention across the way, where she was standing at a corner locker. As this was happening, Terri stopped walking so that she was blocking my friend and pulled Lyndon into a kiss. I tried to look around them, but then Terri stopped kissing Lyndon and proceeded to loudly and intentionally misinterpret what was happening.

"Enjoying the show?" she asked. I raised an eyebrow at her, wondering if this dummy bitch was in fact addressing me like I thought she was. This turned out to be the case when she followed up her first fuck-ass question with another equally fuck-ass question. "Wanna join?"

This time, her antics were met not only with me rolling my eyes but everyone nearby audibly groaning. It was enough to briefly stun Terri. And dissuade her from continuing down a line of questioning that was surely going to end in one of us laying hands on her.

This doesn't seem like a big deal, but consider what's at play. Lyndon and Terri's extended Main Character™ performance aside, they had both *newly* come out as bisexual. It was still kind of a big deal at this time because we're talking about the early 2000s to the early 2010s. And considering both of their backgrounds, it was a small miracle that they had even arrived at these personal realizations about themselves.

Lyndon, for example, started as an extremely devout Christian. Seriously. She was putting my Sky Daddy act to shame. And to make matters worse, her father was a *cop*. A white *conservative Christian cop*. That trio of dreaded Cs was enough to make the standard anti-bigot projectile vomit onto the floor. So, I can only imagine what the hell was going on in that house and what she was subjected to. And it kind of made sense that she eventually snapped, threw caution to the wind, and began to explore bisexuality.

Terri was an even more interesting case. She too was raised as a devout Christian. But she chucked the label as soon as her *pastor* father started distancing himself from her. That's right. The bitch was a PK. An embattled preacher's kid. And the "weirder" she got—which her dad perceived as her appearance (she went back and forth between punk and goth aesthetics), her hair (perpetually multicolored), and her piercings (nose in particular)—the more he acted as if he was no longer interested in knowing her. And eventually, they were fully at odds when she decided to date girls . . . after dropping her boring Christian ex-boyfriend. Who her dad had been *really* fond of.

On one hand, I fundamentally understood their trajectories. Their oppressive parents—fathers really—hadn't allowed them to be themselves. It was hard to please them in general, even when they were being "good Christian girls." So, logic dictates that eventually both of them would get tired of pretending after getting no results and throw caution to the wind.

Perhaps the most fascinating thing about this was the fact that all this shit—including their gym performance—seemed to stem from a weird place that revolved around daddy's approval. Specifically, after chasing their approval for so long, they were now in the mood to reject it. But not just reject it. Rebel against it! Rebel by diving into bisexual exploration . . . and subjecting the rest of us to their impromptu-but-not-really-impromptu make-out sessions.

The issue was never about their (excessive) PDA. Straight motherfuckers do that shit all the time and we're all expected not to care. Or to move along. No. The issue was that both Lyndon and Terri, as white girls, demanded that an audience—the rest of our *very* Black gym class—bear witness to their act of audacious *rebellion* against white patriarchy. A demand that bordered on harassment because none of us were willing participants. And if one of us displayed any obvious or even subtle discomfort with the weird position they were trying to force us into, they'd blow up and either ask us insincerely to "join" or try to spin it like our discomfort squarely stemmed from them being queer.

Which . . . I found *funny*. Funny in the fact that assigning bigotry to our discomfort implied that we, as *Black* girls, were *obviously* "predisposed" to being more homophobic than these so-called free-as-a-bird white girls. It was also funny to me because that meant that they were assuming there were no *queer* Black girls among our ranks. And that if there were, they wouldn't have a problem with their Main Character™ behavior.

Despite the fact that—again—the rest of us were unwilling participants.

I'm not even gonna front. After being subjected to this until the next school year, *bisexual* became a word that I was not very fond of. Every time it was uttered, visuals of wayward white girls who had something to prove came to mind. Between that and the "purity culture" poison I was being fed by Doorway to Heaven Church, I bought into the hype about bisexuality being a limbo stage between heterosexuality and homosexuality. By the time I had truly read up on it right as college began, I didn't care for it. And the small voice in my head that was trying to tell me how ironic that was got obscured by the fact that I was not trying to be associated with it. Even if it turned out that I *was* it.

So.

With all of this context and this extended backstory I just gave you, me stating, *out loud,* to my two girlfriends Eve and Harlow, that I might be bisexual was a big fucking deal. A huge deal. A large milestone in my personal development based on my, ahem, *involuntary* experiences and exposure to bisexuality and what little I initially knew of it. It was a left-turn kind of development for me. But based on the seed that Alyssa's act of coming out had planted, and based on Eve's test calling me out on the truth behind my various "girl crushes" over the last couple of years, I had no choice but to confess to what the tiniest part of me (my burgeoning higher self) had known all along:

That I was a flaming bisexual.

Or rather, I had always been destined to be one.

I found myself back in front of Eve's sectional, staring at them as they stared at me—post–bisexual confession.

"Not that I think you're lying or anything," Harlow began, "but are you sure?"

"I think so," I responded.

Eve shrugged. "Well, *I* think that it makes *a lot* of sense."

I narrowed my eyes. "Explain."

"Oppressive Christian upbringing aside, you haven't once

mentioned meeting any cute niggas at UChicago since you came back. Wait, I take that back. You mentioned one—but you glossed over him, to be honest, and haven't stopped talking about all the cute girls you've met so far."

"Okay, but what's the correlation?"

"I feel like boys bore you, mostly," Eve said. "I mean, there's that and the fact that I have definitely caught you hyperfocusing on girls' lips in general when you're speaking to them—sans Harlow and me."

"I do that???"

"Yeah," Harlow chimed in.

"And y'all didn't think to, I don't know, tell me?" I sighed into my hands. "I was probably coming off as a huge-ass weirdo. Oh my God."

"Eh. Wasn't our business." Eve cocked her head to the side.

"Yeah," Harlow continued. "We figured you'd get there on your own. And look! You have."

"Mmhmm." I rolled my eyes, still very sullen about the whole thing. "So. What happens now? Where do I go to make this shit official."

"I'm not sure about all that," Eve said, "but what I do know is that this should . . . be celebrated. We should all celebrate freeing ourselves from the chains of oppression that is heterosexuality."

"I like where this is going!" Harlow said. "And how will we be celebrating?"

"By doing what we do best: making a 'fuck, marry, kill' list," Eve said, completely stone-faced. "But this time . . . with bitches."

Harlow and I looked at each other and burst into obscene laughter.

"Unbelievable," I managed to cough in between breaths.

"She's a goddamn clown." Harlow pushed her glasses farther up the bridge of her nose and continued to laugh.

"What? I'm serious! Why do y'all always assume that I'm not serious?" Eve crossed her arms, pouting.

MY TRAUMATIC INJURY

Listen to me. The human body is disgustingly fragile. Useless! Flavorless!

Seriously.

Whereas some motherfuckers in nature have scales, poisonous skin, wings, TAILS, talons, hind legs, camouflage skin, beaks, hoofs, lights hanging from their bodies, top speeds that rival Lighting McQueen, literal body armor, and can see colors that we cannot even begin to *imagine* in our human brains, the human body is a smorgasbord of flesh, bones, assorted liquids, and more than a couple of "wires" for posterity.

It's a flawed design for sure. One I will be asking many a deity about when it is finally my time (Anubis? Gaia? I got y'all's tea!). Of course, this flaw is probably intentional since we're not supposed to live *forever*, but the limitations of the human body are never as obvious as when said human body suffers an injury.

My big injury happened in the spring of 2014, in April, during an intramural outdoor soccer game between rival dorms. It was an ACL tear. And later, doctors were surprised that it was still minorly attached to *anything*, much less a bone.

And I'm not being dramatic when I say that my knee going left when it should've gone right in the pursuit of a soccer ball quite literally changed the trajectory of my life. As well as my core beliefs.

But first, let's talk about why I got into intramural sports to begin with, shall we?

My time at the University of Chicago, a PWI (predominantly white institution), was pretty . . . tumultuous. And that's how I would describe it on a good day. Like many (abused) immigrant children, I had found the university's promise of an unnecessarily rigorous education—"where fun goes to die" my ass—to be an alluring one. It had been something I was used to in high school, something that had helped distract from the chaos going on at home. Because, as you know, that meant that I was good at *something*. And being good at something meant that I had permission, no matter how small, to like myself. Or rather, to not totally hate myself. Despite the fuckshit my parents were on. It was also one of the few things that could distract my brain from the war it was waging against my body day in and day out.

Of course, if you're familiar with the difference between academic rigor in *college* versus in high school, then you know that I had a big storm coming—and come it did. By the end of the first quarter of my first year at UChicago, I was flirting with academic probation.

That's right. Your girl thought she was Ms. Smarty McSmartpants, but higher education proceeded to say *sike!* and jump me. Then again, I suppose that my poor academic performance had a lot to do with the fact that I wasn't even in the right major—with me initially being a computer science major who was struggling to nail down all pre-med prerequisites. My parents, like most Nigerian parents, had been hellbent on me going into medicine. It was their dream for me to spend 3092347093 decades studying all the ways to cut people up on an operating table. Never mind that those close to me knew that I had absolutely no interest in doing any of that shit. And plus, in my opinion, you need incredibly *still* hands or need to have the ability to keep them still when the need arises—even if you're just *thinking* about becoming a surgeon. And that's not a skill I had or something I could do. Nor were they things I was concerned about. I had enough trouble concentrating during exceedingly intense "focus" moments in video games where I was expected to stay incredibly still. You expect me to go into an ER with jittery hands that are poised to do the cha-cha slide across someone's aorta?

I don't think so.

The other side of my pending academic failure was the revelation that I was *shit* at time management. Okay, well, not totally shit. I'm gonna give myself partial credit. I mean, in high school I'd found a way to survive my parents, hold down a part-time job, keep my grades straight, and do an ungodly amount of extracurriculars, so I clearly had been *forced* to pick up *some* time management skills. But suddenly, when I went to college, the little I had known and taught myself just kinda flew out the window.

There's that thing that people say where, as a college student, your *aim* is to get a good amount of sleep, get good grades, and maintain a social life. But in reality, you usually only end up accomplishing two out of three of those things.

It's funny because the assumption here that I'm always hit with when I start to tell these stories is that my grades were tanking from jump street because escaping the clutches of an abusively strict immigrant upbringing *and* Christianity meant that I was predestined to party my fucking brains out and go completely off the deep end.

Meanwhile, all I really wanted to do when I got to college was sleep. And get good grades. But it turned out the former wasn't gonna be a consistent thing because I was depressed, and insomnia had been a longtime companion. And the latter definitely wasn't happening because every academic program, as a UChicago undergrad, had been designed to be inhumanly difficult for no reason other than breaking your young spirit. Because they could.

I thought I was smart by skipping around the whole pre-med thing and trying to find some happy medium in computer science. You know. Trying to do things on my own terms while keeping in mind that I still needed to make money after college.

But after a "fun" computer science class about coding had me crying and throwing up well into the wee hours of the morning as my burning eyes squinted at some mathematical formula I had never seen in my *life*, I abandoned that silly mission too and had to go back to career path square one.

Needless to say, losing my ability to bring home an A that didn't cost me a piece of my soul in the process absolutely decimated everything I thought I "knew" about myself. I was Alexandria. And Alexandria was *smart*. Alexandria was capable. Alexandria never returned home with anything lower than a high A. Alexandria could merely glance at a book and tell you what the whole thing was about, down to the damn curtains that the author loved describing so much. Alexandria had struggled in math, but she won in the end—according to her high school GPA. But . . . that version of Alexandria was gone. And so were her grades. Suddenly, all the As had morphed into struggling Cs and Ds. And I remember openly sobbing when I got my first F in one of my math classes.

Pretty melodramatic, I know. But my good grades were all I had at one point. So.

This would be the first in an infinite number of rock bottoms that I hit at that cursed institution. And I took it pretty fucking hard. So hard that I went from being an insomniac to almost instantaneously becoming a narcoleptic. Suddenly, sleeping was the only thing I could do . . . *well*.

Still. Since I was no longer able to rely on good grades to get me through the hellscape that was life at UChicago, I had to pivot to something else pretty quickly. My initial pivot included abandoning the charade of pursuing medicine and computer science and opting to finally start finding my lane in the English and Cinema and Media Studies departments. The other part of my pivot included writing more screenplays, working on a now-defunct blog with Eve, getting absolutely addicted to yelling at people like Frank Grillo on Twitter, becoming even more invested in superhero content (growing up as a Christian meant that the only fucking superhero I was "allowed" was Jesus fucking Christ), and, wouldn't you know, deep-diving into Marvel fan fiction. Which included me writing my own.

And that's all I'll say about that!

This was *enough*. For a while. Moving away from "academic excellence" being the only thing I had going for myself did my psyche some good. Plus, allowing myself to pursue my affinities for film and writing meant that I was getting closer and closer to what I actually wanted to do for the rest of my life.

However.

You've been reading this book long enough to know that the ghost of internalized fatphobia is never too far behind. Especially when I do something as boldly audacious and foolish as *being happy*.

Though I was making headway with my self-esteem in some ways, I found that I had started to put on the dreaded "freshman fifteen" that all the motherfuckers I had talked to about college (before showing up here) wouldn't shut the fuck up about. Mind you, I'm sure they never actually deeped why they themselves had "put on" weight. Like, maybe you were fucking happy and that's how your body just wanted to exist at the time? Or maybe you were depressed and your body was trying to gently @ you about what might be going on in your brain? But no. All analysis stopped at "freshman fifteen bad because fat bad."

And sadly, like so many other times in my life, I ate that shit up. Like Thanksgiving leftovers.

As you can imagine, my anxiety about gaining any type of weight post–high school (particularly after losing so much of it for prom) *spiked*. And like all the other times I did something extreme to fight any inch of weight gain or fat, I decided quickly that I had to find something to fight that same "good fight" here.

Sports turned out to be that thing.

Intramural sports to be exact.

My decision to do so was a little hilarious because, while

I was hyperactive in high school to put off gaining weight, it hadn't occurred to me that I could be doing the same in college—with sports. Sure, the interior of most of the university's gyms had seen me every now and again, but team sports had never really been a thing I was into. You know, because a bitch was on that "I work alone" shit like my parents had been shot in that dirty-ass alley like a certain billionaire we all know.

If only.

The dead parents part, I mean.

But yes. IM sports. They were a thing for me. And you know what? I was actually pretty . . . good? In fact, I was *great* at most sports. It certainly helped that the dorm I belonged to was super competitive. If I remember correctly, we ended up taking home the championship my first year, and that did wonders for my brain and my psyche? Because everyone likes being a winner, right? Right!

After the championship win, I threw myself further into the IM sports world. Hell, I committed to being ultrafit in general. And, once again, like a good Taurus with a Mars in Aries, I *committed*-committed. Like, ferociously so. I even did that Kuvia shit where they had us all up at the crack of dawn, "greeting" the sun and whatnot. Despite sleeping for a concerning amount of hours per week (due to undiagnosed depression, no doubt), I had never felt so sleep-deprived in my life. And yet! I was happy to do it. And happy that that was currently my state of existence.

IM sports gave me an outlet to properly channel a lot of my repressed rage and anger. Granted, it didn't exonerate me of my original, fatphobic logic behind trying it to begin with—because that did remain. I was still determined to keep the extra weight off and not let "my skinny summer" have gone to waste, based on the effects that summer continued to have on me.

Still . . . I'd like to think that my enjoyment of soccer won out over fatphobia.

Anyway. The next year was even more intense—if only due

to the fact that we, as a house, were hellbent on winning the IM championship title twice in a row. For bragging rights, mostly. But also because it was a running joke across the entire campus that no one knew who the fuck our dorm was—in *name*, truthfully. And we all know what happens to our brains instinctually when a bunch of randos try to dismiss you as nobodies; for some reason, you just get in the mood to "prove them wrong" and piss them off. Even though, again, these are a bunch of randos you're dealing with.

But yes! Sports!

So I threw myself into it all. And I was fairly good. Fast too. After showing up to high school prom with a bobblehead, I had learned my lesson about cutting corners where strength training was concerned (regardless of the reason), and proved to be my own little five-foot-six powerhouse in whatever IM sport that I tried my hand at. The only ones I ended up opting out of were water sports because I didn't have a swimming bone in my body.

Fall and winter sports were always fun, too, but spring? Spring had cool shit like soccer, and I was really keen on playing (mixed) soccer. I mean, when you come from a family who worships the ground that the Super Eagles walk on and who are gung ho about screaming at the TV every four years as the World Cup rages on, there is absolutely no way that you are *not* going to like soccer. So, as soon as spring came around, I was one of the first people in line to sign up.

As for the season? Well, it was really, really tough.

The other houses held nothing back. At all. And not to say that our house wasn't great, but many of the athletes (or those that were athletically inclined) that stayed in our house had more expertise in volleyball, Wiffle ball/softball, kickball, dodgeball, and things of the like. Senior players who had been really good at flag football and soccer graduated the year before, so it was on the underclassmen, who were left to step up to the plate to get us to this year's tournament. And we were up against other houses who had an endless supply of lifelong soccer players—both recreational and those aspiring to be professional.

Our season was chock-full of hard-fought wins and incredibly painful losses. But somehow, *somehow*, we made it to the semifinals. And it was a really big deal for us, having lost our stars from last year, save for one.

Initially, if you can believe it, I wasn't planning on going to the semifinals. I had a paper for one of my "core" classes that I just couldn't afford to fuck up on. And going to the game would have cut into the already limited writing time that I had. Still, forces bigger than the game eventually led me there. One of our really good players had to leave town due to a family emergency, and since IM sports were strict about not suddenly adding players to your roster super late into the season, I was the only person qualified at that point to fill in for them—albeit having positions shuffled around since I wasn't a striker.

Fast-forward to our biggest game of the season and I'm subbing in as one of the fullbacks—right-back in particular. Our opposition was talented, and we'd had more than one or two close calls with them goal-wise (on either side), and they were itching to put one in ours. Near the height of the game, during the second half, I ended up being subbed in for one of the center backs, as the last one had almost broken the nil-to-nil tie we had going on.

This is where I tell you I probably should have listened to my gut. Because being a center back ain't no fucking joke. The center back usually has to be a sturdy-ass nigga, and they're responsible for making sure the goalkeeper doesn't have to block potential goals every two seconds. This essentially makes them the final line of defense before a goalkeeper has to put their body on the line for the game. If you know where I'm going with this, you know that I had never played as a center back before and this game would be my first time doing it. I remained anxious about the decision, but the captain trusted me because of my guts and my ability to adapt quickly. So, I went with it.

I would love to say that the game proceeded smoothly after my substitution and that we ended up winning a game that had drained every ounce of energy from us, but . . . the truth of the matter wasn't that neat or triumphant.

As the second half dwindled down, both teams started to get really aggressive about scoring goals. Like, very aggressive. And we found that the opposition was getting closer and closer to making it to ours—which wholly stressed me out. The thing was, though, that the opposition kept swinging left—which was purposeful because that meant avoiding me—a sturdy bitch. However, as the game dragged on, they were eventually forced into my area, which proved to be a highly crucial moment in the match.

I ain't gonna lie to you. That moment happened so fast it feels like a blur now when I look back. I remember this tall-ass white dude running toward me with the ball. *At least* six feet. Handling it and kicking it around as if he was Ronaldo or something. I wasn't necessarily scared, but I knew all five six of me was gonna have to be smart about getting the ball away from him since he was so tall and fast. I hung back for as long as I could, and when he got close enough, I slid my left leg near his and kicked away the ball.

Which . . . cost me dearly. In fact, it cost me my version of *everything* at the time.

I had gotten the ball away as I had planned. But what I didn't plan for was him losing his footing and basically tripping into me. If I had been watching this in slow-motion with some bird's-eye view somewhere, I might have been able to avoid getting tangled with him and falling to my doom. But I wasn't that lucky, and we ended up going down pretty hard.

Yep. All six feet and two hundred and something pounds landed on my ass. And my left leg landed in a very unnatural position.

I don't remember the minute details of what happened during and after the fall. But what I do remember is the sickening *pop* and pausing for a second—like I didn't just hear that shit. You know my thing: denial, denial, denial. But in this case, there was no denying it. I had torn my ACL—I would learn later—and it hurt like a bitch. I'm sure my screaming informed everyone else of such.

Mr. Fee-Fi-Fo-Fum™ ended up scrambling to his feet (he was pretty scratched up himself) to check on me, and he apologized profusely when he put two and two together. I wasn't really paying attention though—the only thing my mind could focus on, much to my misfortune, was how much pain I was in.

The rest of the game just got shittier from there. I was helped off the field by two of my team's favorite players, and everyone present did that thing that people do where they clap you off the field for your valor. And bravery. And guts. And sacrificing your body. I was the "star" that day because I did stop what could have been a morale-killing goal. But I certainly didn't feel like one. Mainly because the opposition did end up getting their goal anyway, with the ending score being 1 to nil.

So essentially, all this shit was for naught. In my case.

I ended up being driven back to my apartment first (I lived off-campus technically, but houses reserved the right to grant former dormmates rights to join up with their sports teams), so I could sit up somewhere safe and prop my leg up as I figured out what to do next. I was silent the whole time.

You'd think I would've immediately gone to the hospital. But in this hellish country, under its absolute toxic dogshit of a "healthcare system," we call that "wishful thinking." I couldn't even afford the ambulance ride there (seriously—it's the reason teammates were driving me around to begin with). So, to me, an *actual* ER visit was simply out of the question. I didn't feel like being reminded that I was poor. Again.

Despite this, one of my teammates ignored my protests and escorted me to the school's ER facility later that evening. Actually, *escorted* is too soft a term. *Dragged* would be more accurate.

While wheeling me into the hospital, my teammate had been hella optimistic about me receiving the proper treatment I needed that night. But by the time the ER staff took in all my paperwork and explained the limits of my TN health insurance plan and what my bill might look like, I was begging my teammate to wheel me back out of the hospital before I launched into a huge bitch fit.

I suppose some of you might be scratching your heads, thinking that this "technical" injustice shouldn't have occurred with the passing of the Patient Protection and Affordable Care Act in 2010. However, full implementation of that law wasn't really a thing until 2014. And even then, based on what we know about money-hungry (and *also* underfunded) hospitals trying to get away with overcharging for things like, I don't know, sharing skin-to-skin contact with your fucking *baby* after it was just born, this, unfortunately, wasn't out of the ordinary.

After that whole ordeal, and because I am supremely unlucky, I had to be helped back up, again, multiple flights of stairs . . . because I lived on the fourth and final floor. With no elevator in sight.

I would end up flying back to Tennessee, much to my dismay, for actual medical assistance. And even then, my parents—with whom I had, unfortunately, had to maintain limited contact for financial reasons—made that hard.

Before I made a decision to come back to Tennessee, my father made it obvious that he blamed me and berated me for what happened. Called me stupid as fuck for playing sports instead of studying, which was highly hypocritical considering his *extreme* love for soccer. Because he blamed me, he refused to pay for my flight home. My mom, who was extremely bad at money management, didn't have any savings to help get me home. And my sister, Kalindi? Lmao. That wasn't an option.

Since my parents were being cartoonishly evil and callous, I ended up having to *work* at a nearby library to raise my own money for a ticket home.

You read that right. I had to *stand* on a *torn* ACL to *work.*
What a hellish country.

What an even more hellish existence.

The only positive note is that I had friends who rose to the occasion to help me. We were all fucking broke, so they couldn't pool enough resources for me to stay in Chicago and undergo ACL reconstruction surgery. But they managed to get enough money to buy me an expensive knee brace in order to tide me over long enough to earn my plane ride money and fly back to Tennessee at the beginning of July that same year.

I'm gonna decline to explain the agony that was traveling back home on my defunct ACL. But I should probably explain some of the events that happened thereafter.

After touching down in Tennessee weeks later, I was relegated to staying with Kalindi in her apartment, as I was not keen on returning to the hellscape of my parents' house. Despite my sister's disdain for me, she opted to accommodate me; I think partially because she felt guilty and also partially because I'm sure my mom used her tried-and-true version of guilt-tripping . . . in a way that only Nigerian mothers are capable of. Soon after, maybe a day or so, I checked in with my PCP about the situation, and before you knew it, I was going into surgery.

There were a lot of unpleasant parts of this process, which, interestingly enough, had less to do with the actual surgery and more to do with before the surgery (and, eventually, after). My mom was hovering all around me at that point. At my appointment with my PCP, right up to the surgery with her walking with the group that wheeled me into the operating room, and smothering me post-surgery when I finally left the hospital.

Reflecting on this now, I realize the highly manipulative thing she was doing here. Playing the part of the parent who was overly concerned because of the amount of pain I was in. Trying to separate herself from my father, who had made it clear that he didn't give a shit. But at the time, I genuinely believed this was her honest attempt at making up for being a bird of a mother—one who had always put her marriage to a man who had done unspeakable things ... before her children. I mean, she was here, right? In my face. Trying to do what a parent is expected to do. So I believed the hype. And took her actions at face value. I still wasn't totally happy about keeping an open mind, because of the bad blood between us, but I knew that if I wanted us to both have a chance at repairing this relationship, I had to try.

Either way, though, this was bullshit.

Perhaps the only silver lining of the process was the surgeon in charge of my operation. I remember being slid onto that OR table and seeing a fairly beautiful man wheel himself over—with a face that looked like a carbon copy of some romance hero ... from a Talia Hibbert novel. Everything about that damn face was chiseled, and he had some brownish-*green* eyes that I'm sure were a hit in that hospital. And he was tan, with really thick, dark hair. A very sexy *tan*. A sultry tan. A tan that reminds me of one of those expensive peanut butter seats you find in luxury cars. I laughed to myself because I'm crass and of course I would be thinking of how a sexy human's face reminded me of a *seat* I'd be delighted to sit on.

His name was Dr. Henderson. He ended up greeting me, lowering his mask, and carefully explaining to me what the fuck was about to happen—including how I would feel when the anesthesia kicked in. I only really caught half of his spiel though because I was fading pretty quickly. Before I could really process what he was saying to me, he got up.

"Ready to patch her up?" He looked down at me and over at my left knee.

"Yes." I was loopy as shit. "But only if you plan on taking me out," I slurred my words.

"Tell you what, let's talk after the surgery." He chuckled. I wanna say I smiled at him after that, but I'm pretty sure I made the weirdest face before a gas mask was placed over it. The surgery team huddled over me and around me like a football team. Except that I was the ground and they were fervently praying over me for favor right before making the game-winning kick. I watched Dr. Henderson pull up his mask and join the huddle.

I smirked after catching that last glimpse of his face. It was kind of nice. Like, in that "well, if I die, at least my final moments include gazing at a stellar piece of Gaia's handiwork ... before my soul goes on a trip and yeets itself into an eternal abyss" kinda way.

Which ... good looking out, Gaia.

At long last, my vision blurred and forces beyond my control tugged my eyes closed. Despite my initial discomfort, I settled into the darkness like it was that old college friend you hadn't seen in a while and were just dying to catch up with. Wondering, silently praying, that my friend would reach out, slip her hands into mine, and take me with her.

MY SUICIDAL TENDENCIES

If you're reading this, then you know that I, unfortunately, did not *perish* on the operating table like I had low-key wanted.

It was a tragedy of sorts. Because that anesthesia was *hitting* and I real-deal thought I was never gonna return. The initial thought of leaving this place had made me hella giddy. I wouldn't have had to worry about my shitty family anymore. Or my shitty university and these shitty student loans I had taken out. Or even the thought of having to deal with this shitty injury and the shitty process that I knew recovery was going to be like. All of it was shit. All of it. Life, to me, felt vastly overrated.

And life unfortunately was going to get infinitely worse.

There's a bunch of fallout that comes with dealing with an injury that will most likely scar you for life. Like this one. The first wave of the fallout has to do with you trying to temporarily readjust. Make some effort to try to do the normal things you did pre-injury without looking silly doing them. The second wave of fallout comes when you finally grasp the fact that there are certain things you may not be able to do again, or there are certain things that will become incredibly harder for you since our society is one that does not give a shit about accessibility. But those are "standard" of course. What usually isn't standard is the third wave of fallout I experienced, where internalized ableism and internalized fatphobia landed me in a weird space with my physical therapist and sent me down a spiral that almost ended with me dying by suicide.

Sounds bonkers? You're absolutely right.

And while it makes for a good story to retell, it sucked donkey ass to have to live it.

Being wheeled back into my hospital room after the surgery was such a mood-killer, with my mom and siblings waiting in there; my father, however, was thankfully nowhere to be found. I was still mad disoriented with everyone crowding me, and I was eternally grateful when Dr. Henderson shooed them all out of the room.

"So, when's our big date?" he said as he dragged a chair closer to the side of my bed. I chuckled, remembering some of my babblings before I had passed out.

"Well, that depends on what this recovery time is looking like," I replied, and then his face got a little more serious. "How long am I gonna be 'down,' doctor?"

"Do you want the short timeline or do you want the long timeline?"

"Surprise me."

He paused. "You're looking at, at the very *least*, six months." He crossed one leg over the other and leaned back. He didn't look happy to be delivering this news. I sat back in my bed, audibly exhaling. "And that depends on how often you go to physical therapy. I know how often I would recommend it, but—"

"Insurance," I finished.

"Yeah."

"How often would you recommend it if that wasn't a factor?"

"Five times a week."

I whistled. "Cool. How often can I get away with considering that insurance *is* a factor?"

"Three times a week. At minimum."

Fuck. Me.

I started to massage my temples and Dr. Henderson offered a sad smile.

"I'm sorry."

"No, no. You're just doing your job." I shrugged. "So, I guess my next question would be how this recovery process is going to go, physical therapy included?"

"Good question."

For the next fifteen minutes, Dr. Henderson explained what the six months were going to look like. He opted not to sugarcoat anything and explained that it would be a very long, grueling process—whether it capped at six months or whether it went even further. He mentioned that the inflammation and swelling in my knee would go away in due time, but that the pain before, during, and after the process was going. to. *suck*. To be clear, the pain was going to fluctuate from day to day, as would my personal pain scale. And it would linger long after the swelling had gone away. He mentioned having prescribed me hydrocodone, with the hope that it would take most of the edge off. I was also supposed to check back in with him if it happened to make me nauseous—which it did when I got back to my sister's house. He eventually ended our conversation by adding that if I stuck to physical therapy at least three times a week, I might be able to hit that six-month recovery mark. But he stressed that the *full* healing process was going to take a lot longer.

"It can take up to two years for you to regain a great deal of your mobility," he said.

"A great deal?" I raised an eyebrow as he met my gaze. When he paused, I sighed again. "I'm . . . not going to regain *all* of the strength and stability in my knee, am I?"

"There's a possibility," he said, "but we won't really know until we can monitor the results of your physical therapy sessions."

"Fair."

I thanked Dr. Henderson for his time, and he took his leave. The rest of my family, that gang of parakeets, took that as an invitation to surge back into the room and bombard me with questions about how I felt, how the surgery went, and what was going to happen after I left the hospital.

I immediately dissociated.

Eventually, that second week in July, I was escorted back to my sister's house and eventually after that, my parents' house. Kalindi happened to be my first "rest stop" because, again, Nigerian mom guilt. It was obvious she wasn't thrilled to have me there, mainly because having to take care of me was *such* a burden and such a *downer* when it came to her dating and social life. And she never let me hear the end of it as long as I was there, particularly because she had to put in time off to make sure she was around often enough to help me because I couldn't fucking *move*. This is classic, really, when it comes to this family. Of course, she would make me feel bad for not being able to move. It probably got her thinking about all the virulently fatphobic shit that she had thrown at me growing up and I just know that she was foaming at the mouth to return to that. Never mind that this was probably the first time in the history of *forever* that she had to lift *one* finger to help me. If I could have suffocated myself with the shitty pillow she gave me to lie with on her shitty pullout sectional, I would have.

Believe it or not, all of the bullshit I mentioned above didn't end up lasting too long. By the time we were going into week three, she had a sudden change of heart. It was almost like she had a come-to-Jesus moment offscreen, you know, because my life is just so fucking *funny*. I remember her giving me this bullshit spiel and a half-assed apology about being a shitty sister and promising to do better if *I* met *her* halfway. I. *Me*. The person who was injured. The sister who hadn't done shit except be born after her. The sister that she had constantly rejected at every turn.

Kalindi sat down next to me one day. "You know, I'm the only sister you have." We were watching a Lakers game while eating an extremely watered-down version of Nigerian beef stew— one my sister had made and claimed was "healthy" because of its inclusion of vegetables that quite frankly had no business being in the stew to begin with. I didn't really want to be watching the game or eating her shitty food, but what I was quickly learning while being mostly immobile was the fact that people, family included, were always going to opt to take full advantage of you. Steamroll right over your wants, needs, and even your rights. She never asked for my input on how I should be cared for, and it was clear that she wasn't going to. "And you're the only sister I have. And despite our differences, we have to stick together. Especially because the rest of the family is . . . you know . . ." She took one of her index fingers and made the universal "crazy" sign by the right side of her head.

"Bold of you to assume that you're not included in that," I responded.

"Ah. Are you still upset about me calling you a bunch of mean names all those years ago?"

"Am I upset about you viciously bullying me over my weight for well over a decade?" I scoffed. "Yeah. I'm assuming any sane person would be."

"That was regrettable." Kalindi sighed. "I do regret that."

"Are you apologizing?" I said slowly, not believing that she was really going to force me to extract this fucking apology from her.

"Yes, yes I am," she said. I waited for her to follow that up with some version of "I'm sorry." But it never came. Instead, she merely smiled like the conversation had ended and went back to watching the game. My mouth slightly dropped open and I had the sudden urge to call her a selfish bitch—though I never verbalized it. I waited for a couple of seconds, only because I didn't think she was serious initially, but when it was clear that she was actually *very, very* serious about not following up her fauxpology with a real one, I opted to do the one thing I had been dreading to do the entire time:

I called my mom to pick me up and, tragically, take me back to her house.

As you can probably guess, dear reader, I was absolutely devastated that I had to return to the circle of hell that was my parents' house. In fact, a piece of my soul died as I was being driven back by my mom—who was on cloud nine about having me back "home" and couldn't wait to tell everyone (her church included). Meanwhile, I continued to silently lay out an array of plans, to myself, about how I was going to off myself in due time. One of those plans included me opening the side door to her SUV and throwing myself out.

Once again, I'm still here, so clearly I didn't do that.

Staying at my parents' house, after a year or so of being in Chicago, was a fucking mind fuck. If I had it my way and the health insurance Ponzi scheme that this country was running wasn't a thing, I'd have flown back ASAP. But since Dr. Henderson had wanted me to start physical therapy right away, like *right away,* I booked an initial "test" session, based on his referral, and got started.

Except that my parents, like most shitty and abusive ones, weren't keen on giving me any peace. Day one of physical therapy was very . . . rough. Mainly due to the pain of moving an injured limb that doesn't want to move. But also because my physical therapist was an older white man who, like most white medical "professionals," was very much indifferent to my pain as a Black patient.

Those stats about white doctors dismissing Black pain? Yeah, that shit is real.

Later that same day, after my brothers helped me onto the couch and handed me a snack, I sat there. Mainly waiting to die, but mostly just hoping the time passed quickly enough for me to magically end up back in Chicago. I'm incredibly unlucky though, so yeah.

Sometime later, my mom came over, presenting pounded yam and ogbono soup on a makeshift desk—one of my favorites. Now, part of me wanted to believe that she did this out of the kindness of her own heart (she's got a big, big Cancer placement), but the other part of me knows that food, in particular, is one of the go-to methods that Nigerian moms apologize with.

Obviously, I don't like being bribed, *but* this was *ogbono soup* we were talking about here. I didn't know how to make this shit yet. And so I just took the food from her and said nothing. She sat down beside me and started talking. I really couldn't hear *clearly* over the sound of me inhaling pounded yam. But from what little I was able to gather between bites, she was going on and on about family. I paused at one point to hear some of her ramblings:

"I do not like how you got here," my mom said. "But I am so happy you are back! We are a family again. I can't wait to tell the church." She seemed giddy. I looked at her, holding a piece of pounded yam directly in front of my mouth, and contemplated spitting on her.

I did. I contemplated just hacking a big ol' loogie and spitting it in her face. In fact, I daydreamed about putting my piece of pounded yam back on the plate with the rest and smashing it into her face. I also contemplated taking the ogbono soup and dumping it over her head like it was slime and it was 1994 and I was on a Nickelodeon show.

It would have been one thing if my mom really wanted me there. But in reality, I knew that she was relieved to have me back home to sit in this miserable pile of shit that was my family. More kids leaving the house meant that my father's cruelty was back to being hyperfocused on her. And my being back home served as a buffer.

Hence my wanting to spit in her face.

But all I managed to do was give a pained smile back. All while angrily stuffing my face. My mom smiled back at me and eventually left me the fuck alone. I thought that would be the only stress I was met with that day and then I quickly found out that I was wrong as fuck.

When night fell later and I was on the verge of taking my 84023740th nap upright, my father slinked down the stairs from his nap (as I mentioned before, he worked the night shift, and unfortunately for me, today was one of his days off). I swear to God, you could see this black smoke cloud following him around and moving around his feet. Like, he was that sinister and evil. And without any of the charm played by, say, any evil Keith David character.

He sauntered over to me and sat down on the coffee table in front of me.

In a just world, I would have gotten to headbutt him.

He greeted me. "How are you doing, Alexandria?"

"What do you want?" I cut straight to the chase.

"I am sure you are upset about me not showing up to the hospital, or me refusing to pay for your ticket here," he said, "but I wanted to teach you an important lesson about not getting distracted and facing your front when it comes to your studies. Do you understand?"

Hmph. What I did understand was the fact that a) I was very blessed to not have had to see him in that hospital, and b) how much of a foolish megalomaniac was he to think that my injury revolved around him and his stupid lessons? Fucking wild.

"No. Get to the point quickly." I glared at him. He looked shocked that I had snapped on him like that.

"I know hearing me say all this is very difficult, but I am your father and you will show me res—"

"Not by choice," I cut him off. "You are not my father, by choice. My choice, to be clear." A dark cloud flashed over his face and eyes. And I was so *sure* that he was going to take this opportunity, while I was functionally immobile, to do his usual thing and slap me upside the head or punch me or whatever sick shit he probably had planned now that I couldn't really *move*.

You hear, all the time, about how "caregivers"—particularly those who are parents or "family"—take full advantage of the disabled person in question. And I always found it so fucking evil, because I knew they were only doing that because of the power imbalance. Only doing that because the disabled person in question couldn't "fight back." Physically, anyway.

It was some sick shit.

But I'd be lying if I pretended like I never thought this would have *ever* happened to me.

"I will forgive you for speaking to me like that. Because I am loving and kind."

Wow.

And there goes the narcissist. Right on time.

"I know we've been through so *much* as a family. And I'm sure you even remember some of it too," he continued. "But we should let the past be the past. Let bygones be bygones. Allow us to help you. Because we are the only family you have. And we must stick together."

If it were possible to projectile vomit in his face, I would have done it.

Instead, I said, "Are you done?"

"What?"

"Are you done?" I repeated. "Because if you're done, I'm going to call Mom now. So she can take me to bed." My father looked at me, sucking his teeth. After a moment, he got up dramatically and stormed off. "Goodnight!" I yelled after him, pleased with myself.

The feeling wouldn't last though. Because like every single time I bucked against my parents and showed them what for, there was a price that was paid.

The next morning, I was awoken by screams and shit being thrown around. And based on the direction of the sound, it sounded like it was happening in the kitchen. My dad was talking loud as fuck about my mom cheating on him with some stranger, and my mom was yelling at the top of her lungs—there was an important distinction between talking loudly and yelling in the Eduwa household—about how sick and tired she was about the allegations. And obviously, my brothers were yelling at both of them to stop—followed by the sounds of what I assume were plates smashing and kitchen chairs being tossed around.

I definitely was hungry and had contemplated calling one of my brothers to grab me a toaster strudel or something, but clearly, that was no longer a good idea. I sighed and decided to go back to sleep.

After this, I resolved that, insurance be damned, I was going to have to get my Black ass back to Chicago.

I didn't say too much to my parents about my plan. I merely stuck it out for the rest of the week and scrounged up all the money I had left—scattered in savings accounts across several banks that I had nearly forgotten about when I left for college—for a plane ticket. I started packing up what I could reach from my bed or from my chair, and asked my youngest brother, Tommy, to help me pack the rest.

The following Monday, I hobbled outside via my crutches, with Tommy walking right behind me with my suitcase and backpack. My Uber was waiting at the foot of my driveway and I honestly couldn't move toward it fast enough.

At the very *last* second, my mom came running out of the house—with my dad standing smugly in the open door-way—and tried to wrestle my stuff away from Tommy, who was twelve at the time. Knocked him down and everything. Which . . . you think she might have had some dignity, but no. My mom finally had me, her co-sufferer of abuse (as a woman), back in the house and she wasn't about to give me up that easily.

Thankfully, my Uber driver, who was a Sikh man, sensed the tense and ridiculous nature of my mother's outburst and got out of the car himself. He went to grab my bags for me and motioned for my mom to stay back—lest he have to call the police. And while, as I mentioned before, they had been called to my parents' house on numerous occasions when I was younger, I knew—and my mom knew—that this wouldn't pan out for them considering that we were much older, and considering that, if *I* wanted to, I could press charges as soon as one of Porky Pig's cousins showed up.

My mom backed up and began to wail dramatically. Loudly. Like I was going off to war. Or like someone had returned, telling her that I had perished in battle. My driver, who was as over it as I was, helped me into the car and tossed my bags into the trunk.

Relief washed over me as the driver pulled off and my parents' house became smaller and smaller in the rearview mirror.

GOING BACK to Chicago for physical therapy was *technically* more peaceful than in Nashville, for one because I didn't have to deal with my insane family; and for two because I wasn't going as much as Dr. Henderson had advised. And who could blame me? His physical therapist referral was shit!

But because this was still the summer months for UChicago (I had returned at the end of July), it was mostly a ghost town. So that meant that I didn't have a lot of help.

One of my friends, Kara Vega, met me at my apartment weekly and helped me get up my colossal flight of stairs, bags and groceries included. She lived deeper in the city and was splitting time between her summer job on campus and one that she had in town.

"You sure you're gonna be okay?" She brought in the last of my stuff and put it down in the living room. I had finally put my crutches to the side and found myself lying down on my rickety couch.

"I'm fine," I said. "I'm gonna be fine. Trevor should be here any minute. And he'll take over from there."

Trevor Fridman was my gay white roommate who I had previously met and befriended in the dorms. He was great. Really sweet, in fact. But he was messy. Incredibly messy. Both in the metaphorical sense and the actual physical sense. Like, he couldn't keep his shit in one place, which would prove to be a severe issue later when I had to leave; because him turning the apartment kitchen (and subsequently living room) into a goddamn science experiment was going to fuck up how much space I even had to be mobile.

"Okay." Kara exhaled, uncrossing her arms. "But you let me know if you need anything, okay?" I looked at her and she repeated herself. "*Okay?*"

"Okay! Okay." I chuckled. "I got you."

"Good." She nodded and then took her leave.

Part of me wishes I had asked her to stay a bit longer, only because I knew that I needed company that wasn't my psychotic, narcissistic family. But at the time, I was adamant about not being a burden to the people around me, regardless of the relationship. I had internalized so much of that from that accursed house. All the fatphobic and colorist abuse. And the internalization had only gotten worse now that I had an additional "liability," a disability, to deal with. I would like to say that I'm well past those issues as I write this, but truth be told, the unlearning continues to this day.

Anyway, I didn't ask Kara to stay. She had her own shit to deal with and she had her own immigrant parents (Somali) that she had to navigate as well. I relaxed and waited for Trevor to show.

Except, he never did.

Not because he had disappeared into the night or something. I learned that he'd had to stay back in his home state longer to help his dad with some ongoing construction project or whatever the fuck. He texted his apologies and that he would be there in *two weeks*. I told him to be safe and added that I hoped to see him soon.

And this, lovelies, is where my *real* hell began.

Having to negotiate being freshly disabled in both my parents' and sister's houses had been bad enough. They were *bad* people. And the only thing bad people could do was make bad situations *worse*. This is a given and it was something I had expected. However, even with me being free of them in Chicago, I had not expected how *agonizingly* lonely this healing process was about to be.

Those two weeks alone meant that I had to essentially fend for *myself*. On occasion, I would ring Kara whenever I needed to do a quick grocery run, and she never *ever* let me come down those flights of stairs, for obvious reasons, and always made sure I had enough "quick" food to eat so I didn't have to stand trying to cook something.

But by and large, I was on my own.

The first week was particularly bad because, pre–ACL tear, I had put my bed on lifts. Of course, that made it very comfortable for me and left me with tons of space. Still, barely having any control or strength over my left knee meant that I literally could not hold myself up long enough to climb onto my bed. Even for napping purposes. And believe me, I did try. But trying to pull myself up there felt like dragging bags upon bags of cement bricks behind me. So I abandoned all hope and made the living room couch my "bed" for the time being.

Losing my ability to sleep *comfortably* wasn't the only indignity that I suffered in those two weeks. Even something as simple as trying to use the bathroom became this almost impossible chore. It's funny because my trips to the bathroom had already been sporadic since I had suffered the tear and had to be bounced around my family's houses post-surgery. Not getting as much movement or activity as I was used to meant that I was in a state of perpetual and painful constipation. TMI, I know, but imagine being really *regular* and then having *nothing* move at all—regardless of the fact that you are still basically eating the same.

That in itself sucked. But on the off chance that I finally had a goddamn bowel movement, walking myself to the bathroom basically became a trip to Mordor. And "walking" myself really meant *dragging* myself down a long-ass hallway with a tiny bathroom at the end of it. I'm not gonna lie; that first day was horrid. And I had gotten my hand on the knob of the bathroom door just as I was about to shit myself.

I would go on to have about four more close calls. Just like that one.

The other thing that I found fairly impossible to deal with was trying to keep myself clean.

I'd had a pretty reliable shower schedule pre-injury. I usually showered once a day and would tack another shower on if I had been playing whatever IM sport on that particular day. Post-injury? Well, let's just say that it was reminiscent of all of these conversations that white people keep subjecting us to on Twitter about not washing their fucking asses. Or legs. Or bodies, period.

Of course, I am *Black*. An *African*. And there was no fucking way I was going to let it get that bad. But my lack of mobility and *help* meant that I was just going to have to make do with what I had.

In regards to actual "bath" time, I mostly used washcloths and bowls of water and wipes, especially on days when it was too painful to make it to the seat in front of my bathroom sink. On easier days, I would take a sink bath. After a week of this, I finally felt well enough to attempt to take an abbreviated bath in an actual tub. Dragged my water-resistant chair in there and everything. But, as you know, because my life is a dramedy, that particular venture ended with me falling over in the shower. With all of the water in the bucket I had filled slapping against me and then spiraling down the drain.

It felt like I was in a Life Alert commercial. But like, a really, really *dark* one. And so I cried, because it was more than appropriate.

Being disabled was not something I was used to. Nor was it something that I wanted to get used to. But it didn't really matter because this was my life now.

And I hated it.

Still, hate aside, I knew I was going to have to find a way to move along with it. And roll with the punches. Whether I had help or not.

I'D STARTED physical therapy as soon as I was back in Chicago, and by the time Trevor returned and started escorting me there himself, my PT sessions were already off to a, let's say, fascinating start.

Around the first week of August, I had finally tracked down a clinic that would take my insurance—for the most part.

But who has time to talk about deductibles and out-of-network shit? Not I. But still. It was a mixed bag.

The upside was that finding the clinic made me feel as if coming back to Chicago had been the right choice. And I was in need of that kind of validation. *Bad*. The downside was that the clinic happened to be near the fucking airport. Midway, if I remember correctly. And that meant that I had to haul my leg onto like 24708320498320 buses before I even got there. Despite the hassle, get there, and get there weekly, I did.

The first time I visited the clinic, I ended up walking in and greeting whoever had been at the front desk hurriedly. I had been running hella late due to a missed bus and some rain. I grabbed my paperwork from the desk, and in about five or so minutes I was getting called over to the other side of the clinic to be evaluated—where a bunch of tables were set up, weights were set out, and the like. Absently, I made my way over, dragging my feet like I would at any doctor's appointment. I kept walking until someone stuck their tattooed hand out in front of me. I glanced at it for a second and realized someone was trying to introduce themselves. I looked up, ready to shake their hand and introduce myself as well. But when I did, all words in the English language evaporated from my brain like that one episode where SpongeBob forgets his name. Besides noticing that a man, with his hair tied back in a jet-black bun, was towering over me (I'm talking like six two or six three), there were a lot of things I loved about his *face* in particular. But the most showstopping thing was his eyes. I saw the deepest pool of brown looking at me, golden flakes peeking out from his pupils.

It's a blur, mainly because I am birdy enough for my brain to start beatboxing when I see someone really hot. But despite my mental fog, I managed to catch that his name was Jason—Dr. Jason P. Manug. *He* was going to be my physical therapist for the foreseeable future. It was good that he mentioned that, because one of his colleagues was standing right next to him. She was hot *too* and I definitely wouldn't have minded getting sessions from her either.

"I didn't catch your name?" Dr. Manug said slowly. I blinked at him before I finally realized that he was talking to me.

"Oh! Oh. My name," I laughed nervously. "My name . . . ? Yes! My name is . . ." He looked at me, waiting expectantly. "My name is Xela! Xela. Wait, no. Alexandria. Sorry. I've been watching too many episodes of *Happy Endings*. My name is Alexandria. Alex or Lex for short!" I continued chuckling like I was off my fucking rocker.

Which . . . looking back on my life, that was always the case. But that's not the point.

"Alex. Alex! Alex." He said my name like he was trying it on for size or something. "Nice to meet you, Alex."

"Uh-huh," I said. "Nice to meet you, Dr. Manug."

"You can call me Jason, by the way." He grinned.

The next couple of weeks, months truth be told, passed like that, with more bird and hopeless romantic behavior leaping out of me whenever this man was around. I always made sure I was immaculately dressed for every appointment. Which was . . . a whole *saga* because I couldn't wear pants or jeans like that anymore. Besides the obvious of not wanting to obstruct my injury and slow down the healing process, I couldn't fucking stand or even sit long enough to squeeze some pants over my ass and hips or do the ass shimmy to pull up my jeans. Nope. I had to switch over to dresses and long skirts for the most part, because I needed that ease of access.

But I pressed on. Perfumed but in a subtle way. Nails perfectly manicured and painted. Not a single strand of hair out of place pre-workout. Post-workout though? A completely different story considering that he worked me to the bone.

To the bone, y'all. To the *bone*.

Of course, the fact that I was dying due to the 42398749837 reps I was expected to finish on every machine (to regain my strength) got kindly obscured by the fact that, once again, *Jason* was incredibly easy on the eyes. So easy that sometimes it proved to be distracting. Case in point, winding down from my workouts every day meant that I had to stretch with him. Which meant, to be clear, him getting on top of me to stretch my leg out in assorted ways. The stretching itself was pretty painful because of the scar tissue in my knee and because my knee was being moved in directions that I most certainly was not familiar with. But the visual I was getting from where I was lying? The way that every time he moved over me, I got a whiff of his cologne? And not to mention the occasional, yet intense eye contact he would hit me with, followed by a kilowatt smile? *My God.* Sometimes I even had to look away because it felt so intimate and kinda raw. But also really tense, in a sexy way?

Describing this now seems like I'm describing some self-insert fan fiction in your standard medical show (a subsection of fan fiction that I certainly wasn't a stranger to, haha), but I'm not kidding you when I say that I was in a *dangerous* situation. This was the *second* fine-ass doctor that had crossed my path since surgery, and I just had to wonder why I was *finally* meeting a bunch of hot people now that I had been fucked up health-wise. And in a position where I couldn't really go *outside* as often as I wanted to and do something about it. It was comical, really. But I tried to focus on the positive.

Rewinding a bit, maybe you think I imagined the "tense" feeling I mentioned but—nope. It was a thing. As time went on, and when I wasn't blushing from *technically* being put in a compromising position on one of the patient beds, both Jason and I began sharing small, relevant tidbits about our lives. The first week, he had started off with real general questions about what had gotten me there and what I planned on doing after college. I told him the obvious about the big IM soccer game and mentioned my writing and film aspirations. He gave me some interesting factoids about how he got into his profession—which included an injury of his own. He'd initially wanted to be a professional basketball player.

"Basketball?" I repeated back at him. "I don't see it."

"'Cause of the Filipino thing?" He chuckled. "Because I get that a lot, unfortunately."

I raised an eyebrow at him. "No? I just thought you looked more like a soccer or baseball person. Don't make it weird." He released my leg for a second and put his hands up in mock surrender.

"Touché!"

Like I said. The first week of PT was pretty basic, because you know, you gotta build rapport with your patient or whatever. But as time went on? *Baby*, things got a little *personal*. Something I hadn't really expected.

We went from discussing the basics of our lives (favorite colors, favorite shows, why pineapple did or did not belong on pizza—it just does not . . . okay?) to deep diving into things like our childhood dreams. For me, it was still being an author. For him? He had real-deal wanted to join the circus. We were both into comics, so I made a joke about the Flying Graysons that was super dark and he ended up guffawing. Eventually, this segued into a talk about our parents.

"How do your parents feel about you being up here by yourself?" he asked. "Are y'all close?"

"Short answer? I'm a functional orphan. Kinda like Dick, but I sorta-kinda had a choice. Which, in my mind, means that my mother and father don't exist and perhaps never existed to me." I shrugged.

"That bad, huh?"

"Yeah."

Jason nodded. "That's very . . . honest."

"I try to be. Most of the time," I said. "You?"

"I can relate somewhat. I grew up here with a really strict Filipino mom—I'm first-gen—"

"As am I. Nigerian."

"Nice!" He continued, "Anyway, she was such a hard-ass. Kinda pretty cold too. But I cut her some slack because she was raising me by herself. Since her early twenties. And now that I'm twenty-six, I can't imagine doing that shit myself."

"Can I ask what happened with your—"

"Father?"

"I was going to say 'other parent,' but that works."

"He was some random white guy that took off. Met my mom when he was still a tourist. And just when it looked like he was gonna stay and shack up with my mom, she told him she was pregnant and he panicked. There's more, but that's the gist of it," he said. "Fun stuff."

"Cool story. I'm sure it's a hit with therapists." More of my dark humor flew out of my mouth uncensored. He looked directly at me and my eyes got really big—as I realized what I had just said. I moved to cover my mouth until I saw him trying to suppress laughter. And failed miserably.

"True. Very true." He laughed. "I feel like everyone should go to therapy at least once, you know?"

I nodded. "Agreed, but who would pay for it?"

He looked at me like he was going to start laughing again. "Obama?"

"Not an Obamacare joke." I snorted.

"I mean—I just think that the government should be paying for this, right? Like, what the *hell* is a deductible?! It should all be free."

"I couldn't agree more!"

This kind of banter continued throughout our sessions, with physical therapy being a constant in my life for the foreseeable future. The funny part was the more we laughed and trained together, the quicker I healed.

EVENTUALLY, classes recommenced for both Trevor and I. And Trevor had to stop tagging along with me to PT due to picking up a new a cappella commitment. He had wanted to move some stuff on his schedule around to keep escorting me, but I let him know that I was a big girl and could take the 2349832098432048 buses that it took to arrive there myself.

On my first day Trevor-less, I came into the clinic after a day full of annoying classes and went to the desk to commence my usual ritual of signing in and moving through the various workout stations for my daily round of torture. Jason was sitting at the front desk, and when he saw that I was alone, he looked concerned.

"That is a long hike to take by yourself." He crossed his arms.

"Sure, but this was what my commute was like when I first got here. So . . ." I shrugged.

"Hmm. Well, hope it's just for today then, but either way, when your boyfriend gets back, I'm gonna have a serious talk with him about—"

"Boyfriend?"

"Yeah? That Trevor fellow?"

"Bold of you to assume that Trevor is my boyfriend. Or that I'm even straight." I mirrored his crossed arms and he quickly uncrossed his.

The additional gag was that, once again, Trevor was a whole flaming homosexual. Like an official card-carrying gay.

"Ah, I'm sorry—that was very un—"

"Even bolder of you to assume that I *have* a boyfriend, to begin with." I smirked. "Which . . . I *currently* don't."

I'm never going to really know Jason's true intentions behind asking me that. And at this point, I can only guess. But I remember this very small but very *bright* twinkle that appeared in his eyes. It was like I had just said something that he had so desperately wanted to hear.

Or *confirm*, in this case.

I didn't really mind either, because, to me, the age gap wasn't that serious. I was close to turning twenty-one. And he was just twenty-six. Nothing older and nothing younger. I had always been taught inadvertently by my sister (who had been very sexually active to the chagrin of my parents) that the no-no age range was about seven (plus) years. As she also had experience dealing with people, men in particular, who happened to be much older. And such experiences always turned out to be . . . not very kosher. Since Jason and I both fell under that range, I didn't mind his curiosity at all. In fact, his curiosity piqued mine.

It was practically all I could think about for the rest of the day. Even throughout my strenuous drills and even when he had me hop onto one of the patient beds for stretches. With my head in the clouds like this, the whole hour and a half flew by, and before I knew it, I was packing up my shit to go home as everyone left was preparing to close the clinic for the day. I said my goodbyes to some of the last lingering employees and started to head out the door.

"Alex! Wait!" someone called out.

I stopped, holding the door open halfway. When I turned, I saw Jason jogging toward me, putting on his jacket hurriedly while slinging his backpack behind him.

"I'll drive you to the station," he said. "You know, so you only have to take one bus." I looked up at him, mildly suspicious that a cishet *man*, with no immediate (blood) connection to me, wanted to do me a favor.

"You don't have to do that." I tried not to squint at him as I weighed his words.

He didn't miss a beat. "I want to."

"The station's not very close, just so you know."

"I'm aware."

"I mean, if this is really how you want to end your workday, then, I guess." This time, I did in fact squint, wondering what he was up to.

He smiled. "I do. In fact, I *insist*. It's on my way home anyway."

From then on, it became part of Jason's end-of-day routine to drop me off at the bus station before heading off on his own. It proved to be an interesting time, mostly because if he was pretty hype at work, he came alive even *more* off the clock.

I remember him driving me to the station one time, and for the first time in like a year, a Big Time Rush song came through the speakers, blaring from the radio. He went to change the song but stopped when I started humming along to it.

"You know this song?" he asked.

I stopped humming, suddenly curious. "Yeah, do you?"

A wry smile spread across his face until it got big as fuck. "I do. I used to watch their show with my sister. I thought it was dumb at first but—"

"Their songs are really catchy, aren't they?" I finished.

"Surprisingly," he admitted.

"Surprisingly? Hmph." I smirked as I turned up the volume.

Together, we proceeded to belt the chorus to "City Is Ours" at the top of our lungs.

BY THE beginning of January 2015, after five months of PT sessions, Chicago had turned into the coldest of frozen tundras. The snow was ceaseless, and it provided an interesting backdrop to my final session with Jason.

The last day proceeded along as any normal day would, but I noticed Jason was a little sadder. Moved a bit slower. And there were several moments he'd steal glances at me, assuming that I hadn't seen him. But one thing about me? I know when people are staring. To be honest, I can feel it on the back of my neck. Even if I don't directly acknowledge it. I thought it was kind of cute that he thought he was so slick.

Hours later, Jason pulled into the bus station and helped me out of the car. I slung my backpack onto my shoulder and turned to bid him farewell.

"Last day," he said, almost in what sounded like a question.

"Last day," I confirmed. "It's been real."

"Yes, it has." He shoved his hands into his pockets. He looked kind of nervous, and while I was curious, I opted not to point it out.

"You've been a great doctor," I said. "I still got some work to do, but I'm off to a dope-ass start. All thanks to you."

"You're welcome. But, just so you know, you did all the work," he said. "None of this would have happened if you didn't want to do the work."

"True . . . but also, take the damn compliment." I laughed.

"Okay, okay. I hear you." We laughed together for a few seconds before I hoisted my backpack up once again and started to head in the direction of the buses.

I waved. "Bye, Jason."

I'm pretty sure I made it, maybe, about a foot away or so before he stopped me. "Alex, wait!"

"Uh, did I forget something?" I looked at him and then started patting my sides like I had dropped my keys or my phone.

"No, no. I did." He stood in front of me. "I . . ."

"You . . . ?" I was trying not to be annoyed, but I had a bus to catch and he was kinda dragging what he wanted to say out.

"I meant to ask you for your number," he said finally. "I thought it would be *weird* for obvious reasons if I had asked earlier—"

"Because you were my doctor—"

"Because I was your doctor. So, I'm asking now."

I looked him up and down. Semi-shocked that he had managed to spit out what I'm sure he was thinking about the entire day. I probably wouldn't have said anything, ever, so I was a little impressed by his guts.

I let a couple of seconds pass, you know, just for the appropriate amount of tension to rise. And then I smiled at him.

"Hand me your phone."

"Yes ma'am." He grinned back.

Moments later, we waved at each other through the window

as the bus pulled out of the station. It was weird. This definitely felt like the conclusion of something, like the very last scene in a movie or like the *final* episode of a TV show. But imagine some Keane song playing in the background as I drove away.

Still, I felt strangely . . . hopeful? Yes. Hopeful. Optimistic even. It'd be interesting to see what would blossom between us now that I wasn't his patient anymore and he wasn't my doctor. And now that our meetings would be happening *outside* of the clinic.

I liked Jason. A lot. Like an embarrassing amount. Who wouldn't? He understood all my niche comic humor, was geeked about knowing an "aspiring writer" and didn't mind making an ass of himself (a little bit anyway) by singing fictional boy band songs with me. He had also taken it upon himself to shorten my commute home from physical therapy—even going as far as lying about it being "on his way home" (oh yes, he did!). And, for fuck's sake, he was *hot!* And into *me!* And this was all reinforced by the fact that he diligently held my hand throughout this entire saga of attempting to repair my torn ACL . . . and my self-esteem.

Dealing with this injury by myself the past summer had been such an isolating experience. Excruciating too. Made worse by the disgusting way my parents and sister had behaved toward me in a bid to regain the power they had lost over me when I moved to Chicago. But the addition of physical therapy, Jason in particular, had helped to alleviate all the really ugly parts and feelings I had about everything. His support and presence inspired me to work on healing the other parts of me that had been shattered when my ACL was torn. Not just the physical ones.

I leaned against the window as Jason got smaller and smaller until he disappeared.

UNFORTUNATELY, Jason never called. Or texted.

I'd love to say that I had expected as much. I'd love to say that I wasn't invested in any type of outcome at all and therefore wasn't really fazed by this development. I'd also love to say that I was one of those girls who was really sure of themselves, didn't give a fuck, and simply shrugged it off after I didn't hear from him within the first forty-eight hours. But the truth of the matter was that . . . I kept waiting. And waiting.

And *waiting*.

As per usual, I was pretty in denial about the whole thing. I even made up a bunch of scenarios about why he hadn't called. A lot of them ended up with him probably being dead in a ditch somewhere. Or his phone spontaneously combusting and him thereby losing my number. Or him having to leave the country in a huff because he had witnessed a violent crime and would thus be in witness protection for the rest of his life.

There were plenty of other scenarios, too, some of which I'm too proud to list here now. But the point was that I was pretty devastated. "Crushed" would be a better word honestly. I scanned my brain, trying to go over the events of the last six months. I tried to identify any points where I could have given mixed signals or he could have given mixed signals. I tried to determine if I had just imagined the whole thing. Hallucinated it after a particularly good trip. I even opted to blame it on my mental illness—since I knew for sure that I was depressed at the time. I considered that I had possibly daydreamed it to escape the cruel reality that I lived in. But even after all that thinking and reminiscing, I couldn't identify a single reason why he'd leave me high and dry like this.

Other than the fact that he was a dickhead. And probably hadn't intended on calling me at all. I mean, who knows? Maybe this was part of his whole routine as a doctor. His shtick! To stoke the fires of sexual tension and keep you coming back for more. Like a drug. Just so you can get off your ass and actively and enthusiastically participate in healing yourself. With the added bonus of regularly seeing his immaculately chiseled face.

I obviously didn't know what happened, and I knew for

certain that I would never know, but I ended up concluding that I was definitely hella gullible. And that I definitely wouldn't be falling for anyone I had to deal with in a professional capacity *ever* again. I would *never* shit where I ate in my life. That was done! That was over with.

I cried a lot after that. Wept. Sobbed! For some time. I mean, I had already been crying pre–ACL injury—mainly because being at UChicago was an insufferable experience in a myriad of ways, and the curriculum continued to beat my fucking ass. And I definitely had been sobbing post–ACL injury because of the loss of my mobility and freedom. And frankly? Respect. So many people were just okay with disrespecting me for taking up additional space—both as a fat person and a disabled person. And while I thought myself to be pretty strong, it still got to me. That and the pain I still had to endure navigating this unbearably inaccessible campus, even after my physical therapy sessions had long ended.

Not to mention all the things I still couldn't do. Or that I probably wouldn't get to do again. Running, *period*, felt like a tall order. But running for long periods of time? Ha. Heels, which I had actually enjoyed wearing, were out too. Even if I dared to try, I almost always wiped out. My knee was too unstable. Swimming (wading and flopping around in the water) was still impossible at this point—with the muscle imbalance still being a thing. And don't get me started on my new aversion to rain. Because while it would normally put me to sleep, it also woke my knee right the fuck up. And the pain would last days on end.

I was tired. This shit was for the birds! And I wanted my old life back.

I was so sick of having to live with this new "strike." I didn't know how anyone could be living like this. With their quality of life being hampered this way. I was so sick of living with this *fresh* new wound that people were using to marginalize me and deny me the full scope of my humanity.

I took it very hard. Very fucking hard. I took it *all* very hard. So hard that I refused to do *any* type of writing. Didn't matter if it was for school or for "fun."

It wouldn't be far-fetched to say that I was grieving. Grieving the fact that I was foolish enough to think that someone like Jason was actually interested in me. And grieving the fact that I still felt so alone despite all this "progress" I had made with training to regain my mobility.

This phase of my grief was fairly contradictory because while I felt alone, this was not the case. In fact, the opposite was true.

I was surrounded by a fair amount of people who wanted to help me heal—despite not knowing anything about my bottomless grief (because I felt too embarrassed to tell them, as a huge chunk of it had to do with Jason). Truly. Since I was going outside even *less* than I had been while attending physical therapy, Trevor still made the time to check on me in between demanding classes and extended a cappella rehearsal sessions. Faithfully. In fact, I'm sure I annoyed him from time to time, seeing as he ended up talking to my door more than I would have liked. But being in the kind of mental state I was in didn't allow me to stretch my empathy that far.

Still, Trevor let it be known that he was available for whatever I needed, which included fielding requests and concerns from other on-campus friends. One such friend was Emiliano Mendoza, a cheeky son of a bitch who shared my love for writing.

I'd met him during my first year, fall of 2012, in an English class and we shared a writing workshop before going our separate first-year ways. We wouldn't really link back up until midway through second year, when he ended up moving off campus, as did I, and we ended up crossing paths in the theater and poetry scene. Or in the streets, while protesting the latest trifling thing that the university had done or said in the last month. Or while defeating each other's houses in varied intramural sports—which, as you know, eventually led to my injury to begin with.

Emiliano ended up, ironically, living only a couple of blocks from my apartment during this extended grieving session of mine. And after he noticed my recurring absences and over-heard from Trevor how close our apartments were at a theater event post-injury, he insisted that I come over to hang out and just vibe. Of course, despite his insistence and Trevor's dili-gence in getting his messages to me (I could not be relied on to answer my phone post–physical therapy), I spurned his initial offers—opting not to allow anyone (be it Trevor or Emiliano) to bear witness to how tired, weary, disgusting, and disheveled I looked in person. I couldn't do it. I wouldn't do it!

However, when I wasn't dodging Trevor or Emiliano from behind my door, I found solace in my friends online, particu-larly on Facebook (yes, I'm that old) and then Twitter. My ACL injury preventing me from leaving the house meant I had even less time to engage my peers, especially where *physical* student organizing was concerned. So naturally, I gravitated toward those spaces online. Feminist spaces in particular.

This was where I met Neal Balasuriyage, who I now refer to as my (chosen) sister.

Neal—short for O'Neal, a nickname she earned after dunk-ing on fully grown niggas on a basketball court—was a ball of chaotic stardust that I met on Facebook in 2014 in a Black femi-nist group, right around the time I got injured. She had a couple of years on me, and I was reminded of that whenever she told me about one of the 3402394083 jobs she had, her main ones being a part-time bartender and a paralegal. While I wouldn't get to officially meet her in the flesh until the very next year, that didn't exactly matter to me. A friend is a friend is a friend, no matter what "medium" the friendship originates in.

Any conversation with Neal was enough to brighten my day and have me laughing until I pissed myself, despite me being holed up in the house like a goddamn mole. That said,

I didn't really shed too much light on the extent of my depression (and how it was affecting my ability to attend classes *and* work the part-time job I had at the time—a bad omen for my pockets), until I told her the briefest version of my misadventures with Jason.

I remember her cussing me the fuck out.

"You fucking bitch," Neal gasped.

"Huh?" I was shocked.

"You heard me," she added. "So not only did this nigga go Houdini on you, but you've been struggling to work and didn't think to say anything until . . . now?"

"I mean . . . yeah?" I shrugged, though she couldn't see me. "Like, it's not your responsibility to take care of me. Plus, we just met each other."

There was a pause on the other side of the line.

"Ouch," Neal said. I quickly realized how dickish of me it was to say that and I tried to correct myself.

"I mean"—I hesitated—"what I *meant* to say is that we haven't been friends for that long and it would have felt weird to come to you with my hand out."

"Okay, but friends can ask friends for help. There shouldn't be any arbitrary rules for that kind of shit."

"Well, I don't know what to tell you, because that's just not something I'm used to, *okay*?" I snapped. "Asking for help makes me feel like shit. It makes me feel helpless. I hate it."

I felt like Neal was ready to argue and tell me how childish I was being (because I was!), but instead, she said the following:

"Give me your Cash App."

"Neal—"

"I said, give me your *fucking* Cash App."

Of course, I ended up indulging her. And from time to time, whether I *asked* for help or not, my Cash App would ding and it would be followed by a lovingly aggressive text from Neal telling me to go "buy some fucking groceries." I was, somewhat begrudgingly, thankful for her help.

Still, my grief remained. I want to pause here and say that grief is not an inherently bad thing, despite the widespread US belief that it should be avoided as long as possible (re: COVID-19), but my particular version of grief felt . . . infinite. A gaping hole in my being. And not even the aforementioned interactions could begin to fill it.

To make matters even direr, my grief was worsened by my already existing depression, the addition of seasonal affective disorder, *undiagnosed* bipolar II disorder, the extreme weight gain I experienced after I left physical therapy and was unable to get to the gym as often as I wanted in the snow, and the fact that it was dark and cold—and these were *peak* months for cuffing season.

Sometime after that, nearing the end of the third week in January, I tried to end my life.

Like, *officially*.

And not in that way when you're like "I'm passively thinking about all the ways I could kill myself" in your head. Nope. I bought a brand-spanking-new bottle of extra-strength Tylenol and gathered all the other cold medicine I had accumulated this far—with the intention of finally taking myself out of the game. Unplugging my shit from the simulation. Getting my "creator" to take the ladder away from my Sim pool and let my fat ass drown.

I remember it being some random Wednesday night or some shit. I intended it that way. Wednesdays meant that Trevor wasn't around and he was either busy with a cappella rehearsal or he was spending the night with his boyfriend. I opted out of the whole note-writing part of it too. I had written so much shit in my few decades of life that I figured the best way to go out was by simply saying nothing. Just leaving existence quietly. Peacefully. Letting my actions speak for themselves.

The only hiccup in my plan, the one thing I hadn't counted on, was Regina, one of my oldest friends, calling me at the time. And I mean *oldest*. We had met at my mom's wack-ass church many moons ago and had somehow managed to stay close and stay in touch.

She rang. Like some weird stroke of divine intervention. Mind you, this happened *moments* after I had downed all of the Tylenol pills, and I remember staring at my phone with the most exasperated look on my face and with a burning feeling of annoyance in the pit of my stomach.

Despite this, however, I answered the phone.

"Hey," I said, trying to act normal.

"Hey," she said. "You good?"

This fucking witch.

"I'm good," I answered quickly, trying not to be defensive. "Why wouldn't I be good?"

"I dunno," Regina replied. "I'm sorry! I'm sorry. That came out weird. I was just trying to say that I've been thinking about you *all day* and since I had some free time after this shitty class ran late."

"Oh," I answered. "That's really nice of you,"

"No, no," she replied. "Don't let me off so easy, Alexandria." To be clear, she was one of only two people on this planet that was still allowed to say my full first name. "I should have called. With what's been going on with you. I'm sorry."

"No, it's okay—"

"It is most certainly not okay." Regina cut me off. "I didn't really know how to show up for you initially, and I figured you might want some space, considering everything that had happened—especially where your family was concerned." She kept talking. Her speaking pace picked up, probably because she had always been so anxious in general. "I realized though that I had never directly *asked* you what you needed. And how I could show up. So. I'm here to ask now."

Honestly, I stared at the phone like I was on an episode of *The Office*. Gaia *must've* had a fucking bonkers sense of humor. Because the timing was both incredible and almost insulting. With the way that it came out of nowhere. What were the chances that someone, a loved one, would reach out to tell me that I didn't have to be lonely anymore? That I didn't have to isolate myself anymore? Or that, rather, they weren't going to let me do that any longer? And what were the chances that this loved one would be someone I spent a considerable amount of time with growing up? Someone who witnessed, firsthand, the depravity of my parents and the specific types of violence they wrought upon me? The violence that had led to this moment?

What bizarre timing indeed.

"Um . . . I'd like to vent. If you have time," I whispered. "I never get to vent. People always vent to me."

"Of course I have time!" she responded. "Let me find somewhere quiet so we can talk."

"No. Not right now," I said hurriedly. "Tomorrow. Tomorrow is good."

"No problem," she confirmed. "I'll call you after class tomorrow. Does this time still work?"

"Yeah," I said absently. "Yeah, it does."

After that, Regina apologized again for not contacting me sooner and *promised* that she would do so tomorrow. I thanked her for calling, wished her goodnight, and promptly hung up the phone.

I ended my night by puking up as many pills as I could.

For those who are curious, no, I didn't end up going to the hospital or calling for help, firstly because of that pesky out-of-network coverage rule. Secondly . . . consider how many states in this country treat mentally ill people during brief (or even extended) moments of distress.

In the state of Illinois, for example, a person with mental illness could be committed to a psychiatric hospital against their will either by court order (I am dead fucking serious), by power of attorney, or by what is called "emergency admission by certification." No court order or POA is necessary for this latter route. Instead, if said mentally ill person even *seems* like they're gonna harm themselves or someone else, any medical professional or police officer who gets involved in the mix can take it upon themselves to file paperwork to get them involuntarily committed.

And since "attempted suicide" definitely indicated that I had intended to harm myself, there was no fucking way on Gaia's green Earth that I was gonna dial 911 on myself or even tell anyone in my immediate circle that I did this shit. I knew more than a handful of organizing associates who had experience with UChicago's brand of "care." And they had told me horror stories of being forcefully detained by campus police during mental health episodes (which included *any* mention of suicide). These stories always ended with them being involuntarily hospitalized in a university psychiatric facility—barely able to reach any loved ones long enough to tell them where the fuck there were being held (a phenomenon that is explained at length in Cassidy Wilson's essay "At the Forefront of Medicine: My Summer Involuntary Hospitalization").

With my support network being as fragmented as it was thanks to my parents, my freedom as a fat, disabled Black girl—however fragile at that point—wasn't something I was willing to risk.

So I laid my ass down to sleep.

Hoping that throwing up everything had done the trick.

MY WOULD-BE PARAMOUR

Why are you so protective of bi and pan boys?"

A good friend of mine asked me this question about a month before Pride 2018. At that point, I was in Knoxville (to be discussed!). We were in some hipster coffee shop whose name I can't remember. But it was nice. Warm. I watched the steam rise from my undisturbed cup of tea and leaned forward to stir it. My friend's brown eyes locked with my own, full of even more questions about my passionate recurring defense of such men. I looked back down at my tea and realized, of course, that I didn't have an answer ready for them. Okay, that's a lie. I said the most cliché line in the history of clichés:

"It's complicated."

And as cliché as that sounds now, it was. It would have been "easy" to respond that "Oh, I'm bi too," so I "get it." But that is not only a woefully underdeveloped take but also an unnecessary one, considering that I had some actual lived experience that explained my commitment to such men. This fierce loyalty to bisexual and pansexual men started with my own ill-fated relationship with a bisexual cis man in college.

Let's call him . . . Bruce.

It was the year 2015. The very beginning of February. Mere weeks after getting my heart broken by Jason *and* attempting suicide. Anyway. It didn't hit me until we eventually got up-close and personal, but Bruce, frankly, was a beautiful man. Striking brown eyes. Facial hair that hugged a particularly strong-ass jaw. Muscles in all the right places. A goofy-ass smile that was enough to derail my thoughts, which is quite the feat considering that, for those who are astrologically inclined, my Mercury is in Gemini, so I literally have thoughts running through my mind a mile a second. At *all* times.

He had this thick, curly black hair all over his body. I had never seen someone *that* hairy. It was as if Wolverine decided to go to college! And it was a look that I wouldn't usually go for. But I couldn't help but be pulled in by it . . . and a very *microscopic* part of me (thanks, demisexuality) pondered the prospect of tugging on it all during *quiet hours*. I imagine he looked like what *Assassin's Creed: Odyssey thought* they were doing with *their* version of Adonis. His only "flaws" were that he was slightly shorter than me (I was more shallow then. I still am, *buuuuuuut* it's something I try to be mindful of every now and again.) and a year and a half younger, but that went out the window when he opened his mouth.

In my first year in college, in 2012, I became way more involved in social justice groundwork. I was trying to seek penance for my previous life as a conservative dickhead who was content to parrot 99.9 percent of my parents' dickheaded rhetoric as it pertained to (American) Blackness. I'd also felt like my life had been snatched from under me when Mike Brown died, knowing that he had been the exact same age as Craig. Of course, all of my advocacy work damn near came to a screeching halt when I fucked up my ACL back in April 2014. And even months after physical therapy ended, my internalized ableism was off the charts at that point and there wasn't much—I thought—I could do from my bed at home or from the couch of the dorm that I frequented at least once a day. And this meant that I was eternally frustrated with the state of the world and its treatment of Black people and, you know, my own inaction because of my injury.

So, one day, I expressed said frustration in my old dorm's common space.

I casually fired off, "Fuck white people," in the dorm, apparently within earshot of Bruce. I was sitting with two of my girlfriends (one nonwhite and one Black) near an unlit fireplace as we stuffed our faces with day-old sushi, lamenting what was going on in Ferguson and Baltimore. Bruce looked up from his homework at a table nearby and agreed. "Oh, totally."

Mind you, Bruce was a white dude. Not the whitest white dude or a white dude's white dude, but still clearly white. And while I would later find out that he was Sicilian and Jewish (and that these identities informed his stances on social justice), in my mind, all of that added up to "spicy white," and at the end of the day, there was still this random white dude I had never met butting into my conversation with my girls. I scrunched up my nose.

"Sorry for intruding." He was suddenly painfully aware of his presence. "It's just that someone here is finally talking about something interesting for once and I got kind of excited."

"Uh-huh." I nodded slowly and went about my business.

My girlfriends practically broke their necks as they started signing at me to continue the conversation with him, but it was too late. I was already checked out and back to my regularly scheduled ranting. But this was far from over. I mentioned the story in jest to my play aunt Gladys Turner (who worked at the dorm) and she chastised me for not entertaining the conversation, which was fair. After all, it was notoriously hard for me to find friends and dates because most of my chosen PWI's population had its head shoved up its ass and thought any part of Chicago that was not overwhelmingly white was "sketchy."

"So a little birdy told me that you met a boy?" Gladys caught me as I was hobbling into the dorm one day.

I made a face. "I don't recognize boys as human beings so you'll have to be very specific about who you're talking about. Like *really* specific."

"One of them white boys who just moved in," she said. "Bruce I think is his name."

"If he's the nosy one who butted into my conversation the other day, then yeah. That's probably him. Although I think the word *met* is very generous."

"Okay, Ms. Smartypants." Gladys smiled at me. "So when are you going to officially 'meet' him?"

"Never sounds like a really good time."

"You joke, but I bet he'd give you a reason to get up out of that apartment you're always cooped up in."

"That's funny, because the last time I checked, I'm always here. At the dorm." I was getting impatient.

"You think that's better?"

Okay. She had me there. I was spending hella time at my old dorm because my friends were still there. But also because it was *really* close by and the thought of being social with other people I didn't know *post*-injury was terrifying. On the other hand, I was hella tempted to roll my eyes at her advice because white boys were very overrepresented at this school and I always felt weird about trying to engage one of them romantically because of the off-chance that I would meet one of those "Jungle Fever" types. But just so she would give it a rest, I agreed to try to get to know the ol' dude better.

"Goddamn. I'll go. Shit," I grumbled.

"And when did I say it was okay to start cussin' at me?" she shot back. I quickly straightened myself up and walked off before I could get myself in more trouble.

So I asked him out for coffee the next time I saw him in the dorm.

Fast-forward some weeks later to me waiting for Bruce in one of the campus coffee shops. The local Einstein Bros. if you will. I'm saying this like I didn't care about the meeting, when in fact I had spent most of the previous night and all of that morning trying to pick out a nice black maxi dress. One that was cute enough but didn't look like I was trying *too* hard. And one that also would be sturdy enough to hide the fact that I had gained nearly fifty pounds since I had torn my ACL. This is fucked, of course, but remember that the words *body positivity* and *fat liberation* were nowhere near my vocabulary then. At that point, I was just a fat Black disabled girl with a host of self-loathing issues that stemmed from carrying those identities around, who was going out on a limb by even entertaining a mayo-saxon, to begin with, and who was hoping that this little boy didn't decide to stand my fat ass up so I wouldn't be tempted to call Neal and tell her to get the bail money ready.

Still, I was excited, which conflicted with my anxiousness. And after waiting about twenty minutes, I was ready to get up, leave, and go make that phone call to my sister—until Bruce finally came running in with flowers, huffing and puffing apologies because a class had let out late and he had missed the bus back to our main campus. I side-eyed him, but since I had been there (CTA buses could be petty like that), I sat back down so we could chat.

We had a really great talk that lasted for *hours*. Our conversation spanned familial backgrounds (we were both first-generation Americans with *demanding* immigrant parents) and passions (what I wanted to do to fix media representation that was "fucked up" with my writing, and his concerns about housing and him wanting to someday head the Department of Housing and Urban Development to "make things right"). I crossed my arms over my gut at one point after we'd smashed a bagel or two together, suddenly feeling self-conscious about my weight the moment my eyes finally registered that he was fine as fuck. If I had been a couple of shades lighter, I'm sure my face would have been beet-ass red. His eyes briefly flickered down at that motion and then back up at my face. I was sure that he had noticed and was prepared to defend myself and my self-antagonistic tendencies when it came to being fat. And then . . . he just smiled at me and kept talking. It was something I took note of and was sure I'd never forget.

We also got so into talking about social justice that the shop basically up and closed on us. But instead of ending things

right there, Bruce asked if I wanted to take a walk with him. It
was a beautiful day out, so I obliged. We walked a large part
of the way in, oddly enough, comfortable silence—which was
confusing to me since I had just met him, but not confusing
to me because, in talking with him, I felt like I had known him
for a long time. After some moments, he finally asked me if I
was dating anyone. My reflex was to say, "That's none of your
goddamn business," but I merely told him "Nah" and then
mentioned a humorous run-in with a hot Black goth girl at a
recent party AND my short and extremely uneventful dating
history with other men and women—my physical therapist
included. His eyes lit up during the party story, and he interrupted me to ask the million-dollar question:

"So, forgive me if this comes off rude as fuck, but . . . are you
bisexual?"

Me, ya girl? I was sweating BULLETS. How DARE he ask me
that? Like, what did he mean by that? Where exactly was this
conversation going? And would I like where it went?

I hesitated. I had been comfortable enough with him to let
the goth girl slip, but I didn't know if he was generally curious or if he was one of those bisexual-voyeuristic cishet male
douchebags who just wanted to watch me make out with other
girls on the off chance that we would magically finger-fuck each
other in front of him.

Of course, I had been looking away the whole time while I
contemplated exposing myself even further. But when I finally
looked back at him, he was staring back at me with the warm-
est eyes. Like, I was expecting something more . . . lecherous.
But it wasn't like that. In fact, he made things worse by having
pretty-ass, long-ass lashes that framed these earnest-looking
eyes, and if I wasn't so captivated by them, I might have just
smacked him on principle. But I admit I was too far gone.
Beguiled even. So, against all common sense, I confirmed his
line of questioning . . . in my own way, of course.

"Yeah," I spat. "What about it?"

He didn't even answer me right away. He let that goofy-ass grin eat up his face for the eleventh time that day and then launched into his own history and mentioned a boy or two that he dated in high school. I, like him, was pleasantly surprised to hear that and returned his question, asking if he was also bisexual.

"Oh wait," I interrupted him. "So you're bi too?"

"Yes." He nodded. "Is that okay?"

It's a question I haven't forgotten to this day. And it left me a little thrown. We weren't in some weird puritan sect. Of course it was okay! Like, I was bi too. Why wouldn't it be okay? Why would it be cool for me to be bi, but weird for him to be? I relayed this much to him.

"I'm confused. What do you mean 'Is that okay?'" I scrunched up my nose. "Why wouldn't it be okay? Who says it's not okay?"

He sighed in relief. "Well, you'd be surprised."

"Hmm." I looked him up and down. "Well, if someone doesn't like it, tell them they can come fight me."

"You can't fight everyone."

"I can most certainly try."

He laughed quietly and left it at that. But I still didn't understand, particularly because I figured it was no one else's business but his and the person he was dating at the time. But what I, a baby gay at the time, didn't comprehend was that Bruce was trying to clue me in to queer and sexual politics and how bisexual (and pansexual) people of different genders were perceived, politicized, and allowed to conduct themselves under this particular banner of queerness.

I didn't get it. But I would.

After that walk, Bruce and I started hanging out more often. Our separate study sessions in the dorm turned into a shared one. This made me nervous because I didn't want to be one of those birds who abandoned their friends for male dick, but my equally horny-ass friends encouraged it and always had a conniption if I tried to cancel on him. Our walks got even longer, which was funny considering my injury. And he was most definitely concerned about that. But I liked the privacy walking granted us, and as Gladys said, it was better than moping around my apartment (plus, I loved Trevor, but your girl needed space). On busier days, we'd meet up at Einstein Bros. to shoot the shit and share what we were doing in terms of organizing—with him focusing more on groundwork and me starting to find my voice online. We also spent a lot of time joking about our mutual crushes and pointed out every person we thought was hot whenever we walked the campus together. He pointed at this dude once and called him "tall, dark, and handsome" and I said, "Tall to you." He told me to shut up and we laughed about it for ten minutes.

Being around him was . . . surprising. It was rare that I felt this comfortable with anyone, much less a man, this fast. I also just don't trust people. As a rule, I think we're the shittiest thing to have ever happened to this planet and believe that Thomas Hobbes's assessment of the brutishness of humanity (a.k.a., if we were to be left to our own devices, we probably wouldn't do the "morally" right thing) was the correct one—even though I also don't really care for listening to dead white men. But there was something about Bruce, some aura that you could feel coming off of him, that made him instantly trustworthy. And equally hot.

I mean, he was *also* a Scorpio, but I'm not gonna get into that.

But I didn't really know what to call what we were doing. A situationship? A flirtation? A *really* intimate friendship? I'm not sure. I am sure that the above occurrences were our more casual encounters. And sometimes things would get *more* intimate. On these walks, we would often hold hands, and the same went for when we were chilling in the common spaces together. I was a sap trying to masquerade as a non-sap, so sometimes I would act like linking hands was such a large inconvenience to me, and he would just smile and rub my hand absently with his thumb. It was such a small gesture, but it was the kind of closeness I started to crave because it made me feel safe. And cherished. Other times, I would fight my inner sap when I'd catch him looking at me with that goofy-ass grin. One time, I asked him about it.

"I'm just casually observing how hot you are. And funny. And smart." He looked up from his book.

"Your white ass needs to stop buttering me up," I scoffed, looking up from mine.

"It's not buttering you up if it's true."

"So you're gassing my head up then?"

"I don't think that applies here either." He shrugged.

"You sicken me," I shot back.

"It's nice to know that I'm growing on you."

Conversations like that just intensified my feelings for him because it became very clear that on top of being a reassuring and attractive presence, he respected my love for humor and banter and gave it right back to me each time. I'm not gonna lie, as someone who is perpetually horny and often has to address that *by myself*, behind closed doors, that *did* things to me.

When we'd hang out in his dorm, Bruce would rope me into a cuddle session, where, to my utmost surprise, he cherished being the big spoon so much. And we often paired our shared love for cuddling with our shared love for movies. I *loved* a good comedy. He *really* liked horror. Or something Tarantino-related. But we often settled on the former, and I would watch the movie through my hands like a five-year-old while he teased me. And each and every time, in the middle of teasing me, he'd tip my head up to face his and kiss me. Ever so softly. But also with enough force to make a bitch dizzy. Most of the time, things wouldn't escalate out of concern for my mobility and because it was almost always a school night, but the Netflix and Chill crowd know these were the perfect conditions for woohoo-ing regardless. As the Simmers know.

And then one day, *it escalated.*

He went in for the kiss, as he always did. As soft and as sweet as always. But on that particular day? A bitch wanted more! So when he pulled back to look me in the eyes, I placed my hands on both sides of his face and gently pulled him back in. But folks, there was nothing *gentle* about this kiss. It was quite the opposite. Messier than usual. Even sloppy. And with me moaning all up in that mouth of his to show him that I wanted *more*. When he finally escaped my vice grip to get some air, his eyes—delirious and full of lust—caught mine.

"Where did that come fr—" he started.

"I want you to stop playing with me, Bruce." I held his gaze. A couple of seconds elapsed.

"Yes ma'am," he replied. He went back down and captured my lips with his again. And just when I thought he was going to intensify that kiss, he pulled back some and moved to dot my neck with gentle kisses. I was agnostic at this point, but you would've thought that I caught the fucking Holy Ghost because this ungodly shudder ripped through my whole body and I honestly thought I was going to combust.

The next thing I knew, we were rolling around on his bed. Swapping spit like a bunch of disgusting-ass, lovesick *youths* with no bills to pay. And of course, I LOVED that shit because it was something I had missed out on doing in high school because I was perpetually obsessed with losing the next ten pounds. And the next ten pounds after that. But my weight be damned, because I was gonna get my back blown out that night.

I managed to snake my fingers toward his belt as quickly as I could and started to unbuckle it when he placed one of his hands over mine and pulled back.

"Are you sure?" he breathed.

"Of course I'm sure. Why would I be tonguing you down like this if I wasn't sure?" I huffed.

"You know what I mean."

"Do I though?"

"Alex."

I mean, I obviously knew what he meant. He had let it slip before that he was most certainly active where the sex was concerned. And considering how quiet I had gotten during those times—particularly because I'm not a bitch who speaks when I don't know what I'm talking about—he had certainly put two and two together. Which is that I had no such experience and could occasionally be bashful about it.

"If you're talking about the whole virgin thing, I'd drop it because I really don't feel like being psychoanalyzed right now and would just like to get this over with." I propped myself up on my elbow. "Okay?"

"Okay." He nodded before looking back at his pants. "Would you like to do the honors?"

"I would actually."

Thus the ceremonial dance of unclothing each other carefully like we were both cans of Pillsbury Cinnamon Rolls commenced, and moments later, we were standing in just our underwear. I was still very hyped up, but the longer we stood in front of each other because of sheer anticipation, the longer my eyes registered, once again, how *fit* he was. And how I just . . . wasn't. He took a step forward, ready to undress the last bit of me, and I took a step back, plopping down on the bed and slouching like this was DeflateGate and someone had just let all the air out of my pussy.

"What's wrong?" he asked.

"On second thought . . . maybe we should finish that movie." My face got tight and my smile was even tighter.

"Are you okay?"

"I'm good." I squirmed under his gaze. "Why?"

"I . . . I'm okay with you being nervous and unsure and changing your mind and us going back out there and whatnot. But . . ."

"But what?"

"I don't think that's what any of this is about."

"Hmm. I didn't know that. What is it about, Bruce?" You could just hear the venom dripping from my voice. I looked him up and down once more before my irritation got the best of me. "What? *Spit it out.*"

He sighed. "I saw how you were looking at me just now."

"And?" I tried to sound nonchalant. He sat down on the bed next to me, taking my hand. And honest to God, I thought about snatching it away because of the foul mood I was in. But I resisted and forced myself to look at him while he continued.

"Sometimes, I overhear you making really slick comments about yourself. About how you look. Or how much you weigh. And my first instinct is to correct you. You know, reinforce how beautiful you are. But I don't wanna overstep. That's something I never want to do, considering who I am and who you are. And also because I have my own body image shit I deal with and that's something you have to work through yourself. So I've tried to find other subtle ways to tell you and show you how phenomenal you look."

"Your point?" I fought the urge to roll my eyes. I'd told him I didn't wanna be psychoanalyzed and sure enough, here I was. Being psychoanalyzed. He could sense that I was getting increasingly agitated, so he leaned in and softly grabbed my chin.

"Why do you think that being fat means I won't want to have sex with you?"

When I tell you my eyes went so fucking wide that they nearly popped out of my head—talk about being caught off guard. I tossed away his hand so fast and turned my body away, grabbing at the sheets to make myself as small as possible. This was years before I would meet Dr. Siddiq, my favorite therapist, and Bruce's question was about the closest I had ever been dragged within an inch of my life . . . and my edges. Having been exposed so clearly and succinctly made me want to disappear. And deny, deny, *deny*. Which was tempting, of course. But I opted not to do that. Instead, I just sat there. Motionless and facing away from him. He tried to put a hand on my shoulder to comfort me, but I pushed it away, clearly deep in thought.

I had had a chip on my shoulder about my weight, about being fat, for the longest time. That much is clear, considering this book. But I think getting slapped in the face with the truth was particularly jarring for me because I hadn't considered that all the terrible things that my family and even (former) friends said about my weight would somehow leak out and seep into my romantic and platonic relationships. It's something I should have anticipated, but I didn't. I thought it was *enough* that I had already cut off like 75 percent of my family and that, outside of therapy, perhaps joking about all of it would be enough to remove the sting. That it would be enough to forget, at least. But nope. They were still around. Still here. Except they were unfortunately locked away in my head and that was the worst thing of all.

Bruce sat there with me for what seemed like an eternity before getting up and slowly collecting his clothes. A last-minute jingle from his belt jolted me to attention like I had been asleep, and I suddenly turned to him.

"People really don't stress enough how badly your family can fuck you up," I said finally.

He stopped in his tracks. "You've never mentioned them."

"For good reason. They're shitty," I snorted. "But I got into college. And I moved as far away as fucking possible. And I always had a rule: if I don't mention them, I don't have to think about them. Seems simple enough, right? It's almost like Voldemort." He sat back down. "But it's never been that simple. Because even with my vow of *silence* when it comes to them," I placed a finger on my right temple, tearing up, "they still live up here. And on the rare occasion when I find myself in front of a mirror or, like, basically naked . . . I hear them. And I see something abhorrent looking back at me." Tears were free-falling from my face. "I wish I didn't feel this way. But I do. And God fucking help me, I get scared sometimes because—"

"You're scared that you'll still hate yourself when the voices are finally gone," he finished.

I looked down at the ground. I didn't know what to say anymore.

"Neither you nor I will be able to make those voices go away in just one night." His voice was soft. "But what I do want to tell you tonight is that they're liars. *All* of them. Every last one. And you don't have to let them dictate how you feel about yourself."

"Like it's that easy."

"It's not. I've lived it." He smiled, but it looked so . . . heavy.

"How do you deal with it?"

"Sporadic therapy," he replied. "But also? I've learned to turn that part of my brain off for just a second. Ignore the shit long enough for me to live my life. Because I'm the only one who can live it. And I don't want some shitty person who's no longer in my life living it for me." He lifted up my head with his finger so that he could meet my gaze. "Does that make sense?"

"Yeah," I whispered.

"Okay. What do you need from me right now? Do you want us to put on our clothes and go back—"

"No."

"No?"

"No. I wanna stay." I breathed in. "I can turn my brain off."

"Okay."

"And . . ."

"And . . . ?" He squinted his eyes at me.

I looked at him, my resolve returning. "I want you to tell me how amazing I am. I could use a new voice up here. One that I actually like."

He smiled at me. "You are probably the most beautiful person I have ever laid eyes on. Pure effervescence. Unparalleled. Unmatched. Incalculable!" he rambled. "You are so fucking brilliant and so fucking funny that I'm constantly on the verge of shitting myself."

"*Probably*?" I teased him.

"See, if I *hadn't* qualified that, you would have said I was blowing smoke up your ass again." He snickered. I burst out laughing, quietly cursing him for being caring enough to make me laugh in the middle of being a blubbering mess. He smirked at me and attacked the side of my face with kisses, which turned my quiet cursing into loud cursing. I tried to act like I wasn't really into it until he grabbed me just enough so that I was finally straddling him. It was an abrupt and risky move, but it was one that quieted my laughter long enough to notice how loving his eyes were and how they felt as they stared into mine. I mean, sure, we wanted to fuck each other's brains out, and sure, he was *very, very* into me. But this was . . . different. This was a look of reassurance. Of safety. And of respect.

I stared right back at him as I took his hands and guided them to my back. He followed my lead and unhooked my bra, letting it fall away from the both of us. He leaned in, sprinkling kisses all over my chest, and I became highly distracted until I felt something poking me in my lower abdomen.

"Oh." I looked down. "So that's how that works."

"Mmhmm. You should say hello. Don't be shy." Bruce looked up at me, winking. I punched him in his shoulder, partly for being so crass, but mainly because he was being absolutely way too endearing and I couldn't handle it. I drew him in for one more kiss before I finally got serious.

I drew back. "Condom."

He nodded. "Condom."

He got up from the bed and walked toward the dresser. I let the comforter fall away from my chest and eagerly waited for him to return and lay down some serious fucking pipe. Of course, my hopes and dreams for good peen were dashed when his bedroom door suddenly swung open and I found myself with the comforter over my head while he dived back beside the bed.

"Oh shit! My bad!" I heard a frantic voice call out. I peeked over the covers long enough to catch the silhouette of his room-mate, Anthony. And this was confirmed when Bruce himself peeked over the side of the bed and started swearing at him.

"Dude! What the fuck?" Bruce exclaimed.

"I'm sorry! I'm sorry!" Anthony tried to avert his eyes. "I didn't even know you were home!"

"And that helps how?!"

"I mean," he spoke nervously before pointing at Bruce's dresser, where the TV remote was sitting. "You always forget to leave the remote by the TV. And usually, I just pop in and grab it. But you just so happened to be home this time, so . . ." He finally noticed me in the bed. "Oh. Hey, Alex!"

"Hi," I managed to say.

There was an awkward-ass silence until Anthony finally cleared his throat.

"So . . . I'm gonna take that remote and leave now." He inched toward the dresser, grabbed the remote, and practically ran away, with the door slamming behind him. Bruce and I probably sat there for like two seconds before we burst into laughter. The moment, for us, was pretty much over, but it didn't take away from what happened (and what nearly happened) in that room. Or how I thought about my body and the voices trying to convince me that I should hate it.

AS FOR hooking up? Well, we experienced a string of almosts. We'd get *just* far enough and then be interrupted by something. Or someone. It was annoying for a bit, but I counted it as one of the many quirks of our relationship. And whenever those interruptions happened, we would laugh again and he would kiss my forehead, my cheek, or my nose (because I had been clear about my insecurities about that too), and I would scrunch it up at him, joking that "My lips are down here!" Eventually, it didn't bother me at all because I wasn't interested in quantifying our feelings for each other based on what fucking base we got to. We were good where we were at.

But as it goes with all good things . . . it didn't last. And one particular situation ensured this would be so:

How we both handled him being groped by a gay friend.

Four months after our first "almost," after grabbing a bite at our favorite coffee spot, we went on one of our walks. Hand-in-hand as per usual. Spring had just barely started. I remember this because I kept getting slapped in the face by assorted petals and because I had to stock up on a shit ton of Claritin like the week before so I didn't morph into Will Smith in *Hitch* when he had that allergic reaction to shellfish. Anyway, on this particular day, Bruce seemed *uncharacteristically* quiet. And I picked up on it right away. As soon as I asked about it, he looked me in the eyes, probably weighing his options and trying to figure out if it would be worth the blowup that he knew was coming.

He sighed. "Don't get mad."

"Uh . . . that's what people always say right before they tell you something that makes you mad." I tightened my grip on his hand. His defeated tone worried me, and I can't lie, I was scared shitless of what he was gonna say next. Did he flunk out? Was he sick? Had this . . . *thing* we had going finally run its course? I had no way of knowing. But I braced myself for the worst anyway. He of course had no idea that I had already run 3240839403928402980493809 scenarios in my head to determine what kind of bad news I was getting. He merely chuckled at my stubbornness and, probably against his better judgment, told me the bad news anyway.

He launched into this story about how he'd been hanging out with friends recently, most of them dude-bros and a lot of them athletes. Or rather, wannabe athletes. He also mentioned his friend Jessie and how Jessie had started getting all touchy-feely with him. Bile materialized in my throat as I had a sense of where this was going. I picked up right away that this was Bruce's main (and straight) group of friends, and while the group was close and not strangers to being touchy-feely in that very cishet male "no homo!" kind of way, Jessie, he stressed, had been taking it a bit far. Like ignoring boundaries. Trying to give him massages without asking. Touching his hand. And occasionally saying some really lewd shit to him whenever he was "drunk."

This had been happening for some time. Months apparently. But I was surprised to hear that Bruce had dismissed it as a joke at first. It didn't make sense to me why he would do that. The Bruce I knew wasn't scared of confrontation and damn sure was very good about respecting boundaries and enforcing his own. I thought about interrupting him to ask, but I decided against it. Which, mayhaps, I shouldn't have, considering what he told me next. The final straw came earlier in the day when they were all hanging out in one of the dorms and Jessie had "accidentally" groped his ass while passing by. Bruce checked him and Jessie smugly laughed it off, calling him "mistaken" at first and then "confused"—a clear yet shady dig at Bruce being bisexual. When he didn't get the reaction he wanted from Bruce, he settled on calling it a minor accident. But then added that it shouldn't even be a big deal considering who Bruce was and what he . . .

Jessie didn't get to finish that sentence because Bruce decked him. Punched him so hard that he himself almost fell over. He wanted blood from Jessie and lots of it, but his bewildered friends held him back while Jessie skittered away. Leaving Bruce to deal with a group of friends, of men, who hadn't seen what happened. Hadn't seen how he was violated . . . and nearly outed. And presumably, because he was too flustered to explain himself, he stormed out, made his way to the coffee shop, and then ended up on this walk with me. I stopped walking immediately, my abrupt halt yanking him back.

"What? You asked what was wrong." He looked back at me. I stared at him for the longest time before I spoke up again.

"Besides Jessie, am I the only one who knows?" I blinked. When Bruce hesitated to say anything, I knew what the answer was. I was the only other person who knew. And the *only* person who wasn't trying to weaponize it against him. I immediately dropped his hand and started to march in the direction of the dorm.

"I am going to KILL Jessie." I stomped. "I'm going to kill that little bitch, I swear to fucking God."

"Alex—" He followed me.

"Actually, I don't swear. I promise. I promise to kill him."

"Alex, stop!"

I should have stopped. I should have. But I was seeing so much red that I didn't hear him. Couldn't even comprehend what he was saying. All I knew was that I wanted to lay hands on Jessie and stop him from ever hurting Bruce, this precious man of mine, again. No matter what that meant. I started to run, but since Bruce was in *way* better shape, he ran ahead of me and blocked my path. I told him to move. He told me to leave it alone. Me being headstrong, I pushed past him. And when I tried to continue walking, that's when the screaming match began.

"Can you listen to me for just one second!?" he shouted.

"Sure. After I kill Jessie. As I said!" I shouted back.

"Jesus Christ, Alex!"

"What?!"

"You don't fucking understand!"

"What do you mean I don't fucking understand?!" I walked toward him. "I'm bi too! People trip me up with their phobic shit, too, okay?"

"It's not—" I could feel the frustration radiating off his body, but I kept going.

"No, I'm not done!" I cut him off. "And I don't appreciate this coming from you of all people because you *know* I've had to deal with people's weird-ass projections on my body and entitlements to my body, gay or straight, because I'm *Black* and I'm *fat* and I'm *bi* so that *obviously* means I'm desperate and super-fuckable, right? *Right*?" I huffed. "Don't tell me I don't fucking understand, Bruce."

He exhaled hard. "It's still not the same. I get that you think you understand, but . . . it's just not the same."

"How?? How is it not the same?" I threw my hands up. "Tell me! How is it not the same?"

"I'm a man."

"Okay . . ." I tried to contain my sarcasm but lost that fight soon enough. "What a groundbreaking observation."

"And I'm closeted, Alex," he added. "You're not. Haven't been for a while."

One thing you should know about me, dear reader, is that I pride myself on the fact that I always know what to say. It may not be kind, it may not be nice, and it may not even be particularly tactful. But I try to have some type of answer to everything. And pride myself on being right like 99.9 percent of the time. But this time around? I had no answer. And then I knew.

He was right.

Biphobia was . . . *slightly* different when it came to our genders. Sure, we both weren't taken seriously because of "confusion" (ugh), but the other bouts of biphobia that we both experienced tended to rear itself in ugly and specific-ass ways. For me, someone who identified as a woman, while my sexuality would always be called into question, it was partially encouraged. Mostly because of that voyeurism I mentioned earlier. Mostly because of fetishism. Mostly because "I'm a girl" and "That's what girls do." We follow each other to the bathroom and sit on each other's laps and hold hands and kiss and get to experiment because it's cute—and by cute, I mean "cute" to tourists and voyeurs, and "hot" to men. This was still grossly biphobic because my sexuality didn't exist to be "cute" or gawked at, but it was on a different level, in a completely different realm than what Bruce had experienced.

For him, as he informed me during the latter part of our screaming match, the rules were different. On top of cishet men not even being able to do anything—like wipe their asses—without it being "gay" (a fault of cishet men no doubt, but bear with me), Bruce had to overperform everything depending on *who* he was with. With his normal friend group, he was "super-manly, athletic, super-bro Bruce." And even *that* probably wouldn't be enough if they were to ever find out he was bisexual. With Jessie (whom he thought he could trust), he found that he had to overperform his queerness so he didn't seem like a fraud for still being into women or other non-men—which Jessie had shaded him about more than once. It clicked for me then. After all the screaming. The shouting. The pointing. And the cursing.

The only person he could really be himself around, his free, uncloseted self, was me.

He begged me to drop the issue. Told me to swear to him that I would drop the issue. And honestly, I started crying. I'm not proud of it, but I didn't know how else to grieve over this . . . *prison* he was trapped in. He had only seen me cry once before, back when we talked about my family, so he was instantly worried. He drew me closer to him, wiping my face.

"What's wrong?" he asked.

"You deserve better," I sobbed. "Don't you think you deserve better?" His usual smile materialized out of nowhere. I presume this was done to comfort me, but it made my heart sink even more because it was empty. Distant. Resigned.

"I don't know." He wiped another tear from my face.

I did not take it well. I was absolutely furious that we lived in a world that made Bruce fearful of standing up for himself. And it's safe to say that my anger was the catalyst in starting the doomsday clock on what had previously been a joyous, once-in-a-lifetime love affair. Bruce assured me that things would be okay as we walked home, but things weren't okay after that.

To this day, I believe that he internalized my anger—like I was disappointed in him. Which wasn't true at all.

That incident changed the trajectory of our relationship. It changed *us*, even.

Our walks got shorter. Study sessions became scarce. Hands touched less. Coffee sessions were skipped. All that until we were pretty much strangers again. We drifted apart, fading back into our respective friend groups. He started dating other girls and I figured it was time to date other people, too, even though my luck in that regard was pretty much shit. We would see each other in passing sometimes and he would softly wave at me. I think it was his way of checking if we were still okay. If I still cared about him. I wish I could tell you that I just completely froze him out after the fact, but that wouldn't be true. Because when you really care about someone like I cared about him? Well, there's no real way to *forget* what happened between you. And what was shared.

So I waved back. It was always quick and I was still hurt. But I thought I would give him that much.

FAST-FORWARD to my final year in college, 2016, and I remember getting a call from him a couple of nights before I was gonna finally walk the stage in June and leave this hellhole. I had been tempted to screen his call, but my gut told me to pick up.

"Hey." I could hear Bruce's smile on the other side of the line.

"Hi," I replied softly.

And just like that, it was like we had never parted ways. He caught me up on all the strange core classes he was being forced to take, his girlfriend of the week, and the latest weird happening in the dorm. I brought him up to speed on my promotion at my library job, all my hilarious-yet-awful dates (including a particularly painful one with an improv guy who was not at all funny and an undercover Republican), my concerns about graduating with no job, and the latest mishaps with my roommates. We talked for hours. Hours upon hours upon hours. Eventually, it got so dark that I finally had to tell him that I needed to go because I had work in the morning. We started to say our goodbyes and then he stopped me.

"Wait." He sounded nervous.

"I . . . what did you really call to talk about, Bruce?" I sighed. "Because I really don't have time to stay up all night with you and reminisce about the good ol' days when we were still together, you know, before you broke my heart and like half-way ghosted me and—"

"I'm sorry," he cut me off. "I am so, so sorry. For everything."

You know. I have a funny relationship with closure in that I really don't believe it exists. But because the prevailing theory is that it does, I've always been a person that fully expects to never get full closure, or rather, the closure that I'm truly looking for. Or searching for. In the case of my old flame Bruce, I had always wondered if I would ever get a proper apology. I had always wondered if he would return from what I perceived as an elongated tantrum or an extended bout of disassociation and declare his love for me, flowers in hand, like during our first date. I had always wondered if he would give the world a middle finger, burn down that closet, and just ... *disappear* with me. I had wondered if it was ever possible for us to just vanish into thin air ... as two bisexual idiots in love. No longer limiting ourselves to society's expectations of who to be and who we should be.

I had wondered if it was possible for us to just ... be. Together.

Bruce's distant voice came back to me. His "Hello? Are you still there?" rang in my ear, rattling it like it was a cage. My wistful (and mental) visit to our shared recent past suddenly inspired anger. And resentment. I wanted to hang up and leave him with as much uncertainty as he had left me with. I was so upset at the way our relationship had just unceremoniously withered away until it was dead. I was heartbroken. I didn't know what I had done to deserve that. I spent so much time over the course of a year crying myself to sleep. Wondering what I could have said differently, what I could have done differently when Bruce told me about Jessie. Maybe I should have just apologized and been there for him. Maybe I should have just listened. But every scenario led me back to the fact that ... I had always wanted better for him. The *best* even. And that was something that he had not wanted for himself.

So I came back to myself. On the phone. With that nervous voice in my ear, waiting for me to answer him or to depart in silence. The temptation to chew him out for leaving me was so vast, but I opted to extend to him the same amount of vulnerability he had extended to me in this moment. Because I knew him parting ways with me a year ago was less about me and more about all the ways he still was uncomfortable with himself. And I wondered if he would ever be comfortable with himself.

"I understand," I said.

There was an audible exhale on the other line and I heard what was probably the beginning of quiet sobs before he finally hung up. Looking back on it now, it still fucks me up, because I know that Bruce assumed I had judged him over the Jessie situation and how he handled it. He probably thought that I—even with me being bi too (after all, bi and lesbian women still can be biphobic toward bi men)—thought he was "confused" and less than a man because he was not yet able to be out in the open. And he probably didn't want to face me after all of that.

But in reality, I wanted justice for him. I wanted to beat Jessie until he was unrecognizable and make him apologize for violating him. In reality, I myself wasn't even all the way "out" because my parents and hometown community still had no idea (now? I don't give a fuck if they care because they're not as relevant to my life as they were then). And in reality? I would have never judged him for it. I merely just wanted him to be able to live his life on his terms.

The thing is, though, while it was nice for me to want those things for him, it was his right to come to all of those conclusions himself. He should have been the one to decide what would happen to Jessie, and he should have been the one to decide how exactly he was gonna live on his own terms. All this because bi and pan boys rarely get the space to do so. Because they're always overperforming for someone else. Always overperforming straightness. Always overperforming queerness. Or in our case, always overperforming the fact that he was "okay" when he really wasn't. All while shouldering the expectations of what a *real man* should be. At the expense of themselves.

Not realizing all of this sooner (and not treating Bruce gentler as a result) is probably one of my only regrets in life.

I TOOK a sip of my tea, which was still pretty warm, and debated whether I would tell my friend about Bruce. They had smirked at my cliché mention of shit being "complicated" and I figured they wanted a real answer. So I racked my brain, trying to turn over some phrase that would be a worthwhile introduction to the short but ultimately tragic love story that I was about to offer up.

"Define 'complicated.'" They leaned forward, mirroring my pensive-ass body language.

"You ever been in love?" I asked. "Or something close?"

"Possibly. Or it could have been gas. But we'll go with love," they replied. I would have chuckled if I wasn't being so serious right then.

"You ever loved someone so much only to realize that they didn't really love themselves? Not as much as you loved them?"

"Yeah." They were quiet.

"Yeah. *That* kind of complicated."

MY LIFE AS A BABY GAY™

After dealing with my tragic almost-but-not-quite ex, Bruce, part of me consciously and also unconsciously decided that I was done with men for a while. Like, I had had *enough*. I needed a break from the chaos, indecisiveness, and tragedy that I was used to. Because, currently, I was playing several roles in multiple coming-of-age movies and I wanted out! I wanted off this goddamn tilt-a-whirl. And I wanted to explore the part of me that was clearly attracted to women.

Of course, this yielded various results.

I should first say that my journey in terms of dating my same gender wasn't linear at all. Nor are most things really. And while a good chunk of my dates with women would happen post-college, there was one mildly hilarious run-in during college that helped me get my feet wet a little. With Lila.

I consider my brief flirtation with Lila one of my most formative experiences. Mainly because it showed me how woefully underprepared I was to free myself from the bondage of heterosexuality. I had no idea *what* to expect now that I wasn't a slave to the regressive bigotry that I had been raised with. I was a newbie. One step above a Baby Gay™.

And I was about to learn that in a very painful, if kinda amusing, way.

I met Lila during my senior year in an intermediate American Sign Language class, which started in January 2016. I signed up for the class after talking with my friend Kara.

There'd been this really competitive intermediate screenwriting class that I was interested in, but Kara mentioned she needed someone to practice ASL with. Considering all the ways she'd shown up for me over the past few years, I opted to take the ASL class with her instead.

It was Monday, the first week of classes. What could I even say about Lila? Well, when I first saw her, I felt like that episode of SpongeBob where Squidward discovered that he liked Krabby Patties and stared at one longingly—licking his nonexistent lips while an intense amount of sweat dripped from his face. THE BITCH WAS FINE. So very fine. So very, very fine that she looked like a Rosario Dawson and Gina Torres clone. A clone I was plotting to risk it all for.

I should pause here and say that there was a particular way that my bisexuality manifested at the time—the main distinction being that I was quite attracted to masculine-presenting women and feminine-presenting men (these days, this matters less). With a couple of exceptions. Pre–having it explained to me that gender was largely bogus.

If you were to ask me why that was, I wouldn't be able to explain a damn thing. Not in-depth anyway. The most I'd probably be able to tell you is that you can *probably* trace the origins of such attractions to the overlap of my longtime crushes like Tommy Oliver or Booboo Stewart. But that *would* also require some deeper analysis about the complex my parents and greater community gave me about hair.

Lila though? She didn't neatly fall into what I call my line of attraction. Nor did she neatly fit into any category that my gender-essentialist parents constantly screamed about. This definitely piqued my interest. She was giving high femme—lipstick lesbian almost—paired with long and wavy brown hair, rich brown skin, and the deepest and richest of voices. With calf muscles carved from marble while sporting black pumps that I one day hoped she would use to squish me like a goddamn bug.

I remember stealing the occasional glance at her, which

consisted of me looking at her and then facing my front again so I wouldn't be caught red-handed by her or our professor.

After about my fifth glance in that direction, I resolved that I was the teeniest bit obsessed. I literally couldn't pay attention to anything else. I just *had* to talk to her. You know, just to see if she was single, possibly. And to check if I even had a chance.

The catch here is that in this ASL class, talking was *not* allowed. At all. Like, the professor did not play. You had to leave that talking bullshit at the door—as you should. Otherwise, what would be the point of the class? Still. I had no issues with this rule usually. But today? Of all days? That would just make getting Lila's attention that much more impossible.

I thought about passing a note, but I decided against it because she was in an entirely different hemisphere of the class. It would have taken it like eight days to get there, like a USPS package. And that would *only* be the case if I was fool-ish enough to trust any of these randos to pass along the note rather than reading it. Plus, I didn't feel like having the profes-sor catch me in the act of trying to mack on Lila. Not because she would get mad at me or anything, but because she got a sick sense of humor and it is very likely that she would force me to sign the content of the notes in front of the class.

And I would rather die.

So, I waited until class let out and made a beeline for the door. As I got there, Lila was exiting and talking to a friend in this pretty cool voice. It was kind of raspy. Anyway, it was some-thing that I needed to hear even closer. And I swear to God, I was *seconds* away from getting her attention in the hallway when the professor stepped in front of me like the biggest cock-blocker alive. She greeted me and started signing, asking how I was liking the second level of this class.

Normally, I would appreciate my professor trying to connect with me and all. Since like 98 percent of undergrad professors here acted like they were too good for that. But today? I was definitely feeling a smidgen ungrateful, to be frank. I had never been more tempted to sign Ludacris's "Move Bitch" to someone's face so bad. Still. I waited. And waited. And waited for her to stop signing. And when she was finally done, I speed-walked so fast to see if I could catch up with Lila. But by the time I got outside, she was gone.

And I was super bummed.

But I didn't let it get to me because surely I would see her in our next class, right? Right.

Sike.

Because as soon as I got there on Wednesday, two days later, Lila was nowhere to be seen. She was gone. The bitch had disappeared like she was some modern version of Carmen Sandiego. And I gotta admit, I gave up at that moment. I mean, it was the first week of classes. It would be *just* my luck that she'd drop this class to make room for one she needed to graduate or some shit. Which is something I would totally do because who wants to spend another year at this intellectual prison? Not I.

Bummed the hell out, I went to the one place I knew would cheer me up: one of the campus coffee shops. The Hot People's Café™. Located in the one and only Mansueto Library.

It was an interesting place. On the outside, the café was straight-up shaped like this weird, egg-looking thing. On the inside? Well, everyone behind the counter in said coffee shop was unrealistically hot and attractive.

After dragging myself across campus, deflated as fuck, I sulked up to the counter and, without looking at the menu, asked the barista for "the most pretentious drink they had available." Hell, why not? Nothing wrong with adding a little sweetness to a shit day. To my surprise, however, the barista replied in a familiar voice, "You'll have to be more specific, as we have a pretty exhaustive list."

My head snapped up and guess who the fuck I saw. Well, if you guessed that it was Ms. Lila I'm-a-Goddamn-Ghost Sandiego cheesing real hard at me, then you would be goddamn right.

If my life was a nineties sitcom, as I sometimes wished it was, rather than a bastardized Greek *dramedy*, I would have passed out and some terrible laugh track would have blared in the background.

But because my life is bordering on parody, I instead said, "Well, of course, you'd be a barista in the super-hot café. Of course!" I was incredulous.

And then I was instantly horrified with myself.

Blessedly, Lila let out the ugliest yet most sincere laugh and took it in stride.

"What do you mean?" She giggled. "I mean, it sounds complimentary, but one can never be too sure." But you know me. I changed the subject. *Immediately*.

"I know I don't know you and you definitely don't know me, but I noticed you missed ASL today. You good?" I replied.

"It's Alex, right?" she said, probably based on the name sign I had made in class on the first day.

"Yeah."

"Lila. I didn't have enough space in the ol' schedule. So, unfortunately, it had to go."

I KNEW IT.

I knew it.

Goddamn it.

Ugh. All I could think about was how comparatively boring the class would be without her. Like, who was going to be the subject of my daily daydreams in that class? Casper the Friendly Ghost? Blech.

"But since I don't wanna leave you hanging," she took out a crumpled piece of paper from her pocket and handed me a flyer for a slam poetry event, "I'm here at the café all the time, but this is where I'll be tonight. You should come." She grinned. "Since you're so worried about me and all."

And this was no regular grin, my friends. This was a *grin*. I'm talking a *wink wink* grin! You know, the type of grin that activates the sapphic particles in the atmosphere. *That* type of grin.

I resisted the urge to giggle like an asshole. Obviously, my instinct was to say *FUCK YES I WILL GO!* Because I was most assuredly gonna be in attendance. But instead, I said, "I'll think about it."

I couldn't come off as thirsty. Or desperate. Which . . . worked? Lila winked at me, gave me a pretentious drink of her choosing, and sent me on my way. While I was walking away, I looked at my cup briefly and saw a message scribbled on it with a black sharpie: "See u tonight ;)". I turned around and caught her looking at me. I smiled.

"See you later, *Alex*," she called after me.

A COUPLE of hours passed, and with the prepping I was doing, you'd think I was about to go to war. I remember having this all-black getup. Like Hot Topic threw up on me. The only thing I was missing was a spiky choker for the occasion. I know this sounds a bit *much,* but I simply wanted to make sure I looked like a snack. A very *moody* and *mysterious* snack.

So the time finally came and I hopped on the shuttle to get to the arts center on the other side of campus. As it usually was during the evening on campus, the shit was packed. Packed as fucked. And I was forced to squeeze myself in the middle like a goddamn sardine. Hell, it was so packed that nothing could prepare me for me *missing* my stop because a) the shuttle smelled like toe and wet dog for obvious reasons, and b) it was too packed for the driver to hear me.

This part is fuzzy because I'm pretty sure I blacked out from rage (and from the fact that I was smack-dab in the middle of the putrid smells I mentioned above). Anyhoo, I vaguely remember turning into Legion™ and cussing loud as fuck about stopping the shuttle bus. And wouldn't you know, the shuttle made an abrupt stop and promptly let me off. But my problems didn't end there. The event was only about an hour long and the shuttle bus shenanigans had already cost me like ten minutes. And was *gonna* cost me ten more since I needed to walk back to the arts center.

Still, I persisted. I was gonna ask this bitch out even if it killed me.

When I got to the arts center, I made my way to the café, where everything was being hosted. As soon as I got in, I located Lila across the room and she immediately waved at me. I waved back and started to make my way to her when the Fire Nation attacked. And by Fire Nation, I mean some more bullshit happened and one of the event organizers intercepted me to ask, "Are you Casey? Because your poem is up next!" Before I could even protest, I was basically pushed onto the stage and had a mic shoved into my hand. Followed obviously by the small crowd in the room falling totally silent.

I started sweating bullets.

It had been a while since I had written poetry in particular. It had been even longer since I had attended one of these events, mainly because my injury had turned me into a hermit. And despite the part where I mention that I've written poetry before, for shiggles, I want to make it clear that, up until this point, I had never performed that shit. Never. It was too late to exit stage left though because Lila was watching. She shot me a super cute thumbs up.

So. I did what any sensible human would do in this situation when their crush looks like Lila and they're two seconds from being sprung. I recited Jonah Hill's "Cynthia" slam poem from *22 Jump Street*. Hoping the audience would realize it was a *joke* and refrain from booing me offstage.

Like seriously. I think I did a shot-by-shot reenactment of whatever the fuck Jonah Hill was doing in that movie. It was, in fact, as terrible as it sounds. Very terrible. But also very funny. In hindsight, of course. I mean, who hasn't mildly embarrassed themselves for love?

Thankfully, it was *also* funny to everyone in the crowd, including Lila, who was laughing and clapping for me offstage. The entire train wreck eventually came to an end and I was finally released from the stage to a round of boisterous applause. As I was coming down, I noticed Lila bringing her phone to her ear and hurriedly ducking out of the room. Naturally, I went looking for her.

I searched the entire arts building for her, including the outside, doing my own version of *"Where in the world is Lila?"* But as it has been with the theme of the story, my version of Carmen Sandiego had disappeared.

Again!

I THOUGHT about Lila and her disappearing act the entire weekend, and when Monday finally came around again, I ran as fast as I could to the Hot People's Café™. I got there at the usual time (1:00 p.m.) and even put like ten more minutes before approaching the counter, lest I get the side-eye from people I KNOW who've seen me here like every day.

And then I waited. Gingerly.

Until it was literally too weird to wait any longer because a whole hour had passed and I hadn't seen her once. She was nowhere to be seen. Just . . . poof. I'm not gonna lie. I was a little frustrated. Confused. Lost? I don't know. All I knew was that I was really geeked about asking her out and it seemed like forces greater than I were *not* trying to make that happen.

Eventually, someone else walked up to the counter and I stepped forward to ask the not-as-hot barista where Lila could be . . . and maybe kinda *lied* that I was supposed to meet her here today.

"Oh, you didn't hear?" he said. "Lila made a short film that got accepted at some film festival in LA. So she flew out there for that. I'm guessing, if she wins, she might stay there for a bit."

Honestly, my face has never fallen to the floor so fast.

Was I happy for her? Hell yeah. Did my luck suck ass? *Fuck yeah!*

"You're Alex, right?" he interrupted my thoughts.

"Yeah ... why do you ask?" I raised an eyebrow.

"Well, Lila talked a lot about you. She thought you were really cute."

"Great. Now, that you say that, she didn't happen to leave her number, did she?"

"Uh ... no. Sorry. She was kind of in a rush ..." He shrugged.

And so I politely put on my best stress smile, you know the ones white people tend to shoot at your Black ass when you pass them because they still can't believe you're allowed outside. And allowed a marginal amount of "freedom." Yeah, that smile!

I asked for my usual pretentious coffee drink, was pissed that the drink wasn't as good as usual, and went about my day silently cursing the cosmos and promising *never* to love again. Well, the latter part is not quite true since it was very debatable *then* whether I'd actually been in love. I think my closest guesses as to what I'd actually experienced would be between *deep like* or just simple horniness.

Still. For the rest of that day, I reflected on every single moment I hadn't gotten to ask for Lila's number, and I concluded that timing is truly everything.

And that my timing, and sapphic instincts, sucked ass. I probably should have just asked for her fucking number when I had first met her at that accursed counter. That makes the most sense, right? Any sane lover of women would have done just that. They would have cut straight to the chase and probably named a place, a time, and a day that they would be picking her up for some hot date.

But not I!

Now that I think about it though, in the present, I think it had less to do with me being a dumbass and an ignoramus and more to do with me just ... not knowing what the fuck I was doing?

Think about it. While I had accepted I was bisexual and demisexual some time ago, truth be told, I had never gotten to flex that muscle. Hell, the fact that I even had that muscle was news to me! Christianity had stolen quite a lot of time from me, and that time contained experience that I couldn't go back and collect.

The "demisexual" part was an even greater obstacle to grapple with in terms of "same gender" dating, mainly because, even now, people are still trying to determine if it's a "real thing" and whether it's just *diet* asexuality or an indication of a "low" sex drive. Meanwhile, the same people can't even properly define what asexuality is and regularly *dismiss* how vast and diverse the asexuality spectrum is.

That said, I'm not writing this for them. I'm writing this for me.

And in *my* case, my mind still registered "physical" attraction in terms of *aesthetics* or certain physical traits. A strong Henry Cavill jaw here. A full head of hair there. A muscular back. Maybe they had a symmetrical face. Or nice titties. Or long eyelashes. Or Angela Bassett arms. Or a surprisingly and perfectly round ass. Or Amazonian legs like Gwendoline Christie. I could absolutely and immediately tell you if I found someone "objectively" attractive or "hot."

Like Lila.

However, the demisexuality part kicked in for me when the issue of *sexual* attraction popped up. There was no revving the engine called my pussy unless we were emotionally vibing. No surface-level shit! Truly. I couldn't even *fantasize* about doing the dance with no pants with someone if I hadn't formed any sort of strong emotional bond with them. Like I damn near needed to know what your *soul* looked like before my hot pocket could resurrect itself long enough to even *experience* sexual attraction. And that bond didn't necessarily have to be "romantic" initially ... as I *soon* learned with Emiliano.

Because of *all* this, calling myself a late bloomer didn't even cut it. I didn't know how to do *any* of this shit! I had no idea how to ask another woman out on a date. Had no idea how to explain "demisexuality" to someone on said date. Had no idea how to even conduct myself if I were to miraculously talk my way into a date. Had no idea how to flirt with them or when to notice they were flirting with *you*. And I no longer had any idea whether a woman complimenting you on anything meant that they were simply just complimenting you . . . or that they really wanted a piece of your ass.

Greater still, gender bias and the act of shaking off outdated gender roles were kicking my ass. And you may think it was just me doing the projecting. But baby?

Haha.

No.

I would learn this lesson the hard way when dating a Lebanese woman in 2017, about a year after graduating, in Knoxville, Tennessee. I cannot go into extreme detail because it was actually quite traumatic for me. But lemme just tell you this.

Honestly, the first red flag of this short-lived affair should have been her raving about *that* "Birthright Trip" that she had just recently returned from. But the subsequent and deal-breaking flag would come when I realized that she was treating me like a stand-in . . . for a man.

Yes, it's true!

I found myself holding doors open for her. Opening car doors for her. Closing car doors for her. She had always *looked* to *me* to pay for the few dates we went on and other assorted outings. And even then, the responsibility fell on me to pick her up and drop her off at home. Instead of us just meeting up somewhere. I had even stopped at her house once or twice to fix something or haul something heavy inside.

I know you're probably thinking that I should have just said something. And it's true that all of these things alone aren't *technically* enough to say with certainty that I was being regarded as some sort of cisgender male understudy. And believe me, I thought the same thing. I thought I was fucking *tweaking*. I didn't really trust my instinct that something was off about this dynamic. Mostly due to inexperience, but also partially because I didn't want to screw myself out of a chance to experience the glory that was . . . pussy.

However, I quickly discovered that my instinct was right when we were on some double date with one of her girlfriends, and she, I shit you not, accidentally referred to me as her "big, strong man" when raving to her friend about how "helpful" and attentive I was. She quickly patted my arm (I have no idea how that was supposed to help) and corrected herself and subbed in "Alex" for man, but for me? The damage was already done. I had been forced to see what the fuck was in my face the entire time.

I ended up dropping her off at home. And then never called her again.

To be clear, I never should have gone along with that shit. *Never*. Inexperience be damned. But this was an incredible learning experience. I'd also learn, with time, that women weren't *automatically* easier to date or understand *just because* we were women. And I'd also learn that women were also fully capable of projecting weird gender shit onto other people, just like everyone else. And it gets even dicier when you consider how I was built (sturdy and fat) and what I looked like and who I was—which was dark-skinned and Black. Which all meant, for obvious reasons, that I was very likely to still come up against gendered expectations, even if I opted to *never* date men again.

That hasn't deterred me from dating women though. Or from loving *us*. Nor will it ever.

I'm still learning. And unlearning.

As I'm sure the rest of us are too.

MY RANDOM ACCESS MEMORY

My problems, whether they had to do with navigating the minefield that was love and gender or surviving impending economic instability, would not cease after leaving UChicago—and hotties like Lila—behind.

In fact, these problems, what I'd call Big Girl Problems™—ADULT problems—were only just beginning.

Starting with my Big Move™ to California.

I find that I don't like to discuss my time in California often. Attempting to do so, even with my recent therapists, always has me on the verge of throwing up. This is because it was an experience that was deeply enlightening yet undeniably traumatic for me.

I moved to California in 2018. August, to be specific. The decision was born from one part whim, another part desire to put even more distance between myself and the radioactive Lazarus Pit that was my family, and the last part having to do with the fact that I was determined to put the UChicago degree that I nearly died for to good use.

Right before this decision, I'd spent the hottest of minutes in Knoxville after leaving Chicago in 2016. Not being able to find a job right away led to my friend Eve hiding me in her summer dorm at the University of Tennessee, Knoxville, like a scene out of Bong Joon-ho's *Parasite*. And things only got more ridiculous there. The pressing need to maintain a roof over my head created some interesting dilemmas in the job department—both for Eve and myself since we lived together. My extended stint there was marked by a myriad of misadventures in the service industry that included working for First Tennessee Bank *and* my gay-ass attempting to fly under the radar at Chick-fil-A. This was also before I'd gotten well-acquainted with the hell that was freelance writing in the entertainment media sector.

Like so many people before me, the service industry thoroughly whooped my ass, and I figured, after getting yelled at one too many times about rogue overdraft charges and "incorrect" sandwich orders that the customer dictated to me in real time, I figured it was time for a change.

Of course, this was gonna be a doozy, merely because, to paraphrase one of my favorite comedians (TikTok star Scott Seiss), I had gotten a cinema and media studies and English degree. So essentially, I did, in fact, double down on being broke and unemployed. A nasty combination of things to be if I was to make it in the increasingly expensive state of California. Particularly in Los Angeles.

Still, I pressed on.

The *act* of moving itself was a rather dramatic one, mainly because that decision hinged on an honest initial conversation—rife with the undertones of what I would learn later was separation anxiety—between Eve and I. Earlier that summer, after a visit to one of our favorite pizza joints, I came clean to Eve that I felt myself withering away in Knoxville. That while it had its charms, the city was way too *small* for me. It also didn't help that I was starting to experience some burnout from living with her in Knoxville, mainly because the sinister stronghold that was poverty had created some tension between us. I had grown tired of the mounting pressure of running a now-defunct blog we started together and tired of being accidentally snapped on one too many times. And undiagnosed bipolar II disorder was about to make me snap *back*.

Eve was both understanding and apologetic, and supported my desire to leave the state. The idea of moving to a new coast was a daunting thought, but it became clear very quickly that she was willing to try "The Golden State" on for size.

"I mean, shit, it's not like I have anything going on right now." Eve shrugged on our way home from the pizza joint. "It's dry as hell here."

Her openness and willingness to move made me optimistic about the direction my life was moving in. Giddy even. I was excited to finally be that girl who was chasing her dreams with wild abandon.

Past that initial conversation, however, the *physical* act of moving morphed into a trip to Mordor . . . on legendary mode.

Armed with a Budget moving truck and the little Ford sedan that could, me, Eve, and our younger brothers embarked on a thirty-three-hour journey . . . that we so delusionally thought that we could straight-shot in carefully coordinated driving shifts every four hours. It wasn't until sleep deprivation almost took me out like Hilary Duff's brother in *Raise Your Voice* during one of my truck shifts that we eventually stopped to rest and resume the trek later.

We found ourselves in California—Anaheim to be specific— that August. Some of you are probably side-eyeing me as we speak, mostly because y'all are keenly aware of the shitty cesspool that exists in the underbelly of Orange County. Of course, shitty credit (thanks to financial abuse on my parents' part) had severely limited my options during my quest to leave Knoxville. And while I had applied to more than a couple of apartments, both owned by rental management companies and private individuals in Los Angeles, the *only* apartment that eventually got back to me was the one in Anaheim. So the plan was to land in Anaheim, get our shit together, and then move to Los Angeles as quickly as humanly possible.

Of course, nothing could quite prepare me for how bad 2018 was going to get for me—considering the culture shock of moving out west from the Appalachian South.

From the *moment* I landed on California soil, I found myself on the brink of death. I was, quite literally, fighting for my life. That year, or rather the rest of it, was painful. Bill Jenga™ became a way of life, courtesy of the highest rent price I had ever laid my eyes on. I went from paying like $600 per month to live in a pretty nice and *spacious* place in Tennessee to $2,200 a month. For a place that didn't even fucking have central A/C, didn't have a goddamn fridge upon our arrival, and had the shittiest parking "arrangements" that I had seen thus far. And remember, this was *just* the rent. *Just the rent.*

To make matters worse, I took on nearly 100 percent of the financial burden for the apartment in those beginning months. I no longer had the shitty "safety net" of my parents (I had had to cut them *completely* off before the move . . . no way would I beg a narcissist and his lackey—my mom—for money) and asking my brother Craig was out of the question. Mainly because he was younger, but mostly because he had morphed into an immigrant child/survivor of a strict parent cliché by refusing to get it together, partying too hard, and flunking out of college in Miami.

So I learned quickly how to fend for myself. This meant that until Eve and I both got reliable daytime jobs, I was going to have to pump out an inhuman amount of articles and essays as I ventured further into freelance writing where entertainment media was concerned.

I suppose that there should have been more than one discussion of how bills were going to be handled while we both attempted to find our footing in a new place. But because of some of the guilt that I was holding on to, the guilt that I felt at convincing one of my oldest friends to join me on what was quickly becoming a suicide mission, I opted to not call for an additional discussion and proceeded to channel my freelance paychecks toward all apartment expenses. It just felt wrong to me to continue such discussions, partly because Eve had her own shit going on, was still struggling to get it together, and was just beginning to realize—as I was—all the ways that her parents had failed her and simultaneously adultified her. In retrospect, taking on this load in its totality probably didn't help her get it together any quicker, but I couldn't stand to see her struggle, no matter how much that probably enabled her to get it together with seemingly less urgency.

A bitch still kept it moving, though, and despite that tenacity, I was staring at a "girl, you are about to be evicted, pay the fuck up" notice on my front door every month. This continued even when I was successfully able to find that respectable day job at a local FedEx Office facility. I would spend the day in a dingy black-and-purple uniform blatantly designed to hide any and all fat. And titties. And ass cheeks. The soles of my feet an angry red. Always. Nearly bleeding. Then I would go home and spend my weeknights and entire weekends mass-producing freelance articles like a good little member of the proletariat. It made the other side of my life quite perplexing, honestly. Because I gradually got trusted with more important articles. Articles that would get me onto certain sets. Into certain screenings. In front of certain, and "relevant," people in the "biz." And eventually away from that horrendous FedEx job and away from Anaheim (and finally *to* Los Angeles). Yet my pay and my life reflected no such thing.

I wasn't happy. At all.

I slowly built my California friend group and community the first few months after the move, which improved things for me by maybe one percent, but ultimately, I was at my most suicidal during that time. I'm talking like "If I die, I die" while crossing the street in the most dangerous ways. Or contemplating crashing my car into a divider on the 91, the 605, or the 405. Or contemplating chugging some pills, again, as a grand exit from November 2018, and that time that I spent an entire month in bed, eating the only meal that my 489732984723 reemerging eating disorders and paltry pockets would allow: Thai yellow curry and rice.

I barely made it out of that month. I don't know nor do I

remember how I did. But I slowly, sluggishly, and mindlessly dragged my starved ass through December 2018, in some odd and misguided hope that somehow, someway this month, I would get a lucky break. That something might happen that would encourage me to hang on for a bit longer. That hope lingered in my head, as did my searing pessimism and disgust at myself for even hoping.

My *true* lucky break would eventually come that month, in the form of my friend Emiliano. But before that, I began to grapple with the social and psychological effects that my California move was having on my life as reflected back to me by an unexpected source: Kalindi.

BEFORE I got too deep into the war I was waging against the cost of living in California, my sister, Kalindi, surprisingly made one last-ditch effort to rekindle our relationship. A relationship that she had so thoroughly shot in the face and ran through a meat grinder like Pedro Pascal in *Kingsman: The Golden Circle*.

Under completely normal circumstances, I would have told my sister to go fuck herself and die. I had told the entire family just as much when I left for California, and I was fresh off of calling my mom an abject failure, coward, and enabler as a parent for pretending as if The Terrible Thing That No One Talked About™ never happened.

Buuuuuuut, I didn't do that for, like, three reasons.

The first was that I was in a fairly vulnerable place, particularly where my finances were concerned. And, truth be told, the reintroduction of Kalindi into my life meant that some Guilt Money™ would likely follow—considering that that was the way the Eduwas tended to fix their problems and make up for their shortcomings.

The second was that I had made a lot of headway with my favorite therapist of all time, Dr. Meera Siddiq. She was a sweet, petite Pakistani-Indian woman. Late thirties or early forties. Dark-skinned and with a potty mouth just like mine! A match made in the twelfth circle of hell that I was currently residing in. And she knew a thing or two about abusive immigrant families and the twisted obligation you can still feel toward them because of their "sacrifice." Despite the abuse.

It was because of her incisive insight and these shared characteristics and experiences that I kept an open mind when she suggested that I consider talking to Kalindi again.

"You gotta be shitting me." I sat forward in my seat, glaring at her.

"Before you bite my head off—"

"Bite your head off? That'd be light work," I scoffed, raising my voice. "I should just stop fucking coming if you're going to suggest doing shit that is bad for my health—like talking to my demon of a sister."

"Now hold on. This is still my goddamn office, *Alex*. So you need to take your voice down a few decibels." She leaned forward, matching my glare with ease. I sat back, effectively chastised.

"Sorry."

"Yeah, you had better be." She leaned back as well, exhaling. A couple of seconds elapsed, with me simply crossing my arms and staring out the window.

"Now." Dr. Siddiq broke the silence. "Would you like to hear my rationale for speaking with your 'demon of a sister'? Or are you content with pouting silently for the last fifteen minutes of our session? Because I get paid either way. As you've so graciously pointed out."

"Fuck you," I responded.

"Likewise." She crossed one leg over the other.

We engaged in an intense stare-off . . . until we both burst out laughing.

"You are very, *very* lucky I like you as a client." She smiled. "Or else I would have tossed you out of my office by now."

"I hear you. I'm sorry." I returned the smile. "But, yes, let's hear your rationale."

"So. Let me start off by saying that I think that 'hurt people hurt people' is a bullshit saying. People get away with *so* much by simply throwing their hands in the air and stating that they, too, like many others on this stupid space rock, have trauma. Which is not an excuse for bullshit at all." She rolled her eyes. "But what I will say is that abuse like what your sister endured . . . is often very . . . poisonous. It . . . doesn't really leave any room for love to grow. Or kindness to germinate, for that matter. Unless it is properly dealt with."

"So you're suggesting that I be the one to 'properly' help her deal with it?"

"That's not what I'm saying, because that's not your responsibility. She can get her own therapist for that shit." She raised an eyebrow and I laughed. "But I *am* saying that it could be healing to understand the origins of her . . . *wickedness*. To put together that timeline. Your family's timeline—if we're talking generational bullshit. And its effect on you. Then and now." She finished, "Don't ask me how I know." I nodded, remembering the few times that Dr. Siddiq mentioned her own experiences with her very light-skinned and very childish eldest sister.

She wasn't wrong though. Kalindi was quite a nasty person. With a repugnant spirit. And she was disgustingly wicked and cruel to me growing up at times that she absolutely did not need to be. But unfortunately, she was not the first abuse victim, nor would she be the last, to channel all her rage into subsequently abusing others. Was it fair that she did that? Nope. And was it fair that she decided that I was the easiest target to do that to? Fuck no. Like, I still want to stab the bitch for it *to this day!*

Yet . . . the psychological, spiritual, mental, emotional, and physical effects of *sexual* abuse complicate how Black girls like Kalindi navigate the world. And how they relate to others and the people who love them. That doesn't make it right. But that's the reality.

The idea of welcoming Kalindi back into my life made my

asshole pucker, but I figured that an abuse survivor like myself should hear another abuse victim out.

"You won't regret this!" Kalindi sounded relieved during our first call, which occurred a day after my appointment with Dr. Siddiq.

"Somehow, I highly doubt that," I muttered under my breath.

And dear reader, as you probably know, I almost instantly regretted it. As she would, in just under *two* months, shoot our relationship in the face one final time when she "advised" me to lose some weight in response to feeling out of breath while I was sick with pneumonia.

Pneumonia.

Prior to that endmost violation, my third reason for reengaging her just so happened to coincide with Janelle Monáe's 2018 album, *Dirty Computer*, finding its way to my Spotify playlist.

In a lot of ways, Kalindi reminded me of Janelle Monáe. For me, Janelle is cool as *fuck*. From the top of their head to the bottom of their toes. They always have been. And they'll probably always be. And despite her cruelty, Kalindi was effortlessly cool as well. And she was cool in a way that only Black girls—in all the magic we conjure here in the now, in the past, and in the future—are capable of. Of course, part of this "coolness" was rooted in my sister's ongoing struggle with engaging with or even accepting her feminine side. While the rejection of the "feminine" always creates some sort of imbalance in all people, that imbalance—in my opinion—is always a bit more pronounced and *visible* in young girls and women. Who seemingly have to rage against it to be taken "seriously," since any positive association with the feminine is written off as "weakness."

Yet I can't really blame Kalindi. Growing up under the oppressive regime that is our family and its gender-essentialist propaganda meant that the only real options were to a) conform to and subsequently be swallowed whole by and crushed under the binary, or b) revolt and take up arms against the binary while risking ostracism and ridicule.

So, my sister chose the latter, opting to endure being referred to as "mannish" both by family and folks at the extremely fanatical Doorway to Heaven church—something that was cemented by her cutting her hair short as fuck. I was reminded of the former occurrences when I heard Janelle confronting such attitudes on "Django Jane." And I was definitely reminded of the latter and all-related religious bullshit when Janelle spoke about their experiences with the church in their 2018 *Rolling Stone* profile.

Kalindi took a page out of Janelle's book back in 1999 and onward. Or rather, I was finally old enough to register it (and general existence) with me being five at the time. I watched her fuse several clothing styles she had observed on women like Aaliyah, Alicia Keys, and the girl group TLC. And to be clear, the influence TLC's Tionne "T-Boz" Watkins, Lisa "Left Eye" Lopes, and Rozonda "Chilli" Thomas had on her life became even more pronounced as time went on. And it was something I was briefly reminded of when I heard "a little crazy, little sexy, little cool" in "I Like That," the tenth track on *Dirty Computer*.

Kalindi also wasn't too into "cooking and cleaning," and you'd *never* see her set foot in a kitchen if it wasn't to grab a quick snack, steal *my* leftovers, or stash some of her own. She also got aggressively good at sports and regularly broke the ankles of the resident alpha-male niggas at our local gyms and parks and embarrassed a rich çråqüêr or three on the tennis court. Sports—as became the case for me—proved to be an incredible grounding force for her.

In fact, one of the few aspirations she informed me of while growing up was a sports-related desire to ascend to the WNBA and give her idol, Lisa Leslie, hell. But, of course, since it was a cardinal sin in the Eduwa family to dream, my father quickly quelled that fantasy—with more than eager backup from my fuck-ass mom. My father also *hated* the fact that Kalindi raged so hard against being what he would consider a "proper lady" (which, how *dare* he?) and was sure to take the most biting of sideswipes at her whenever possible.

"For all this *nonsense* you're doing and *wearing*, you might as well have been a man," my father sneered at her as she walked by one time. She was seventeen at the time. My father was sitting on his favorite forest-green loveseat in the living room, pulling up his argyle socks in preparation for leaving for his night shift. He didn't really have a particular reason to be saying this to her on that particular day and didn't really need one either, but I'm sure he was tempted to do so because of the new oversized white-and-red Michael Jordan jersey she was sporting, as well as the shoes to match.

Kalindi, who had been reaching for the handle to the front door, froze.

She turned. "Be grateful that I'm not a man, because if I was, one of us wouldn't be here. And I think you know who that would be." This is pretty ironic, as my sister would go on to put my father in a well-deserved headlock and nearly end his life a couple of years later. But at the present moment, my father paused and looked up from his socks and gulped. Then Kalindi slammed the door behind her and was gone.

I had been peering out at the scene from the edge of the kitchen, making use of the sporadic invisibility that seemed to befall me every so often in this household. Having said that, witnessing this short exchange was probably one of the first times I saw the fear of God cross my father's face. It was the briefest reminder of the power, while unaware, that my sister actually *did* possess. It was *also* really fucked up, and frankly, sad, that she couldn't see that because of oppressive ideas about gender.

This wouldn't be the first or last time that my father or mother weaponized jabs—big or small—that were meant to deride my sister's "confusion" about gender roles or, eventually, sexuality. There were repeated remarks about my sister's "mannish ways" and eventually accusations of "lesbianism" leveled at her from my father (who enjoyed using "lesbian" like it was a dirty word) for her close relationship with her Black American best friend at the time, Cierra, who she had met while playing on her high school's basketball team. Cierra was also the first and *last* friend Kalindi brought around, and I'm like 99.9 percent sure their friendship crumbled under the weight of my father's aggressive homophobia and lesbophobia.

As time marched on and my sister finally caved under the pressure and chokehold that *marriage and children* had on Nigerian customs, my sister's style would morph from overtly "mannish" to something a bit softer, perhaps more along the lines of androgynous, with a slight touch of the feminine. This was done so certain men felt "comfortable" approaching her. And technically, this did end up working for her, as she got married to the typical Edo—or shall we call it Benin? Bini? Clearly, I'm a bad Nigerian—chauvinist of a man about a year before I left for California.

This is perhaps why her coming out to me about being bisexual as well was of particular note. Firstly because, I shit you not, the confession came *one* month (re: September) after I had arrived in California, *five* months after Janelle themself had come out as pansexual (and a day before the release of *Dirty Computer*), and *two* weeks after I started listening to the aforementioned album at the recommendation of my friend Eve (who had always had great taste in music). The timing remains odd to me, but it is one of many moments in my life that remind me that kismet—or providence to some—is very much a thing.

The reveal came right after I had lamented to Kalindi about my continued difficulties dating women who were determined to push me into a more masculine role in the relationship due to their hangups about colorism and gender. I had just closed my laptop for the day after sending in one of many freelanced articles I was slaving away on.

"I hate it here," I remember bitching into the phone. "Like

you really want me to be your 'man' because I'm darker than you? How delusional."

"I suppose it is *quite* fucking annoying, isn't it?" My sister chuckled. "And don't be a bitch with muscles either. Then it gets even weirder." I paused for a moment. Well, a moment would be a lie. I paused long enough that my sister noticed and then added: "Yeah. I'm bisexual too. Surprise, surprise."

I know she couldn't see me, but I immediately narrowed my eyes like she could. It was never like me to deny someone's experience or their own personal life story. It never has been. But, dear reader, I was definitely skeptical that day. Not because I thought she was lying but because my sister had a track record of suddenly being interested in things when I showed a burgeoning interest.

The most egregious of these examples happened when I put unique spins on the shitty hand-me-downs she threw at me when I was moving into high school. She would suddenly want them back because I had somehow made them look even better. The next example happened at the height of my disordered eating in high school. My obsessive consumption of mono-unsaturated and polyunsaturated fats by way of peanut butter and avocados made it so that I always had at least one of each in the fridge. And soon after I had started that, my sister decided that peanut butter and avocados were her new favorite foods *too*.

The last annoying example happened when I started writing little paper books with Regina at church while I was in elementary school. It was at that point, "coincidentally," my sister took up writing—with a focus on poetry. Eventually, I'd venture into poetry as I entered middle school just to spite her for her decision to compete with me. And . . . I would end up better at it, too, much to her chagrin.

When she couldn't successfully compete with me, she would punish me by purposely getting me into trouble. One such occurrence happened when I was twelve and had successfully convinced my very strict Nigerian mother to buy *The Sims*

(2000) for me from GameStop, despite its *teen* rating. All OG *Sims* players know that the inaugural game was actually pretty *tame* in comparison to what's out there now (shoutout to one particular *Sims 4* sex mod!). But that didn't particularly matter to my childish sister. Nope. She would go on to grossly embellish what "woohoo" meant and argue that I had gotten the game just to do that.

This incident ended with me getting beat viciously and being forced to return the game—with my mom staring me down at the very same GameStop and my sister probably somewhere laughing her ass off.

So that's why, dear reader, her well-timed confession this time around didn't initially move me.

"I know what you're thinking—" Kalindi started, my continued silence getting to her.

"Well, that's interesting because if your guess isn't that this wouldn't be the first time you decided to be an abject weirdo that plays weird 'nigga-see-nigga-do' games with her baby sister, then no, you absolutely do not know what I'm thinking."

There was another pause.

"I deserve that."

"Yeah. And more."

"*All right.* I get it, no need to rub it in."

"No, actually, you don't get it." I could feel myself getting increasingly irate. "I spent, despite my better judgment, years looking up to you. *Years.* Years thinking if I toned down the 'annoying' younger sibling behavior, you'd hang out with me more in public. Years thinking that maybe if I was, I don't know, less *fat,* you'd finally not hate me as much. Years thinking that one day you were gonna wake up and realize that we had a common enemy in our ain't-shit father and that we could literally fuck up this man's life if we just did it together." I'm not gonna lie. I was yelling at this point, despite how much I myself hated yelling. "But no. Instead, you singled me out just like that nigga and then had the weird and twisted audacity to then compete with me. Who the fuck are you? And who the fuck do you think you are? And why come to me with this shit now like we're supposed to be some on some bi Wonder Twin shit?"

I exhaled after my extended and much overdue rant. As soon as I was able to calm myself down, I heard quiet cries on the other side of the line.

"You should know by now that tears don't move me like they used to," I said. "But I apologize for yelling. I don't like it. Mom used to do it too much and I don't want to be like that," I added. "But that doesn't mean I'm gonna apologize for—"

"For being right?" Kalindi finished. "Good. You shouldn't apologize for being right. Because *you* are right." I raised an eyebrow as she continued. "I . . . have always been envious of you."

I rolled my eyes. "Shocker, and for what reason, I have no idea."

"Well, if you'd let me finish, I'd say that the envy existed for a couple of reasons."

"Like?"

"Like . . . the fact that you didn't let Dad beat writing out of you," she said. "Or the fact that you literally, and quite hilariously, gaslit them about applying to Vanderbilt and then got on a plane to UChicago—"

"Excuse you, I definitely did apply—"

"Sure, but I don't remember you paying that application fee—"

"Did you just admit to going through my fucking mail—"

"Yeah, but that's beside the point—"

"I think that's very much part of the point—"

"The *point* is," my sister cut me off for the last time, "that you weren't *actually* afraid of him. Somehow. Despite everything he did or said to you. I mean, sure, you were 'scared' in a way that most little kids are 'scared' of their parents. But you weren't *afraid*. But despite all the abuse he put you through, you still did . . . well, *you*."

"This is an odd thing to say coming from the person who rioted against everything he and Mom ever said."

"Yeah. Yeah. I did. But I did a lot of that shit to piss them off. Rather than simply doing it for me." She sighed. "Because if I truly didn't give a fuck, I might have, you know, really tried my hand at that WNBA thing. It was a pipe dream, yeah, but . . . I don't know, I think I could have done it. I don't know."

I paused before I answered. "So . . . exactly which category does this . . . bisexual 'admission' of yours fall under?"

"Well, it definitely falls under the things I was too afraid to admit out loud. Or within earshot of Mom and Dad." I imagined her shrugging on the other side of the phone. "Things that my kid sister once again beat me to." She paused, probably expecting me to chuckle or something, but I remained dead silent.

"I wasn't really a good sister to you," Kalindi said after some time.

"Understatement of the year, ladies and gentlemen," I replied.

"But if I want you to learn anything from me . . . I want you to know that, um, there's this boldness in you that is very . . . aggravating. Um, very uncontrollable. Gutsy, so to speak. And it has absolutely no regard or respect for people who would call themselves your authority figure. But it's also very . . . encouraging." She struggled to get it out, which, I don't blame her. It's one of the few positive things she *ever* said to me *about* me. "Your bravery inspires courage in others. Me even now. It makes you special." Kalindi exhaled. "And I'm sorry I had a part in trying to crush that. I hope you *never* allow anyone to crush that. Anyone, okay? Promise me."

I allowed my mind to wander a bit. What she was asking for was a tall order. One of the *tallest* in my life at that point. I had already felt myself weakening under the mind-numbing grip that fatphobia had on this place. And on me. I found my will being eroded by the intense diet culture lurking around the corners of both Anaheim and Los Angeles. Fad after fad after fad. That was paired with the religion of fitness and had every other person on every dating app boasting about their love for "gym dates" or "love affairs" with hiking. Indeed, things were so bad that about 99.9 percent of conversations that I had the displeasure of overhearing mentioned some new crash diet one of the speakers had just recently waded into. I was also losing the fight against disordered eating once more, a sleeping demon that was once again awakened by poverty and not being able to hold on to a *dime* in this state.

Additionally, I was already in the thick of, as I told her, dealing with how colorism had ramped up its powers of invisibility in terms of my romantic run-ins with cis Black men locally. The type of shameless colorism perpetuated by them in this place was so abhorrent that even *light-skinned* Black women were beginning to complain. Seriously. And this was made abundantly clear when I spoke with two Fenty 220 publicists—who both were straight as an arrow—at a press junket. The conversation ended with one of them stating that she had "given up on niggas here" and opted to date "finer brothas" out of state. And unfortunately for my gay ass, colorism also found me outside of men and proved to be the most violent and obscene turn-off in my quest to date Black women or other nonwhite women who were, to be frank, really looking for *fathers* and not the partners they *pretended* to be searching for. And most certainly not the "man" that they continued to project onto me.

Truly. I was getting *wailed on* from all sides. All sides. And at the moment, it felt disingenuous to pretend that I could ensure that my spirit would not be broken here. It felt blatantly insincere to act like I could keep reinforcing all my resolve to survive in spite of what was going on around me. It was giving . . . *mendacious*—thinking that this place wasn't going to be successful in *fundamentally* changing me.

And still, I said:

"I promise."

MY BEST DATE EVER

As we've established, my dating life tends to be pretty much ... shit. Hot shit. And not the good shit. *Horse* shit. There have been some assorted moments here or there when it's been somewhat exciting. Somewhat sexy. Somewhat ... *something*, I guess. But then, it's always fallen back on its ass, smirking at me in a very "bitch, you thought!" manner. And this would pretty much be the pattern of my life—like the *supreme* pattern of my life à la *Groundhog Day*—for a solid two decades. Until I had nearly arrived at my 25th birthday (celebrating two and a half decades of life on this ghetto space rock). And during my 25th year, I became romantically involved with one of my good friends. An old friend. And the kind of person—meaning *a parent*—that I swore I would never ever date or get entangled with in my youth ... until now.

I feel like this is the part where I'm supposed to put out this general disclaimer saying that I (technically) have nothing against parents. Other than the immutable beef I have with my own. Like they can be a fine group of people. And they have the capacity to shape entire nations. Entire worlds. Just by the mere fact that someone, somewhere in the universe, is placing a rather baseless trust in the standard parent and their ability to literally usher in and be the eternal guardian of another human being. A human *soul* really, that just so happens to be called a "child." A smaller human. A little one.

But based on my own experiences and the experiences of

some of my peers, parents' potential to do harm ... is infinite. And nigh-impossible to counteract, mainly because many parents have succumbed to the high that comes with being in charge of another human being. Truly. The standard human being tends to crave power and respect. The amount that they want does tend to vary, but there's a craving for it nonetheless. And this craving, if unchecked in the standard human, completely evolves into a full-blown God complex once *children* enter the picture. And that's where it gets dicey too, because I am definitely one of those people who count children themselves as a marginalized and unprotected group of people and thereby don't really care for the God complexes that such guardians lord over them.

So, I just tend to ... not be around parents, so to speak. Because, clearly, I believe the bad ones outnumber the good ones. The only exceptions to this rule, for me, have happened recently, with more and more of my friends becoming parents. And observing that the goodness I have observed in these people has transferred to their burgeoning skills in parenting ... and properly caring for the tiny humans they have birthed.

This is why my decision to *date* and subsequently *fuck* a parent on the cusp of my 25th/26th year is fucking hilarious and completely contradictory to everything I just said here. But fear not, dear reader. I sorta kinda promise that the contradiction will be worth it.

Anyway, when did this shit even start?

Well, please see my extended rant on *2018* in the last chapter ... up until *November* 2018. Because, at that time, I was quite literally on my last leg "hope-wise."

Miraculously, my hope, that *last* sliver of optimism, was rewarded when my friend Emiliano came to LA that December.

Emiliano's visit shouldn't have come as a surprise. We had been pinging each other every so often over multiple platforms since leaving college. Granted, the frequency of such encounters varied—as my professional and social life duked it out over my well-being and as his life also threw random calamities at him while he raised a family. Eventually, we landed at complete radio silence in the bottom half of 2017. Save for a random tweet in January 2018 and a DM in June 2018, when he decided to drop in my Twitter DMs to remind me that I was a bad bitch. With a *fire* pen to match. Which was heartwarming. I've never told him that. And I'm not sure I will. But it was heartwarming nonetheless. Then there was a brief update right before my move to Anaheim in August, where he informed me that he had moved to San Francisco, and then silence once more.

That radio silence was broken when he hit me up at the beginning of December to let me know that he'd be around to visit another friend of his in LA. And by the end of that month, we were meeting up to watch *Spider-Man: Into the Spider-Verse* and chopping it up at a surprisingly fancy Dave & Buster's. Granted, I hadn't stepped into one in like a decade. But fancy nonetheless.

The lead-up to us getting together wasn't anything spectacular, but it did remind me of why Emiliano and I had become friends in college in the first place. Having similar tastes meant that we were able to choose a movie, time, and venue with relative ease. The location happened to be a tiny AMC theater in Los Angeles. I remember him asking what time he should swing by to pick me up and, in hindsight, I should've a) clocked that this wasn't totally a platonic meetup, and b) not been such a prideful asshole. But I turned down the ride like an idiot and told him I'd meet him at the theater instead.

After *Into the Spider-Verse* concluded, I found myself sitting across from my old friend at Dave & Buster's; he was sitting casually on one of the barstools, while I sat in a booth (because those stools weren't built for fat bitches, okay?) a short distance away, throwing back a disgusting amount of happy-hour drinks and trading barbs and factoids about Miles Morales and Peter Parker over fried-chicken-and-waffle sliders—which were fucking delicious by the way. *Everything* about the outing could be summed up as nostalgia, vibes, and superheroes. Until that age-old question was uttered and the record player called the universe screeched to a halt:

"So. How have you been?"

I literally can't tell you who asked that question. Not because I don't want to. But because I don't even remember. And writing this during a pandemic hasn't necessarily helped my memory recall it any better or quicker, to be honest. Although I am tempted to blame the happy-hour drinks. Still, because this is *my* story, I'm just gonna assume that I'm the one who asked that *goofy-ass* question.

And what a loaded question it is. So many of the answers you can give 100 percent depend on who is present at the moment. If you don't really give a shit, you're likely to throw a "good" or an "okay, I guess" just to move the conversation along. But if you do happen to be in the unfortunate position of giving a fuck, then the answers can branch off into some sick butterfly-effect map. You can opt for raw and uncut honesty or give an answer that won't make you look as pathetic as you are currently feeling at the moment.

Emiliano leaned back against the bar and crossed his arms, trying to contemplate how to answer this question. I couldn't blame him. There are not enough words in the world to answer a "how have you been"–ass question. To my utmost surprise, however, he leaned forward, seemingly eager to fill me in.

"Hmm. Well, I've been in school . . ."

"Again?!" I was incredulous. "What, you weren't tortured enough the first go-around?"

"Relax." He laughed. "This isn't UChicago anymore. This is Stanford. Which is . . . slightly less stressful."

"Only slightly?" I questioned him.

"I mean, these are academic institutions we're talking about, Lex. There's bound to be some sort of stress on account of bureaucratic bullshit."

"Fair." I nodded. "What are you studying toward?"

"A PhD in anthropology."

"Oh my God. You're gonna be in school forever!"

"Hey, if that means I can keep deferring on my student loans, so be it." He laughed.

"You're such a glutton for punishment, I swear. Why anthropology?"

"Humans are shit. But we're also kind of *interesting* pieces of shit when you zoom out and observe us as a whole."

"By 'interesting,' I'm assuming you mean 'messy'?"

"That's an oversimplification, but . . . yeah." He shrugged. "I'm on the culture and society track and so far so good. I've been wanting to study things like sovereignty and the idea of borders and what makes a 'state' or a 'society' and a 'culture,' and I've always been interested in things like climate change and our role in it and—"

"This nigga thinks he's Captain Planet." I chuckled to myself.

"Yo, fuck off," he shot back, laughing too.

"I didn't think you heard that . . ."

"Eh, you've always been a loud whisperer."

"I resent that." I eyed him as I prepped a return-fire quip in my head in case he decided to try me again. He opted not to continue. "How about Stanford the city? Do you like it there?"

"I live in San Francisco actually," Emiliano corrected me. "Which I have mixed feelings about because of all the white dudebros moving there for their tech startups." I stuck my finger in my mouth like I was going to puke at his mention of "tech startups" and he smiled.

"Funny, I never pegged you as the San Francisco type," I said.

"I didn't either. Just there so I don't get fined."

"You're funny." I grinned. "How did Tiana and el bebé feel about the move?"

Emiliano paused. For a brief second, distress, awkwardness, and confusion duked it out on his face. After that second passed, he donned an impressive poker face that could have fooled everybody in the tristate area. Either way, it was a question I almost immediately regretted asking.

"Great question. Because that's definitely the elephant in the room."

"Elephant?" I raised an eyebrow. "You mean . . ." I pointed at myself in jest and he gave me an impatient look. I threw my hands up in mock surrender and settled down.

"I am now . . . legally separated. And in the process of filing for divorce."

Now, I have the shittiest poker face known to man. So I am pretty sure a wave of shock moved across my face at lightning speed, which he acknowledged with a "Yeah, I know." To cap things off he said, "Suffice to say that she wasn't very thrilled. And neither was my daughter, Lia. But you know."

I paused before answering.

"I'm not judging you, if that's what you're thinking," I said as a precaution.

"I know." He shrugged. "But I'm guessing you're still surprised?"

"Am I legally required to answer that question?" I drew in my lips and made a farting noise to ease some of the tension, which caused him to chuckle a bit.

"That's your call." He smiled.

"Well, yes. But also no."

"Oh?"

"Yeah."

"You gonna elaborate?" Emiliano looked amused.

"Nope. I don't think I should. And I don't think I will," I added.

"Touché."

"Touché indeed," I replied. "So . . . how is Lia? How is that perpetual troublemaker?"

"Ah. Well, she is, um . . . growing up fast. *Super* fast. Faster than I can personally process," Emiliano said. "Which is another reason why this whole divorce thing is so stressful."

"I'm sorry."

"No . . . it's fine." He shrugged. "It was a long time coming."

"Do you want to talk about it?"

"Nope. I don't think I should. And I don't think I will." He parroted me from earlier as I rolled my eyes in humored disgust. "For now, at least. But forget about that. I want to know about you. How have *you* been?"

So.

Following an "I'm getting a divorce" announcement is . . . terrible. It's like being in an early 2000s sitcom, during the special "talent show" episode. And during that same show, you come right after the kid who just so happened to secure a surprise guest performance from Coolio (RIP) in his prime because *why the fuck not*? Which suffice to say . . . that's not an act you want to immediately follow, because anything you do or say is gonna be highly insignificant in comparison. But, you know, since I lacked embarrassment for the most part, I decided to answer honestly.

"Uh. Well. Not great, actually," I said slowly. Emiliano looked curious. "I'm still writing, of course. As evidenced by some of the articles you've seen. But . . . I have *not* had the best year. And if I'm being 100, this is one of the few times I've actually been able to force myself to leave my home—well, apartment—and bed in like the last month. Truthfully."

"Damn."

"Yeah. November was really rough. Like . . . 2014 to 2015 rough."

Emiliano made a hissing noise like he had stepped on the *sharpest* Lego.

Which . . . appropriate.

I was of course referencing my terrible junior year, which was absolute hell due to my busted-ass ACL injury, and Emiliano had been around for all that.

If you remember, of course, I pretty much ignored like half of his initial invites to hang out while I was deeply depressed post-Jason. Well, that was until my brush with suicide—and the possibility of being involuntarily committed—rattled me enough to get my shit together.

To this day, I ponder what exactly prompted him to extend the very first invitation to me. I mean, we were friends, of course. But at the time, if I were to put it on a scale from 1 to 10, I would have said that we were at a safe . . . 5.5. Like we knew each other *kinda* and enjoyed each other's company in passing because of shared interests like protesting or theater or poetry. But there was never any extended time spent together to just . . . talk and be. And get to *know* the other person.

Maybe he genuinely wanted to see me and catch up with me. Like, I don't toot my own little horn often, but, I mean, I was and am awesome. And funny. And semi-mysterious when my gums weren't flapping loud as fuck. And, you know, maybe, just maybe he had become smitten with me in passing and just had to know more. Which . . . that was straight out of my 2003 to 2005 rom-com brain, and I knew better than to let myself get carried away by such lofty, wishful thinking.

But sometimes, I wonder if the invitation was out of pity. Like, I wonder if he was like, "She looks like a sad sack. I should make like Spike Lee and do the right thing" or some shit like that. I wonder if he knew that I technically needed the extra company. I'd hit several rock bottoms post–ACL injury and was looking at a fourth one by the time the invitation came.

It was a thought that lingered in the back of my mind often. Not because of anything that Emiliano did or said in particular (except maybe because of how he looked, which as I said, was very *fine*). But because I had been met with that a lot at the height of my injury. Pity existed all around me. You could see glints of it in their eyes whenever my friends had to hang back so I could catch up with them on the sidewalk. You could see it in the happy-turned-limp waves of my old dormmates whenever I showed up to cheer them on from the sidelines at an IM sport event. You could also see it in the pained smiles of anyone who had the most dramatic misfortune of walking ahead of me at any given time of day and would end up either holding a door or elevator for me. You could also feel it in the air whenever I sat in the dining hall to catch up with old dormmates. I'd walk through and people would part like the fucking Red Sea, but not in the cool "LET MY PEOPLE GO" way. Obviously.

So, yeah. Pity was very familiar. And I suspected that all interactions post–ACL injury amounted to that. Emiliano's invitation included.

But, of course, crediting pity for that whole interaction would invite me and my already chaotic psyche to question the validity of a friend and a friendship I still retain to this day. And was quite fond of. And that's not necessarily a path that I wanted to venture down unprompted.

"Well now I'm sorry." Emiliano looked pained.

"No, it's okay." I shrugged. "Leaving Tennessee was bound to be that dramatic."

"Funny. I felt the same way about leaving Ohio," he added. "But . . . don't stop telling your story on my account. Continue."

I proceeded to tell him about my big move to California. And what happened thereafter.

"Is that everything?" His eyes were wide.

"I believe I covered everything, yes." I shrugged again. Emiliano sat back on his stool again and looked at me, carefully contemplating what to say next.

"Your sister sounds like a bitch."

"She is."

"But she was right."

"About . . . ?" I stared at him, ready to fight.

"About you being brave," he finished. "I'm sorry life has been so hard on you. And for you. I hate that for you."

"I hate that too." My disposition softened. "But, anyway, fuck all that. We did not come here to . . . purely lament our shitty lives. We are in the adult version of a Chuck E. Cheese right now. We should go play some motherfucking games."

"I am inclined to agree with you." He smiled as he hopped off his stool. "Are you ready to get whooped?"

"Oooooh. How kinky of you!" I teased him as I got up.

"Wait, I—" His voice caught in his throat.

"Relax." I stopped him, laughing. "I'm just fucking with you."

"Mmmhm." He rolled his eyes as we both started walking toward the gaming section. "Fucking asshole."

"Aht aht!" I replied. "Don't get pissy because I caught you in a genuine 'that's what she said' moment."

"*Ha ha ha,* nigga." He laughed mockingly.

"And a hardy *har har,* nigga!" I quipped, to which we broke out into full-on guffaws as we rounded the corner.

NOTHING MUCH happened after that. At least not that day. We left right before Dave & Buster's closed, and since Emiliano has always been the type to worry about me, particularly post-ACL injury, he insisted on walking me back to my car in the parking lot. He's fairly well-mannered too, so I also remember him helping me into my car. Right before that, however, he brought me into the tightest and longest hug and I happily obliged him.

And that's when something slightly out of the ordinary for us happened. I closed my eyes and deeply inhaled like the unhinged bitch I am. While inhaling, I noticed that he smelled ridiculously good—like if sandalwood, leather, and a dash of vanilla all decided to have a baby—and I could not believe that I didn't catch it before: mainly because a nigga smelling real nice is one of my unofficial love languages.

Obviously, I like living in denial, so I quickly pushed the thought out of my mind and focused on the hug at hand. Except my mind wasn't having any of that because then I noticed his arms were a tad bit . . . firmer than the last time I saw him, and usually I'd ignore that, but it was hard to ignore it this time around seeing as they were currently wrapped around my person. Emiliano had never been very muscular or bulky. He'd always been pretty lean, actually, and that had always worked for him. This is why the *slight* change in muscle tone was very much, ahem, noticeable.

For a second, while I was still hugging this nigga, I briefly wondered if he, too, was experiencing the extended psychosis that I was by virtue of being this up-close-and-personal with me. I mean, after all, I had gained at least twenty or twenty-five pounds since leaving college. I had always feared that that would happen upon exiting Chicago, and I'm sure the stress of moving accelerated the, for lack of better terminology, *fattening* process. Some of it shot straight to my gut. Some of it miraculously made it to my ass. But much of it had made it up to my titties. Seriously, I went from a simple C to a fucking triple D as soon as I set foot on Californian soil. And even that was in flux with me being back on a cycle of starving and bingeing and occasionally purging. Not because I wanted to but rather because I perpetually had like three dollars to my name—so food was . . . almost a luxury, to be honest.

The point is, being close to him definitely made me wonder about how he was perceiving me after all these years and I was instantly anxious and self-conscious. But before I could even parse all of the thoughts that had flooded my mind as soon as he touched me, he broke our hug and smiled warmly at me. I shot one of my stock smiles back and proceeded to act like I wasn't on the cusp of spiraling in my brain.

After that, we both said our goodbyes and he got on the road back to San Francisco. While I got on the road to head back to my shitty LA apartment.

Except my drive home wasn't as smooth as I'd hoped. No, instead, my insipid brain decided to bring up literally every memory of me and Emiliano hanging out. As well as revisit my sentiments and feelings toward him over the past couple of years. Which I guess was to be expected.

After all, I somewhat regrettably and nigh-immediately had a crush on him as soon as we met in that English class.

Seriously. I remember occasionally stealing glances at him anytime our professor went on one of his "back when I was in college" tangents during the first two weeks of school. Until he caught me looking one day and smiled back. After that, I spent the rest of that quarter staring a hole into the whiteboard in the room out of sheer embarrassment.

My crush tapered off after that and we settled into a pretty rad-ass friendship.

Okay, well. Mostly, anyway. Except for that brief moment in time when I started coming over to Emiliano's apartment, by his invitation, and we would spend time watching movies and shooting the shit.

One of those memories included him introducing me to the cultural phenomenon known as Guillermo del Toro's *Pacific Rim*.

Now, one thing about me? I love me some fucking robots. And well-placed and well-done explosions. It was why I had been obsessed with *Transformers* (the show) as a kid for the longest time. It was also the main reason I wanted to be a Power Ranger too, so I could stomp out evil motherfuckers with a Megazord.

Anyway. *Pacific Rim*. There were monsters (Kaiju), giant robots (Jaegers), Ron Perlman, and Idris Elba in a mustache he borrowed from Tom Selleck. Plus I was super invested in Charlie Hunnam and Rinko Kikuchi's romance, of course.

They should have fucking kissed, by the way. The fuck am I supposed to do with a *hug* after officially canceling the apocalypse?!

Exactly.

You should be tongue-fucking me, motherfucker!

Anyway, while I was staring at the film with wide-eyed wonder and excitement, I felt someone staring at *me*. I opted to ignore it at first. And the feeling did dissipate for a moment. But when I felt it again, I looked away from the TV to search for a source and ran straight into Emiliano looking at me. Not in a creepy way. But definitely in an "I am currently studying you" way, and it definitely caught me off guard.

Because Emiliano is Emiliano, he didn't look away either. He wasn't the type to get embarrassed easily, so he merely put his hands up, realizing he had been caught.

"You okay?" I raised my eyebrow, half-contemplating whether or not I should ask him what the fuck he was looking at.

"Yeah, I'm fine." He put his hands back down. "Never better."

"You sure? Because you're literally missing the best part of the movie." Which he was.

Mako had just pulled out a fucking sword, and here he was trying to summon a crater at the side of my face.

"Not necessarily," he answered, his lips curling into a small grin. I opened my mouth to ask him about the nonsensical answer he just gave me, but before any sound exited, he went back to watching the movie. And playfully nodded his head in the direction of the movie, motioning me to get back to watching it as well. I rolled my eyes at him and proceeded to finish the movie.

I hadn't been prepared for that memory to pop into my head. It was a doozy for sure. And I am absolutely shocked that I didn't veer off the road while my mind was clearly somewhere else.

And yet, I continued to ponder and piece together memories and moments like the one I had just snapped out of. I quietly wondered if, maybe, just maybe, my crush on Emiliano hadn't died. That maybe it merely transmuted itself into something ... else. And now that I was seeing him after an extended period of time, it had decided to rear its ugly head up like a UTI that clearly has a vendetta against you and your lack of cranberry consumption.

No, that couldn't be it. I drew stark lines when it came to my relationships in life. So that had to be way out of the question, right?

That was it. I was comfortably back in my safe space of denial. And then I sped off to my exit, continuing the journey "home."

I DIDN'T really expect to hear from Emiliano for a while after that. Or I assumed I wouldn't, mainly because I tend to take extended breaks from my friendships in general after a really big visit like the one we just shared. Still, I wasn't a rude bitch. So I texted him.

"Just made it back. It was nice seeing you. I had a great time. We have to do it again soon. And not years later :)"

"Ha ha ha. It was a fun time. And it was great seeing you as well." I smiled and went over to my favorite sofa to put my phone down and decompress. But then I stopped when my phone buzzed again. I turned it around to reveal one more message from he who would soon reveal his true self as Rico Suave:

"Goodnight :*"

Indeed. He did in fact bid me a good evening and then topped it off with the unambiguous kissy-face emoji. I stared at it like I had just been smacked.

Now to be clear, I had no idea what to do in this situation. Like, we had always had banter that just barely escaped being flirtatious. It's true. We knew just enough about each other to trade Great Value *Pride and Prejudice* jabs back and forth, but it all remained platonic for the most part. But . . . this was NOT that. Definitely not. No. This was . . . bolder. Riskier, so to speak.

And he knew that. And I knew that. And he very much knew that. But then again . . . did I know that?

I plopped onto the sofa, staring at my phone like it was an abyss. Was I supposed to respond? How was I supposed to respond? I had to respond, right? Like, not responding would be rude, I think. And yet, not responding seemed like the most viable solution. Like I could literally just pretend that I had fallen asleep and then I could forget even seeing the message and then text him several months from now on some "Oh shit! I didn't see this until now" shit. That seemed pretty safe to me. And I almost did.

The only issue with that plan was the fact that my birdy, reptilian brain instantly switched to autopilot and sent the following in response:

"Goodnight ;)"

I sent a *winky* face. A *fucking* winky face.

I was honestly so disgusted with myself. I could have projectile vomited into the TV; that's how embarrassed I was. I wanted to melt into the floor. I wanted the rinky-dink couch that had somehow made it on my journey to California to open its cushions wide and swallow me whole. A winky face? Really? What was I, a fucking preteen in a 2004 rom-com? No. No, I wasn't. And yet my brain decided that the only "smooth" thing I could conjure up to text this man back with was a fucking winky face. I flopped farther into the couch, facedown, hoping that I might suffocate on this musty couch and finally be done with this iteration of existence.

Because Gaia is occasionally merciful, Emiliano didn't answer. Which was a good and bad thing. Firstly because that meant that I didn't have to acknowledge that I sent that bullshit emoji; secondly because though I had been spared the additional embarrassment of continuing the conversation, I already knew that I was going to spend the whole night wondering how Emiliano reacted to said emoji.

And spend the whole night torturing myself over one emoticon, I did. Ha, who am I kidding? Fuck a night. Because a night became two. Then it became four. And then I basically spent the next WEEK turning over the whole thing in my head. The texts. The hug. My despotic hormones picking up on his cologne. Our . . . *outing*? If one would call it that anyway; because I was not even prepared to process the thought of it having accidentally been a date. Like a *date* date.

Sigh.

By the time I had arrived at my seventh day on this bull-shit, which was the third day of the new year, I concluded that something had to give. Because I was not about to approach week two in this same pitiful, hyperfixating condition. I thought about texting Emiliano to maybe catch up some more and release some of this tension that was constricting my brain and the little common sense that paid rent up there. But I ended up chickening out and resigned myself to mindlessly scroll-ing through Twitter. As one does. And as fortune would have it, there he was.

Coming up my timeline. I was tempted to scroll on right past him and mind my business. But I've always been nosy as fuck, so obviously, that's not what went down. I scrolled back up and squinted at his mini-thread and what he had tweeted:

"Yo I'm so BORED"

Followed by:

"Hmm. I'd like to meet someone I can play *Black Ops 4* with. Been a while since I done that. Met someone worthwhile, not the *Black Ops* part. To be clear."

I stared at his tweets for a few seconds while the light bulb in the far corner of my head threatened to switch on. If I had the classic Angel v. Devil duo standing on my shoulders while eyeballing this tweet, their dialogue might have gone like this:

Devil: Oh, bitch. This is the moment you've been waiting for. Go ahead and roll up on his lil' tweet and say "when." Trust me. You'll be sucking his dick before you know it.

Me: Excuse you, I'll be doing *what* now?

Devil: You don't suck dick??? Okay, okay. Fine. That's all right. We're still in this. (Pause.) Does the phrase "getting your back blown out" mean anything to you?

Me: Jesus.

Angel: Lex, you're always so freaking crass—

Devil: *Fucking*, Alex. Just say "fucking"; it's not hard—

Angel: ANYWAY. Listen, Alexandria. This isn't a good idea. Not because I don't think there's something there—

Me: Something where???

Angel: But because . . . is this really a road you want to go down? Like, do you trust yourself when it comes to navigating the whole dynamic between you and Emiliano changing?

Me: I just literally wanted to tell him that I would be down with playing *Black Ops 4* with him. Why are you reading into this?

Angel: Well. It's because—

Devil: You know, I feel like "Black Ops 4" would be a great name for a really complicated sex position—

Me: Oh my God, can you STOP thinking about sex for one fucking minute!

Devil: I could. I really could. But I won't. Because that's no fun.

Angel: BACK to what I was saying; we all know that this urge you have to comment on his basically open invitation is not as platonic as you're trying to convince yourself it is.

Me: All right. I just won't comment then.

Angel: I'm not saying not to—

Me: Then WHAT are you saying?

Devil: She's asking you if you like him. Basically. Like you know . . . *like*. And if you do, in fact, *like* like him . . . then you already know what to do.

Angel: . . . How did you know I was going to say that?

Devil: Pfft. Of course, I knew you were going to say that. I'm you. But better. And sexier.

Angel: Jesus, you're insufferable.

Devil: Yeah, and you can suck my ass as per usual.

Me: Please go the fuck away. I'm *begging* y'all at this point.

I focused back in on his tweet and inhaled, wracking my brain for something that would signal that I was interested and curious, but kinda still . . . mysterious or semi-aloof.

The end result?

I reposted his tweet in his DMs . . . followed by THE two-eyed emoji.

I know what you're thinking. Because I too thought it the second I saw the words "Tweet sent" on my screen. The dreaded two-eyed emoji? How corny. How childish! Like, was that really the best I could do when it came to attempting a flirtation without giving away that it was indeed a flirtation???

Once again, I was sick of myself. But before I could even sit with that disgust, my phone vibrated. And I was staring at a two-eyed emoji that he had replied with right back. Just as quickly as I had tweeted mine.

"Oh shit," I said to myself. "That actually ... worked?" I was stunned for a brief moment. But I knew I had to capitalize on what was quickly looking like it was going to become a worthwhile exchange.

"Still looking for someone to play *Black Ops* with?" I sent off and resisted closing out of the app entirely. I stared at three bubbles buffering until he finally populated a response.

"... Maybe. Who's asking?" He punctuated his question with an emoji that had its hand on its chin.

"... What if *I* was asking?"

"Oh. Well then, I would just say that we could—wait." I smirked a little as I watched three bubbles buffer again. "I'm assuming you read the rest of that tweet."

"I did."

"So ... uh, are you saying that, um."

"I like you?" I smiled to myself, gaining back a bit of confidence. "Yes. Yes, I am."

"I ..."

":)"

"No, you gotta be joking. Ain't no way," he kept typing. "Are you serious?"

"Clearly, I have a track record of being aggressively unserious when I want to be, but in this case ... yes, I am *very* serious."

"I ... uh. I don't know what to say ..."

And just like that, the sliver of confidence that had suddenly spawned in my brain vaporized itself. Anxiety gripped my fingers. And suddenly, my mind was racing for the 324893463503478th time in the last month. What if telling him was a mistake? What if I had just pissed away nearly a decade of friendship on some delusional crush? The thought of it honestly almost made me want to vomit again and I considered just hitting him with a nicely timed "jk." Yeah, yeah, I know that would be cruel, but at that moment, I didn't give a shit; I was in fight-or-flight mode, and I was hellbent on surviving this soon-to-be disastrous moment.

I went to sign out of Twitter when my phone dinged once more.

"I . . . like you too :)" he typed. "Never thought I'd get to say that to you, to be honest. Sorry, I'm still kind of in shock so don't be surprised if my answers are sporadic."

"Wait, how long have you felt this way?"

"No, actually, how long have *you* felt this way?"

"Nah, don't flip this back on me. You've been sitting on this!"

"And you haven't?"

"Pfft, you niggas are oblivious! I was clearly putting out . . . *vibes* that I was into you."

"All I'm hearing is that you thought you were Professor X the whole time and felt as if attempting to address your feelings would best be done . . . telepathically? Is this correct?"

"I mean, more or less."

"You're nuts."

"As are you."

"True, true. That's a given. But I've been nuts about you for a while." I paused when I read that response. My past delusions aside, I had never expected to hear something like that from him. And now that I was reading this in real time . . .

It almost felt like I was frozen in time. But it wasn't about anything traumatic like usual. This was . . .

This was, dare I say, a good moment. A great moment. I stifled a big-ass smile as I went to reply.

"Nuts?" I responded.

"Yeah, nuts," he continued. "I thought it was all in my head. Thought I was being weird. But now that I know? Well . . ."

"What stopped you from saying anything?"

"Well, you know how niggas move. Real grimy and shit. Using friendship to Trojan-horse their way into pussy. And . . . I didn't want to be that person. No matter how much I *thought* I liked you."

"*Thought?*" I was amused.

"Excuse the past tense. I currently do like you, to be absolutely clear," he clarified.

"Good :)"

"So."

"So."

"What now?"

"I don't know," I typed. And then I followed it up with an "I didn't think I'd get this far" Plankton GIF. He sent a couple of laugh emojis back before I saw buffering bubbles again.

"Well, let's start here: Can I take you out on a date? Like, a *real* one. Officially."

My eyes got so big, but I pressed on.

"Uh . . . yes. Yes, you can." I finally let my goofy-ass smile take the wheel. "I thought you'd never ask."

"Oh, and Lex?"

"Yeah?"

"The kissy face emoji . . . was on purpose."

"I fucking knew it!"

AS YOU know, I am used to my life being a shitty sitcom where everyone is in on the joke except me. However, this was not the case with my, well, burgeoning love affair with *Emiliano*.

Ugh.

Can you hear me gagging?

Love affair? Who the fuck am I, Jeanne Tournier? In the so-called obscene film *The Lovers*? I'm not, clearly, but that's an interesting thought now that I actually think about it.

Anyway, dating suddenly became . . . awesome? I felt great. High, even! Like I was definitely romanticizing the fuck out of this shit—to like every single track on *Dirty Computer*. And for good reason too.

Other than Bruce, it had been a *long* time since I dated someone who I found super attractive and also super . . . intriguing. And somewhat challenging. Someone who could go toe-to-toe with my caustic wit. Or better yet, someone who didn't mind one-upping me every now and again. To keep me on my toes. And, you know, Emiliano himself was extraordinary, like truly a pretty motherfucker with an oversized brain to match, but I think what really drew me in was how our longtime friendship had just effortlessly shifted into this new dynamic.

Now, I know what you're thinking. "It's not gonna stay that way forever, girl!" And, of course, you are *very* right. But that's not my point right now. My point right now is that as someone who was still navigating the ins and outs of demisexuality . . . this was quite literally my dream scenario—despite whatever fate awaited me and this relationship in question.

Three weeks had passed since we exchanged confessions of *like*. And at risk of sounding like the syrupiest and most stupendously saccharine bitch around, I gotta say—it felt kinda heavenly. It turns out that talking to someone you'd already put in time with and who equally had the hots for you was *euphoric*.

We talked. so. fucking. much.

Seriously.

Every single day.

Sometimes, it'd be in the form of a random "hey, I saw this and thought of you" meme. Or a funny tweet that had me choking on air. Or a cheeky text. Or a call that simultaneously went on for hours and concluded in the blink of an eye.

It was . . . an experience I was not used to. Being enraptured by someone else's genuine curiosity and affection. And, hell, mutual *obsession*. Some of y'all are too scared to own that, but not this bipolar-ass bitch. No, I was obsessed! But so was he. Which made the experience even sweeter. And addictive.

And as for what we talked about? The list was endless! No topic was out of the question in terms of exploring. Sometimes, we revisited our time at UChicago. And how young and unprepared we were for that hellscape. How attending that school as Black people felt like floating around in the twilight zone. How fucking cold it was there. How that city irrevocably changed us at our cores forever.

We talked about trauma too. Eventually. As one does. Emiliano wasn't shy about discussing the precarious nature of growing up as both Black and Peruvian and perpetually trying to escape the jaws of anti-Blackness. Nor was he shy about discussing how that impacted what he thought about his own identity in real time. Nor was he shy about how that factored into how he was raising Lia and being hypervigilant about keeping her and his soon-to-be ex-wife from any anti-Black family members that decided to pop up on any given day. And he was very open about sharing how attending an institution like UChicago had completely shifted the power balance in his previous household. Both for better and for worse.

"The Peruvian side of my family took bets on if I'd live to twenty-two. Like, *bet* bets. Like *cash money* bets. Jail and death were the top bets. Like maybe I'd end up rotting in a ditch somewhere from some gang shit or a drug deal gone wrong." I pressed my ear to the phone as he continued to speak. "Somebody threw in the college dropout option for good measure. So, it goes without saying that a lot of niggas had egg on their fucking faces when I came back with an overpriced piece of paper."

Me? In the spirit of reciprocity, I also decided to share some of my shit with him. And it was a really big one too:

"My relationship with food is not . . . great right now," I confessed.

"Okay. Do you want to—"

"I'm gonna talk. I just want you to listen."

Saying that my relationship with food was in the shitter right now was tame in comparison to what was actually happening.

After leaving high school, I managed to get my weight together in college for the most part by genuinely getting into sports and just allowing my body to do its thing. And even after my stint of downright horrible eating and straight-up disrespect to my body post–ACL injury and at the height of that edition of depression, I still kept it together for the most part in Knoxville—poverty aside. But when I got to California? Shieeeet. All bets were off.

The kind of poverty I had lived in upon moving there was unparalleled to anything I had ever experienced. And what had started out as a personal food shortage due to money soon morphed into the disordered eating that I knew and loathed. It was sick, I know. But anyone who has ever lived with an eating disorder knows why: it is often the only way we can retain some control in our lives. And I was very much in need of some control in this new *Californian* hellscape.

I explained the origins of my disordered eating to Emiliano. I explained how it reared its ugly head again when I moved out West. I painted a whole picture and elaborated on how Los Angeles in particular, and its aggressive diet, excessive fitness, and Lighter Than a Paper Bag supremacy culture had been beating my ass the whole time. Jumping my ass like the Avengers jumped Thanos while he was living out his own Farmville fantasy. Making it infinitely that much easier to backslide into my old ways and fuck up my relationship with food once again.

"And you wanna know the worst part?" I sighed into the phone.

"What?"

"I hate guacamole now. And avocado in general, to be honest," I confessed. "They put it in everything and anything and if I have to hear a whole spiel again about how *good* it is for you and how it's full of all these good monounsaturated and polyunsaturated fats—"

"NO—"

"Yep. Hate it. Can't stand it. Wish it never existed."

"We can't have that," he said. "I can't have that."

"So . . . what are you proposing?"

"I must take you on a date. A proper one! At once. You know, after I get the babysitter sorted," he explained. "And since I've clearly been charged with righting a cosmic wrong, I'm going to take you to one of my favorite restaurants on the planet."

"Which is?"

"None of your goddamn business," he responded. "Until . . . next weekend?" I let out the most dramatic and annoyed groan, causing Emiliano to laugh because he knew he had me. "Don't be like that! You know I gotta move some stuff around so you can come up here to San Francisco and we can hang out . . . *unimpeded*."

"I GUESS I can swing next weekend." We both laughed.

I WAS no stranger to dating. I had been on dates before. Most ranging from fair to middling to completely ass. And obviously, some nervousness always preceded said date.

This time, however? Going on the date that shall henceforth be known as Thee Date™? Nervousness was pushed aside in favor of the bigger gun: anxiety.

None of it had to do with my long February drive up to San Francisco, blasting "Take a Byte" through the speaker ad nauseam. Or even the fact that Emiliano refused to tell me which restaurant he was taking me to after we dropped my stuff off at his place (and in the spare room he had gussied up for me). Nope. All of it had to do with the fact that this was the first time I had seen him in person post-sliding into his DMs. I was also apprehensive about how I looked, as always; how I was supposed to act; or what I was supposed to say or do—given that this was my first *official* date with my friend.

Hell, it even felt a little weird realizing that I was on a *date*

date with him, rather than the standard friendship date where you catch up and whatnot.

But I'm no punk! I made sure I was there and right on time. Plus, I couldn't chicken out after like six hours of driving. Do you think I'm mad??? No!

Twenty-five minutes after my arrival, we were seated in booths across from each other. And in this hole-in-the-wall, ma-and-pa Mexican restaurant that he had been so secretive about. It was small, intimate, and cozy. And yet? I felt over-dressed in what I called my golden-brown "Lion Bae" wig and my black two-piece skirt set. You know, like the one Mariah wore to the MTV Awards in 1997? Yeah. Anyway, that senti-ment was put to bed rather quickly:

"You look—" Emiliano started.

"Em, respectfully, if you say beautiful or gorgeous—"

"Incredibly sexy."

"Huh?"

"You look incredibly sexy." He was cheesing like such a dork. "I'm sure you already know that, but I also wanted to say it."

"Touché, Mr. Silky." I let some of my guard down. "You look quite . . . dashing yourself."

"Dashing?" He tried not to laugh.

"What??? Calling you handsome would have been cliché as fuck too."

"Dashing though? Come on, you can do better than that, *writer*."

"Fine. Fine! Shit." I rolled my eyes and then got serious. "You look very . . . hot."

And he did. He truly did. He was wearing this dark suit. If you were squinting at it in the dark, you'd have guessed that it might be black. But nope. It was brown. The darkest brown. One that highlighted the lengthy hair adorning his shoulders. One that complemented his eyes—which were currently eating me up like my name was Fufu and I was sexily laid out across a bowl of Egusi soup.

It helped that he smelled good too. Again.

"Was that so hard?"

"*Incredibly* so, actually," I said. "I'm sorry, does this not feel *weird* to you?" I sat back in the booth. "Sitting here, like this, *romantically*, after all these years?"

"I mean, yeah. Kinda. But it doesn't have to actually *be* weird." He reached across the table and placed a hand over mine. I stared at it and God help me, I had to fight the 489632409842398 people that live in my brain just so I could resist the urge to ease it away—which would only make things weirder. Instead, I shot him a wry smile and turned myself back "on."

"All right. Okay. I'll play ball," I breathed. "But first things first: Where is this splendiferous food I was promised?"

"Splendiferous?"

"Sounds like something you would say in one of your good but possibly wordy papers." I laughed.

"Oh fuck off." He joined in on my laughter.

Shortly thereafter, Emiliano put in orders for both of us in Spanish, and because I had forsaken Duolingo and its borderline homicidal reminders to brush up on my Spanish, I had absolutely no idea what was headed for our table and just had to trust that everything was gonna be okay.

And that trust was absolutely taken to the brink when *multiple* dishes with avocado made it to our table. I looked at him as anyone who had just been betrayed would look. As expected, he avoided my gaze, thanked the server, and then began to list off the dishes in front of us.

"So, what we have here is seared scallop tacos with spring mango salsa and avocado cream, seedy arepas with black beans and avocado, bacon avocado fries, and fully loaded black bean nachos with red and green salsas—"

"Em—" I glared at him.

"Before you decide—"

"Nope. This is a setup. I've been shanghaied! Bamboozled," I interrupted him again. "Besides, how is *aggressively* exposing me to avocado going to *cure* my aversion to avocado?"

"Oh, well, that's easy. The dishes will actually be good this time!" He stared at my blank face and then continued, "Okay. How about this: if you try just a *bite* of all of these dishes and you still hate avocado, I'll order something completely different and you can retain your avocado beef. Deal?"

"Deal." I narrowed my eyes at him and then looked over at our collection of plates. ". . . Is that bacon wrapped around an avocado slice?"

"Yep and it's been deep-fried," he added. "Want some?"

"Yes." I reached toward the plate. Emiliano stopped me midway and brought the "fry" in question to my mouth. I hit him with a "really?" look and he shrugged. I thus allowed him to feed me. And he waited, with bated breath, for me to give my verdict.

"It's not . . . terrible."

"Pfft. Okay, Lex." Emiliano started laughing. "You know you liked it!"

"'Like' is a very strong word," I replied, joining in on the laughter. "Anyway, stop hogging the tacos!"

THE REST of the dinner continued without a hitch. By the time we were done eating and drinking, both of us had been reduced to both tears and obnoxious laughter. And it wasn't long before we decided to bounce and continue our date elsewhere.

Emiliano drove me to a spot overlooking most of the city and the lake below. I glanced over at him as he put the car in park.

"Do you bring *all* your lovers up here?" I cooed. He squinted at me and I laughed. "What? I'm just trying to make conversation. You don't have to answer that, by the way. I'm just fucking with you."

"Uh-huh," he added. "So. Tell me. How are we feeling about date number one?"

"Good," I started. "Well, great actually. You know, if I leave out the part where you ambushed me with avocados."

"You're never gonna let me live that down, are you?"

"Nope," I teased him. "But seriously. It's been a long time since I've been out on . . . one of these. And I had fun. Thank you." I grinned before letting my eyes wander down to the lights reflecting off of the lake.

"You're welcome," he responded. "*Had* though?"

"Yeah." I shrugged. "Why?"

"Date's not over, Lex."

"You and your technicalities." I rolled my eyes. "So what's next then?"

Some seconds passed, and when I didn't hear a response, I looked back over and found Emiliano staring at me. Not in a creepy way, either, but it was . . . it reminded me of that *Pacific Rim* movie night all those years ago. He was back in studying mode, except it was a million times more intense. He threw in a brief glance at my lips for good measure and then held that inescapable gaze of his with my eyes once again. I resisted the urge to open the passenger door and flop out. Instead, I looked down into my lap and tried to ignore the heat that was crawling up both sides of my face. I was absolutely relieved when I heard his phone vibrating, figuring that it would serve as a momentary distraction.

"Anyway. I want to thank you for urging me to try avocados again." I capitalized on the distraction by blurting out the first thing that my brain could conjure up. "It's safe to say that I like avocados again. And that I no longer have the desire to start dry heaving when I see them or any variation of them. Sort of. In small doses," I rambled. "And small dishes. It can totally be part of the meal, but I would prefer it if it wasn't the star, you know? I mean—"

I had finally managed to lift my head long enough to address Emiliano to his face and as soon as I did, his lips met mine.

I had two choices here.

I could act as if I was scandalized, lean back, and slap him like I was in yet another 1950s film or. OR. I could stop pretending as if I hadn't wanted to suck on his face after sharing *that* amorous hug outside of Dave & Buster's.

I most assuredly chose the latter.

At this point, the dam broke. And this regular-shmegular overlook turned into Make-Out Overlook™. Neither of us could unbuckle our seatbelts fast enough. I honestly lost track of where his face ended and mine began. Not to mention the fact that the telltale sign of a make-out session going, that is, foggy windows and mirrors, was hot on our heels.

Emiliano pulled back for a couple of seconds and grinned at me. He placed his forefinger under my chin so that my face was tipped toward his.

"I love hearing you talk. Absolutely adore the sound of your voice." He looked at me. "But sometimes . . . you talk too much."

"That's so rich coming from you, *academic*," I whispered back. He smiled at me again and proceeded to brush his lips just inches away from mine. I moved toward him to kiss him once more and he pulled back again. I tried to suppress an ugly face from emerging. And I get it. He was definitely teasing me. But when you find yourself in a make-out session that is this fucking fantastic, that can be slightly annoying. And of course, he felt my simmering annoyance because soon, he leaned back in and proceeded to dot the side of my neck with the softest kisses. A wanting sigh—no, a deliriously and dangerously horny sigh—escaped my mouth. He only paused to breathe against my skin and I'm not gonna lie. I thought he was about to do some freaky vampire shit with how much attention he was paying to my neck, but seeing as it felt this good? Who was I to ruin the fun?

"Jesus . . ." I closed my eyes once the neck kissing resumed.

"I could do this all night," he whispered.

"Yeah, no kidding." I was breathless. "Come here . . ."

I took his face into my hands and kissed him as fervently as I knew how. And he responded by easing me toward him and into his lap. I have no idea how much time had elapsed between me being transported from the passenger's seat, but I do know that said passage of time was accompanied by Emiliano's mouth finding its way to one of my nipples. I was about to take off the whole fucking crop top when his phone buzzed in his pocket again and ripped us out of our cloudy stupor. And certainly gave me quite the unexpected-but-very-much-appreciated shock.

Wink, wink.

"Oh shit." He glanced at a text.

"What?"

"We're late." He glanced at the confused look on my face and figured he needed to elaborate. "I mean, *I'm* late. Gotta go say goodnight to Lia."

"Ah!"

"I'm sorry about this." He rubbed the back of his head.

"There's nothing to be sorry about—"

"It's just, being a parent? All of this can be so hard and you have to strike the right balance or you'll fuck your kid up and—"

"You have responsibilities and Lia is one of them." I shrugged, returning to my seat. "It's late. Like really, *really* late. Our . . . side excursion aside." I offered him a smile. Emiliano looked relieved and proceeded to start the car, our destination set for his place. But mostly, I let my mind wander to the fact that, just moments ago, I was tonguing down someone's *father* right before he stuck one of my tits in his mouth.

Freaky shit, right?

MY NECK,
MY BACK,
MY VIRGINITY,
MY FAT

I know you.

I know that you're probably wondering whether Emiliano and I ended up sleeping together after our avocado excursion, a.k.a. Thee Date™.

And that is most certainly the right question to be asking.

I modeled the title of this chapter after the Khia song "My Neck, My Back." Yeah, I know. Obvious! But something about holding the chaotic and arid entity known as my sex life in conversation with such an incredibly vulgar and fun song speaks to me. Probably because it's what I wished my sex life was like for the longest time.

Imagine me, the Black female protagonist assertively telling her lover how to perform cunnilingus on her and spelling out exactly how to do it—correctly. And in great detail. Imagine me empowering myself, a Black woman, and imploring myself not to settle for a subpar sex life.

It was so tempting to live in this alternate reality in my head. Mostly because my own sex life was the exact opposite of all that ... for a long time. I found it hard to start my sexual journey. I'd been dealing with the baggage of fluctuating self-esteem as I tried to learn not to hate myself or my body at least a little bit. And having sex meant that I had to figure out how to not be terrified at the mere thought of removing my clothes and showing what lies beneath to another living and breathing human being.

So, if you've made it this far, you *know* that there is quite literally no part in this book where I indicate that I have *successfully* had sex. And part of that is because many times in life, it is way funnier to make a list of Ls over a list of wins—even though it sounds counterintuitive. My reasoning behind it mainly concerns "staying humble," but as I grow older, "humble" is a word I see weaponized far too often against the baddest bitches alive. Merely because they, indeed, recognize that they are, in fact, bad bitches.

That said, listing my Ls and mishaps where it concerns dating and sex, in particular, tends to remind me of how far I've come (no, I didn't make that pun on purpose, but hey). And how much I still need to learn to become the sexual demon that I've always wanted to Digivolve into, particularly as I approach my thirties.

So, before I get into whether Emiliano and I even did the deed, I'm gonna have to backtrack a couple of years. Probably a decade too. And pretend I never said any of the shit above this sentence.

Ahem.

I'll start with the fact that, as the title of this chapter suggests, I am, in fact, a virgin. Or was. For like twenty-four and a half years.

As I'm writing this, I'm currently twenty-seven (what a difference two and a half years make), and I don't know why it was such a big deal to me at the time that I was twenty-four and hadn't had sex yet. But Back Then™, it was a *huge* deal to me. I wasn't necessarily ashamed about not having had sex, but I didn't like that it was something I just had to carry around. And be stuck with. And have to explain and contextualize, lest I get jackhammered to death. Plus, I fucking hated the whole concept of being a "late bloomer." Both in name and description.

Of course, such attitudes were inspired by the horseshit I had swallowed for two decades about the concept of virginity. And sex in general. Thanks to good ol' Christianity.

I can't talk enough about how *efficient* Christianity was in its attempt to erase every fiber of me, the person currently writing this. My sense of self? Eroded. Confidence in my abilities as a person in general? Nonexistent. Self-respect? Shredded. My self-worth? HA.

And what Christianity did not thoroughly destroy, colorism and fatphobia tried to finish off. Every separate demon took turns trying to explain to me why I should be denied love—someone else's love and someone's *touch*. America's spin on Christianity already made sex a *vile* thing and stated that desiring it at all—even before one was to "have" it—was probably the greatest sin of all. Look at you. Sinner! But adding fatness to the mix? Oh boy.

To be clear, fat people be *fucking*! This is indisputable. And has been so since the beginning of time. And yet, the general populace could *never* fathom fat people engaging in the act of sex because they see us as "disgusting." Fatness was "disgusting." Is "disgusting." It was seen as a punishment for excess and one of the deadliest sins of all: gluttony. And as an already disgusting being, as the physical manifestation of an already reprehensible sin, how dare *I* even dare to *think* about engaging in the sin of (premarital) sex?

That was the other thing too. The impossible task of saving sex for "marriage." If marriage was even something you were into. Never mind that it's something that is really only applied to women to serve as some sort of testament to our tenacity or purity or righteousness or whatever the fuck. But somehow, saving it, virginity I mean, as something to break open like a fuck-ass present upon consummation of the marriage was somehow supposed to make the whole thing magical? Like you were supposed to get some sex power-up for waiting like a *true* lady.

Mind you, marriage is not gonna somehow unfuck your brain when it comes to these, frankly, demented religious attitudes about sex here. So many times, I witnessed folks I knew fighting for their lives every day as it pertained to having sex—even after they said "I do."

It's all a setup. And as you can imagine, it was the driving force behind the delay in my, for lack of a term that doesn't agitate me, sexual exploration journey.

The other part of it was navigating the obstacle course that was constructed by fatphobia doing the Charleston with colorism (AND featurism AND texturism). Even after I had cleared the religious hurdle. Dating sob stories aside, fatphobia in this context meant I should be *grateful* for crumbs and absolutely *ecstatic* if someone expressed even a sliver of desire for me. I should be *overcome* with feelings of *joy* for someone being *brave* enough to touch me! Adding colorism to the mix meant that I *had* to be "realistic" about my options and how to move if I encountered someone my shade who wasn't "into" someone *dating* my shade. And this circle of hell was intensified particularly because of LA's hard-on for the paper bag test.

It was a double negative practically. It's one thing to be fat. And another thing to be a darkie. But both? The horror.

Then. Then! I also had to be on the lookout for potential fetishists, even if I felt like I had done my homework about everything else. Because let's be honest. There are some that only desire that which they hate. Who they hate. Who they've been taught to abhor or despise.

Sometimes because it's fun (for them). Gets them off. Sometimes because it makes them feel better about their own "shortcomings" (because obviously being dark and being fat were the worst things one could ever be, right?). Sometimes because they just wanna feel like they're rebelling against something. Be it mommy. Daddy. Society? Whatever the fuck have you.

And I didn't want anyone's love or desire for me to have its origins in hate. I deserved better.

Or did I? After all, the summation of all this existed to teach me that I wasn't worth a damn. Wasn't worth "love." And definitely wasn't worth "laying with."

You know, biblical sex euphemisms and whatnot.

The debate on my worthiness, despite everything I mentioned above, raged in my head for years. It still makes its presence known every once in a while. But giving up the ghost (ha) with Christianity meant that I was going to find a way to yeet the oppressive box known as "virginity" into space and have to claw my way toward sexual liberation. Even if it killed me.

Even if it made my demisexual self want to curl up and *die*.

So, after college (which in itself had been a wash besides my dealings with Bruce), I tried to be aggressive—read: *intentional*—about "losing" it.

And it all started with a failed Tinder hookup.

NEARLY A year after graduating college and illegally co-bunking with Eve in her summer dorm in Knoxville for the next couple of months, I decided to "put" myself out there again.

By downloading Tinder.

As every sane person knows, this was my first mistake. Because doing so, firstly, meant that I was putting myself in the direct line of fire when it came to dealing with fetishists and generally unwell people. Cisgender men especially. And I mean fetishists of all kinds. BBW bandits and chubby chasers were bad enough, but now I had to contend with all the "I've never dated a Black girl" freaks and "You're pretty for a dark-skinned girl" lowlifes. Or someone who was just straight-up obsessed with the idea of me joining them in their jungle fever fantasies.

Disaster bisexuals like myself also knew the ramifications of declaring they were such as they braved this cesspool of a dating app. There were many downsides that discouraged announcing oneself as bi, particularly because you would almost exclusively be pursued by people looking for a third—either to experiment or oftentimes to save their marriage. But even if you just so happened to be into threesomes, the biggest potential downside of all was the threat of being bamboozled into one with a truly effervescent woman . . . who happened to be dating a sentient toe of a man.

And you can always see these types coming from far away too because all their profile pictures will be of the woman and be in 4K HD, while there's one blurry-ass picture of the man looking like a PS1 graphic.

Whatever the case, my dumb ass braved the app anyway and experienced every single scenario I mentioned above and then some. It truly tested the bounds of my own personal brand of masochism. And it took *months* for me to find a decent person to rid myself of my virginity with. I was determined to lose this shit. And I was determined to have a good time doing it.

Except they all turned out to be duds. To my utmost dismay.

The first dud happened when I met this fine-ass Black man. He was a lawyer. He was good with money. He was beautiful. Dark! Had this low-cut fade and this luscious beard that made his brown eyes pop. He took me out for drinks at a quiet and beautiful bar. I was *very* excited to get to know him and *also* sleep with him. He had been upfront about letting me know that being casual was all he could handle right now. Which worked for me.

The only hiccup was that, as it turned out, he wasn't a fan of eating pussy.

"You don't eat *what?!*" I exclaimed, jumping out of his bed and his Egyptian cotton (sigh) sheets.

I don't think I've ever pulled up my pants so fast. It was a tragedy! And a *waste* of a really good beard!!!

The second Tinder dud happened when I met this white man (don't start) at this almost excessively nice French restaurant. He was a bit older. Had some silver hair coming in among his dark black hair. But he was pretty handsome and had lips that looked like he stole them off Tom Hardy's face. He had been upfront about his intentions, too, like my last failed shag-mate, but he thought a little food and wine would be good. "Would loosen us up," I believe were his words.

Everything was going well—until he tried to order for me. *After* he didn't like what I ordered for myself. That in itself is a red flag, but it was exacerbated by the fact that I know, without a shadow of a doubt, that he did that because I had ordered what was, to him, probably an excessive amount of food. Because my several side dishes turned into a *glorified* salad.

And I was not amused.

"I was *fat* when you were talking to me on that stupid fucking app, you stupid fucking fatphobic cracker." I got up, grabbing my purse. "Don't let me see you again around here. Okay?"

The last dud came when I straight-up skipped the wine-and-dine portion of things and opted to meet this beautiful Black woman at a five-star hotel. She was dark, like me. And fat. She had long locs in—with the sides of her head shaved and a striking smile that was flanked with cute-ass dimples.

I remember knocking on the door, super excited that I was finally going to get this over with. She answered—sporting that same smile that had drawn me to her profile. I greeted her, ready to step inside.

And that's when the door opened wider and revealed her surprise toe-of-a-white-boyfriend. I looked up at him and then back at her.

I couldn't believe it. I had been hit with the ol' bait-and-switch-a-bi throuple scam and it had almost worked. I looked them up and down. Disgusted at their audacity and pissed that they had wasted my time.

"On second thought, you can go fuck yourselves!" I smirked, before walking off.

I know three tried-and-true Tinder dates might not feel like a lot to some of you, but I was fucking tired. Partly because dating in general took so much out of me emotionally. But also because time had made it increasingly obvious that my bisexuality had company: demisexuality.

Like, sure, the quality of my potential hookups turned out to be mid as fuck. But the added ingredient of what I considered a physical, sexual, and emotional burden at the time dialed up the difficulty to an eleven.

And I couldn't believe it! I could not *believe* how *impossible* this was proving to be.

I mean, I had crossed *multiple* state lines to get laid (I moved a lot in three years), and nothing was happening! My sex well was all dried up. Barren even!

By the time Emiliano reentered the picture, I was weary. Beaten down. Pessimistic. Dejected! On the cusp of a deep-seated bitterness. I had all but given up on trying to get laid and written it off as something that would just have to happen later in life. But his reemergence, which I now suspect wasn't a coincidence, sparked something for me and in me (don't be nasty). And our mutual confession of "like" meant that maybe, just maybe, I was gonna finally be able to remove the technically fictitious albatross known as virginity from around my neck.

I know what you're thinking.

How serendipitous of Emiliano to show up and make this all infinitely easier for me. Particularly for bi me. Which, you know, isn't exactly the most erroneous line of thinking. But our emotional compatibility still faced some additional hurdles on my end.

The main one?

You may think it was him being a dad, but nope. Emiliano was a Lite-Brite. A Fenty 220 through and through. With the hair to match. I'm talking high-end weave bundles. If you're into that? And while he was fit, he was, once again, on the slimmer side.

I know. ¡Escándalo! And it *sure* did produce several ideological conflicts for me. Not on some "It doesn't align with my politics" kind of shit, because politics fluctuate based on what you know and what you're willing to be educated on. But because it meant that I *did* have to have an honest conversation with myself about *who* I was attracted to, or rather *what* I was attracted to.

Living in this crackerjack hellscape had me *constantly* questioning if what I "liked" was *genuinely* what I "liked" or various forms of self-hatred manifesting into a "like." I sat with myself and asked if I was only attracted to him because he was much lighter and the optics of that. Or if I only wanted to jump into bed with him because I wouldn't have a part of myself that I had been trained to loathe for so long mirrored back to me. Or if I only wanted to fuck him because the combination of all this arbitrary-yet-very-real bullshit meant that he was "attractive" and sleeping with him meant that I would potentially look or feel attractive by proxy.

You think I'm joking, but I'm not. All desire is political. All dating preferences are political. And I did want those things at one point. I'm not afraid to admit that. These were the standards that had been held up for me to chase all the way back to childhood. But I *wasn't* a child anymore. And if I wanted to have a good time fucking, I wanted it to be for the right reasons. Not because I was being *told* what to want and just blindly going with it.

Hell, this was one of the top three reasons that I had sat on my feelings for Emiliano for so long. I needed to know that the part of me that was fighting to live above these oppressive forces . . . was also the part of me that wanted to fuck the shit outta him.

And as it turns out, months of getting to re-know each other revealed that yes, I did in fact like-like him for reasons that remained true to the best version of myself.

But don't think that I was out of the woods yet. Finding the right person for the right reasons was just *half* of the battle. Clueing Emiliano in on the various psychoses that I was contending with sexually was gonna be the other half of the battle. As was being forthcoming about my virginity and how I felt about it. Because I wanted both of us to be prepared.

It took me a minute to work all of this into one of our hours-long talks, where we discussed *everything*. I didn't want to randomly go "Hey, I'm a virgin! How do you feel about that?" But I admit that I kind of painted myself into a corner with the fact that a) I was exceedingly knowledgeable about sex and hella curious about it too, and b) I had been very vocal about what I wanted to do sexually, what I wanted to be done to me sexually, and what I wanted to try sexually. Plus, Twitter was chock-full of funny tweets and memes about sex, and since our lines of communication contained like 60 percent of both of those things, I threw that in too. Except that I sorta kinda went overboard with it.

Basically, I was trying—was I necessarily succeeding? Who knows—to project this sexually mature version of myself to the world . . . while also trying to collect as much intel on sex as I could so I could avert any and all sexual disasters—big or small.

Case in point, I knew, as someone who had a vagina and was new to fucking, that I *had* to be aware of his dick size. For my own safety, comfort, and enjoyment. I'm not going to get into the politics or potential ramifications of what it means for it to be "bigger" or "smaller." But what I will say is that, on one hand, I wanted to *feel* something during sex. And on the other hand, I wasn't quite ready to feel said *thing* in my *chest*. Particularly because a lot of you motherfuckers out there don't know what to do with a *thing* of that size.

Plus, part of the reason I was so knowledgeable was that I was very much into doing research. Which meant that I had purchased many a sex toy—including dildos—to simulate the actual experience and make sure I was, ahem, well-equipped to *handle* whatever Emiliano whipped out. And, full disclosure, my experimenting made it abundantly clear that I was not quite ready for, say, an *anaconda*. Or an Arizona Iced Tea can. In literally every sexual way you can think of.

I didn't necessarily know how to bring all of this up with him.

While we'd shared some slightly saucy pictures of ourselves, we hadn't shared full-on nudes yet. And I'm sure it's because neither of us wanted to be *that person* and be the *first* person to ask. But I was running out of time . . . and patience.

So. It turned out to be me.

It happened on a random day. Like a Thursday. I was sprawled out across my bed, half-dressed and wig chilling beside me because why the fuck not? Yet again, we were talking each other's ears off well into the morning. We caught each other up on our respective days and then it quickly morphed into one of our "getting to know each other" sessions. This edition taking the form of a sexual twenty-one questions. The beginning consisted of sharing some of our tamest and wildest fantasies. Later we delved into favorite body parts, as in parts we liked about ourselves. I chose my hips. He chose his lips, which, touché.

But as time passed, I was running out of, well, "appropriate" questions to ask. So, I eventually decided to pull out the big gun and just get it over with.

"So. I kinda don't wanna be that person, but since we *are* planning to fuck each other's brains out, there's something I want to ask you. You know, for logistics purposes," I said.

"Go on . . ."

"Uh, so. I'm trying to ask this in a way that's not . . . trashy."

"It can't be that bad."

"Okay, but you haven't heard me say it yet." I hesitated. "So. What I want to ask you is—"

"You wanna know how big my dick is?" He finished my sentence.

If I had not been so hyperfocused on my own anxiety about asking this question, I might have gasped. Instead, I opted for momentary silence while I tried to frantically reassemble my thoughts.

"It didn't sound as crass in my head." I coughed. "But now that you've said it—"

"It's okay. I figured it was something you'd want to know." He chuckled.

"So?"

"On one hand, size is relative and varies from person to person, you know?" he started. "But it's easy for me to say that as the person it's attached to."

"Right." I nodded.

"*I* think it's a perfect size," he added. "A good size. Not cartoonishly disproportionate on either side of the scale as far as dick sizes go. But . . . I'm biased."

"Which means?"

"Short answer? Dissuade yourself from believing that I'm packing, say, an eggplant. Because I'm not. But . . . I will say that Señor Senior is, ahem, still in the family of everyone's favorite fruit."

"I have several questions." I laughed. "But first . . . vegetable."

"Perdón?" he replied.

"Vegetable. Eggplant is a *vegetable*."

"Um. No, it's not. It's a fruit."

"You're a liar."

"Oh? So what do you call something that grows from a flowering plant and contains seeds?" He kept talking before I could interject. "Exactly. Go look it up."

"Nope. Wrong again." I rolled my eyes. "It's a *nightshade vegetable*. Like peppers or tomatoes or potatoes—"

"Hey, Lex?"

"Yeah?"

"Look at your phone."

I raised an eyebrow. "Why?"

"You'll see."

I made a face before putting him on speaker and tapping the message banner on my phone where his name had just popped up. My eyes got super big upon looking at its contents.

What awaited me, ladies and gentlemen, people of the world, was Emiliano's dick.

Was I caught off guard? Not totally. I mean, the photo was more than relevant considering what we had just been discussing. I just didn't think he would've sent it so fast. It did make me feel slightly less awkward about bringing it up though!

I continued to stare at the photo and turn it over in my thoughts. It pained me to say it, but it probably was one of the prettiest dicks I'd ever seen. And I say that in complete earnest, particularly because I had always found dicks to be . . . kinda fugly; I'm not gonna lie. And it didn't help that I had received so many *unsolicited* dick pics from cishet men in my minuscule twenty-four years on this planet. To the point that I could make a whole fuck-ass collage of them. But, no, he looked . . . really good. Wasn't too big. Wasn't too small. Perfectly manicured, perfectly tanned, with great posture, and *highly* photogenic. It was a dick that I was now very interested in sucking. And sticking in other places. Obviously.

I smirked. "You don't disappoint."

"Don't jinx it, there's still time," Emiliano quipped.

"If you just don't take the compliment!"

The conversation didn't end there either. As I said, we enjoyed talking until one of us felt the urge to pass out for the night. But on this night, there wasn't a lick of sleep in either of our bones or voices. So the talking continued. It went on for so long that eventually, we circled back to something more serious. Something that was time for me to share.

"Can I say something?" I piped up.

"Anything."

"Before we do this—"

"Sex, you mean—"

"Yes, sex; I gotta fill you in on some shit," I continued. "Like, you know. Baggage shit."

"I feel that. Go right ahead."

So, I gave him the good ol' spiel, dear reader, that I gave you at the start of this chapter.

I talked about how I had constantly had to absorb violent

fatphobia and passive-aggressive colorism from nearly every single "family" member just because they happened to be having a bad day that day. And even from my greater "community." I shared all the ugly shit: Starvation. The binge eating. The *purging*. The period where I was exercising way more than I was actually eating. The nagging thought that if I lost enough weight, people would not necessarily "love me" per se—even though that is part of it. Don't let anyone lie to you. That's always part of it. There is absolutely nothing wrong with wanting to be loved.

But nah, that wasn't quite what I wanted. Honestly? I just wanted to be left alone. Not ignored (because God knows colorism and fatphobia simultaneously grant you both invisibility and [self-]revilement), but very much free of the torment wrought upon me by my "family." Free of niggas both telling me to "finish every fucking crumb" on my plate or "cut back on eating" and "save some for the rest of us" if I ever wanted to be "marriage material."

I also got into how religion had exacerbated it all. Or rather, how being an ex-Christian was still a mindfuck in its own right. That shitty-ass Abrahamic religion had shaved years off my life. Stole my youth. And gave me quite the complex about having sex in general.

All because of what was considered "sinful" and worthy of so-called shame.

I talked about the latter topic for quite a while. It spanned a day or two. And he listened. And because he was consistently perceptive, he did eventually ask me about how that affected my desire to sleep with him. To which I answered:

"That is an excellent question."

"Is it a question you plan on answering?" I swear I could hear him raising an eyebrow through the phone.

I took a breath, while he quickly added, "Not to say that I'm *demanding* to know or something. I'm not nosy and I would never pry. But I just want to make sure I know all there is to know about this. And that I don't accidentally pile on any other negative experience that you've had in terms of sex or even discussing sex."

"I have no problem discussing *intercourse* with you if that's what you're asking. The prudent and sex-repulsed Jesus Freak in me died long ago. Was shot dead even," I finished, as I heard him chuckle on the other side. "But your question is a valid one and I do have something to say as it pertains to that."

"Oh?"

" . . . Yeah."

"Should I be afraid? Or . . . worried?"

"I mean, it depends." I sighed. "I . . . honestly don't know how to say this, but I just know it needs to be said. It needs to be something you're aware of."

"Okay. Just lay it on me, Lex. I'm here. I'm listening."

Oh, how good it felt to hear those words and feel them floating around in my ears like the most infectiously good song. I wanted to grab hold of them forever and not have to say what I needed to say next. But the moment came and went. And I knew I had to be a big girl and spit it the fuck out.

And that's what I did.

"I'm a virgin," I nearly coughed.

When I tell you that the deadliest silence gripped my phone line. And to be clear, in hindsight, I'm sure said silence wasn't more than three or four seconds long. But to me? Someone who *loathed* sharing anything remotely vulnerable about myself? It felt like whole eons were zooming past me.

"Come again?" Emiliano finally answered.

"If you're having second thoughts about this whole thing, it is perfectly fine to say that." I immediately regretted opening up and started to walk everything back. "I'd rather you say it now and we just end things here than fuck me over later."

"No, no, it's not that. It's not like that—"

"So, what is it?"

"I just thought—"

"You just thought—"

"Lex."

"Em."

Some more seconds passed.

"Fine. Go ahead. Speak. You have the floor," I said.

"You telling me this doesn't scare me. If that's what you're worried about."

"So what does it do then?"

"It's . . . I *am* a little surprised. If I'm being candid."

"Why?"

"You're just so—"

"Forward? Vulgar? Horny?" I laughed.

"No. Worldly."

"Elaborate."

"I mean, besides being very, no, *exceedingly* educated about sex, you just strike me as someone who *knows* what she's doing and someone who has bedded—is that a word? Bedded her share of lovers." He laughed. "I mean, that is to say, I made an assumption, which I shouldn't have, considering things like asexuality exist and all that shit. But in my defense, you're quite charming. And irresistible. I just—I imagined people throwing themselves at you, to be frank."

I smiled.

"Flattery isn't going to get you laid faster; I hope you know that." I giggled.

"But is it flattery if it's true though?"

"I'd say so." I laughed louder.

"Of course you would." He joined in.

SO BACK to Thee Date™. Our night most assuredly did not end after driving away from my new favorite make-out spot. Nor was Emiliano about to let it.

Sometime later, after everything had gotten sorted and it was confirmed that Lia was going to be staying with his cousin, Adoncia, for the night, Emiliano and I made out in his living room for some time. With *The Haunting of Hill House* playing to an audience of no one in the background. Our second lip-lock session had started with me poking fun at the red lipstick prints I left on his neck in the car and before you knew it, we were *gone*. It wasn't until I finally said that I needed to change into something more . . . *comfortable* that he finally let me go.

I remember what he was wearing. What we both were wearing. Right before we ripped each other's clothes off. Well, not exactly ripped. More like gingerly yanked off, if I'm being completely honest. I had snuck off to the bathroom to put on this lacy red number and when I returned, he was waiting on the bed with some impressively silky gold shorts. I raised an eyebrow as I hit the light switch by the door, made my way over, and started to crawl toward him on the bed.

"You sure about this?" He met my raised eyebrow with his own. I nodded, flattered by his concern.

"Is that for me?" I motioned at his shorts. "You shouldn't have."

"I feel like it would have been rude not to." I smirked as I reached for the lamp next to his bed. As I was about to flip the switch to turn it off, his hand gently came over mine.

"I wanna see you."

"No, you really don't."

"Lex—"

"It doesn't even matter because *I* don't."

"Do you *really* want your first time to be in pitch-black darkness?"

"No," I responded, sitting back on my heels. "But I'm . . . scared. I'm scared! There. I said it. I'm fucking scared, okay?"

"Of what?" Emiliano looked even more concerned.

I *really* wanted to tell him that my mortification when it came to being *completely* naked in front of someone else was still alive and well. I thought me gassing myself for the last week would have finally put the shit to rest, but here we were.

I was frightened. I was feeling the kind of *raw* fear that Janelle described in "Don't Judge Me."

"I don't know what you're thinking. But I could probably make a good guess." His voice cut in on my thoughts. "But if my guess is correct, I'd say that . . . you shouldn't think about any of that. Just . . . focus on *how* you feel and *what* you feel and what feels . . . *good.*"

"And how am I supposed to do that? Since you know everything." I eyed him. Emiliano eyed me right back, and I cleared my throat, knowing that the last part of my statement hadn't been necessary. "Sorry."

"It's okay. As I was saying, the fastest and most efficient way to disconnect from any physical insecurities you might have during sex is to remember one thing: no one *technically* looks 'good' during sex."

"I'm not sure I follow . . . ?"

"Listen. It's one thing to look aesthetically pleasing in general, pre–hitting the sack, but that's not the point. The point is that getting down and dirty means that you're gonna be making a lot of ugly or downright atrocious faces. Or making really *weird* fucking sounds. Or contorting your body in ways that you didn't think possible." He tilted his head to the side. "But none of that shit matters because most motherfuckers aren't having sex because of *aesthetics.* They're having sex because *it feels good.*" I glanced at him, taking in his words.

"Feels good, huh?" I weighed his words. "Fine. Then show me."

"All right. You asked for it." He smirked.

Emiliano wasted no time. He laid me down on the bed and I caught this fleeting look of, for lack of a better phrase, devilish horniness flash across both eyes. And to be fair, I was absolutely *terrified!* Scared shitless. I had no fucking idea what to expect. And yet . . . I was like 200 percent sure that I was in the right hands.

He leaned back down and our lips and tongues met in the

middle, forming hungry, frenetic, and urgent kisses. But also soft. *Light.* Like feathers.

Seriously, this guy had pillows for lips.

How dare he!

I flipped us both over at lightning speed until I was on top of him. He peered at me with a face both full of bewilderment and anticipation. Right as he was about to bring his lips together to form a sentence, I put my finger on them and smiled.

"Shhh," I whispered as I eased my face farther and farther down his chest, his stomach, and his waist until my mouth found its target.

"Oh—whoa!" he yelled out. "Where did you—*when* did you—"

"I've been practicing." I tilted my head up briefly. I just knew I had the smuggest look on my face and it honestly brought me sheer joy. "With bananas and dildos, nigga."

"Yes. Yes, you have." Emiliano chuckled before I went back down.

I'm gonna be honest. I barely have any recollection of when my lingerie came off after that. But by the time I realized it had happened, this nigga was gleefully and proudly wearing my legs as earmuffs. Chowing down and going to *town.* Worshipping whatever god he had found between my legs.

It's kind of difficult to sum up what it was like having sex with someone like Emiliano. But right off the bat? I'd say that it was . . . *dark.* Holy! Loving. Nasty. PRIMAL!

In fact, if I was to give this romp a theme, I probably would say *balance.* Mostly because thanks to his lead, we both did this sexily precarious dance between fucking like we were auditioning for WWE and making love like we were in a scene straight from *The Notebook.* Case in point, I softly kissed his lips, his nose, and his forehead before basically leapfrogging onto his face . . . and waiting tongue. There was also a moment when Emiliano left a trail of light kisses down my back. Kissing it as delicately as one might kiss their lover's forehead . . . right as he had me pinned down in quite the position. And one that simultaneously left his bed frame, ahem, loose and crooked as hell and would be one of the reasons I was fond of backshots from that point forward.

It wasn't all serious though. There was a moment when I was riding him so fervently that my knee made this weird creaking noise and then subsequently gave out. I felt so self-conscious about it, but I remember Emiliano placing his hands back on my hips and asking if my knee needed an oil break. I called him a dickhead and he laughed. There was another moment where we were so eager to tongue each other down while our bits were interlocked that we accidentally knocked teeth and it left both of us stunned for like two seconds. I'm sure any normal person or persons might be slightly embarrassed by such. But both of us looked at each other and burst into the ugliest laughs known to man. Then we got right back down to business when he grabbed me by the throat with gusto! And in a sudden display of strength. I raised my eyebrow in a "touché" way and before I knew it, we sank back into the bed, ready to devour each other some more.

Devour is an apt word here, too, mainly because that's what Emiliano did to all the parts of my body that I was anxious about seeing in action. My love handles lived up to the term; he was insistent on reaching for them, as if to anchor me from floating away. My famous pendulum-like breasts found their way into his hands and his mouth more than once—a win-win for both of us. And he kissed my large belly just as fervently as he kissed my lips—if not more so. It was an interesting paradox for me. Having someone adore the parts of my body I had been taught to despise for the longest time.

I'm not embarrassed to say that I made some ungodly noises. Just like he said I would. Seriously. Some sounds happened to be the kind that could potentially trigger a 911 call. Other sounds one might have mistaken as sound bites from *The Exorcist* if you just so happened to be passing through the neighborhood. Of course, every noise I made seemed to get Emiliano going even more so than the last noise, and pretty soon he was making his own—right into my waiting ears. His were soft moans, just barely above a whisper. Intertwined with the filthiest string of expletives I had ever heard. All punctuated by the sound of my name. Waves of shivers washed down my spine. Weak in the knees didn't even begin to describe it. I nipped at his face, thankful for his vulnerability.

By the time we were "done," in the climactic sense anyway, we had become a pile of sweat, nakedness, disheveled hair, and tangled limbs.

Did I mention that I love how sex smells too? Never thought I would be typing this shit, but here I am.

I wrapped a lock of Emiliano's hair around my finger, curiously peering up at him. And by the looks of it, he was peering right back. As always, he had settled back into "studying" me with his eyes, except this time that meant he was moving his eyes along my face, with his thumb following close behind. With his other hand on my stomach.

My mind was hazy. But it was a *good* kind of hazy. Like when you hit a really good blunt and ascend into space. Focused, for once, not on how stressful it was for me to be comfortably naked by myself or naked around another person, but instead on the fact that postcoital bliss was *real*. And that I was happy to be sharing that kind of euphoria with someone I had liked and respected for a long time.

My eyes drifted over to the window. Inch by inch, sunlight was seeping into the bedroom, making both of us keenly aware that the next day had arrived. I looked back at Emiliano with the tiniest frown. He gave me a reassuring smile before kissing me lightly. A smile, despite its bitterest of undertones, tugged at the corner of my mouth.

"Good morning." He leaned back. His voice was soft.

"Good morning," I whispered. "Enjoying the view?"

"I am."

"Good," I replied, before issuing the question that was at the forefront of my already-delirious mind:

"Would you like to do it again?"

"I thought you'd never ask."

Emiliano grinned, his mouth capturing mine in a surprise but welcome kiss. We kissed slowly. Deliberately. Letting the words he had just shared sink between us. His lips instinctively moved to my neck and I let out a familiar sigh. His hands floated down my back, caressing my love handles and dancing down its curvature until he grabbed my backside in such an authoritative manner that I paused to look at him.

"Oh, so it's like that?" I smirked.

"It most certainly is." His grip tightened. "Do you mind?"

"No," I replied, letting my hand wander down his sweaty body and light happy trail. I was met with a sharp inhale, his eyes finding my mischievous ones. "Do you mind?"

"Not at all." He smiled and before I knew it he had pulled me on top of him. I happily obliged him, pouncing on him before deepening our kiss.

MY UNOFFICIAL GOODBYE

That was *quite* the end to a chapter, wasn't it?

I'm sure it was. And it's an experience that remains burned into my brain now that it's done cooking—with me being twenty-seven and all.

In fact, it was such an enjoyable and memorable experience for me that I would love to say that it eventually led to something more, I'd say, tangible. I'd love to lie to you all and say that our fling had some sort of happy ending. That it took the form of some whirlwind romance that eventually resulted in us declaring our endless love for each other.

Which, as you know, is peak rom-com brain.

Still, that's not how things proceeded. Because that's not how life is. Which is okay! Completely normal in fact. But I'm not afraid to look at my past self and my past experiences and tell you that our fling only got bumpy from there.

I was primarily concerned with the fact that I had just been let go from a Prestigious Magazine™ job and lived in a city where the cost of living is a crime against humanity. But my other concerns included my increasingly fragile mental state. Besides the money/survival aspect, I *still* had a lot of conflicting feelings about sex. As someone who had just been *officially* introduced to the act, I was still struggling with "virginity" propaganda floating around in my head. And my continued experimenting with "casual" sex was exacerbating that.

On the flip side, Emiliano was dealing with the mounting pressures of being a custodial parent and a student who was three seconds from finalizing their divorce. There were things, time-sensitive things, that he had to tend to—like figuring out custodial arrangements for Lia. Figuring out how he was going to pay for his second mortgage—a.k.a., daycare. And trying to navigate exactly where he was going with his degree. Trying to figure out the point of it all.

Naturally, that meant that he wasn't overly concerned with *centering* my feelings. Nor should he have been—considering what the hell he had on his plate. That much I will admit. I *was* pretty selfish when it came to trying to get his attention and monopolize his time. But I wasn't alone in my selfish behavior.

You see, we had never really had a *real nigga* conversation about what had gone down. You know, the post-sex talk. Like a legitimate decompression session. Even though we had already had sex a couple of more times after that first night. There were small tidbits and throwaway lines of "How did it feel?" or "Did you like it?" or "Could I have done anything better?" from both sides. But there was never really a conversation about how introducing sex into the equation that was our relationship was sure to change things.

Whether we liked it or not.

Sure. I would never forget how it felt to share what turned out to be such a beautiful moment with a friend like Emiliano. It was phenomenal. And still serves to be a benchmark *today* in terms of weeding out motherfuckers who want me to accept anything less than stellar sex. And sure, my friend had gotten to see a completely different side of me. One that he liked *very much*. And one that he had figured he missed out on when neither of us said shit about our feelings to begin with.

But as a pair, we were shitty at trying to discuss those things. Things like boundaries. Expectations. Needs. Plus, my behavior was getting increasingly erratic (keep reading). Too erratic to have a mature discussion about changing dynamics. And I was two seconds from being a clingy dumpster fire of a person. On Emiliano's end, he opted to go the avoidant route, both in discussion and action. He didn't want to get *too* into discussing any possibly *intensified feelings* in the aftermath, and he avoided the topic aggressively if it sounded like it was about to come up. I'm sure this was because it was something he couldn't even *afford* to think about right now (i.e., his divorce), even if he did have feelings. There was an acknowledgment of what happened between us, but no clear acknowledgment of what was to happen *next*.

So we both just opted to *try* to keep it simple. Very casual. Be completely detached from any and all outcomes, lest anyone be disappointed.

And I'm not saying that that was a bad plan. But I am saying that it was a *shitty* plan for people like me. People like Emiliano. People who had a multitude of feelings that weren't exactly easy to suppress or detach from—no matter how these emotions *physically* manifested.

It ended up putting an *incredible* amount of strain on our relationship. I wasn't fond of his casual dismissal and avoidantly attached approach, which always happened when conversations got too "personal." And he wasn't thrilled about my anxiously attached ways and my insistence on spending a certain amount of time with him.

All in all, it eventually led to a big fight that summer in June 2019, where words were exchanged and feelings were hurt.

"I don't know what you want me to say. I've been *busy*, okay?" Emiliano snapped.

"Busy is *not* the same as *avoidant!*" I remember screaming into my phone. I had just come back from a really exhausting press junket. And was sitting in my car. "You don't care about me at all, do you?!"

"That's really what you think?" Emiliano scoffed.

"Well, that's really how you act!"

"I can say the same thing about you!"

That was just the tip of the iceberg that was this argument, to be clear. Both of us kept it going and some shit was said that I won't even write here because it damn near almost ended our friendship.

Still, eventually, and *miraculously*, the anger in our words died down and we proceeded to end the argument and try to talk about what we were really upset about.

"There's no winning with you lately." Emiliano sighed into the phone. "Or me, if I'm being honest. What gives? What happened here?"

"I don't know. You tell me. Since you like avoiding everything," I snarked. I heard Emiliano sigh again. "I'm sorry. I'm just . . . angrier than usual."

"Because of us?"

"No? Well, not just because of us. It's everything," I said. "It's work. It's my apartment. It's . . . me." I paused. "I've . . . kinda been purging again. And throwing up. And also starving myself. You know, that depression-weight yo-yo is a bitch, amirite?" I lightly chuckled and then stopped myself. "So, it's safe to say that I'm not doing great *and* that what's going on between us is definitely not . . . helping."

"Alex . . ."

"Yeah."

"I'm so sorry," he added.

"Yeah."

My vulnerability subsequently got us started on a conversation about how Emiliano wasn't doing so hot either—with all his school and parental responsibilities bearing down on him. He had felt odd about sharing how stressed out he was with me post-sex, but hearing me speak on my shit prompted him to speak on his. I of course hoped the conversation was going to end with some happy conclusion or resolution.

But eventually, we both decided that we needed an extended break.

From each other.

I CAN'T say that I wasn't devastated. Or that I wasn't heartbroken. Because I was. I was both of those things. I remember crying and dry heaving in my bed because I had internalized it somewhat. And with me being in the thick of a resurgence of several eating disorders, I had resorted to blaming my body, my fat, as the primary reason that my friend didn't want me. I felt horrible. Absolutely worthless. And I was quickly approaching a very dark place.

A place that I hadn't been in since I tried to commit suicide during college.

Thankfully, Taurean pride kicked in. And my Taurean pride wasn't about to let me even *think* about offing myself again this time around. And it's a good thing it kicked in, too, because many, *many* months had passed and your girl was down . . . catastrophically bad.

At the time, any fluctuation in happiness or even sadness was quickly followed by excessive spending I couldn't afford or the delicate balance of paying all my bills on time crumbling underneath me once again. These poor money-making decisions—and the stress of them—immediately translated into a change in appetite. Less money to work with because of emotionally charged stupidity translated into less food in my mind. And I didn't even think to question it, even as it damaged my already fraught relationship with food and body, and drove my increasingly erratic behavior.

My nerves were fried, man. I was anxious. Irritable! The littlest shit would set me off. I remember thinking—prior to our break—that Emiliano was making fun of me after he sent a particular emoji, one with its tongue sticking out, punctuating my telling him about a harrowing parking story. When in actuality, upon reading it back, he was poking fun at a time when the same thing had happened to him.

My libido, which had been thoroughly—ahem—*awakened* post-romp with Emiliano, died. Shriveled up like a raisin in the sun and nothing could revive it. I tried to fill its absence by rechanneling my creativity into TV scripts I was working on—effectively distracting myself. The lack of sleep I was experiencing also fueled my need to creatively redirect. Insomnia had been a lifelong, annoying-ass roommate for sure, but these days? It had worsened. Like, I used to be able to nap, at the very least, but even that joy evaporated. I was just raw-dogging the day now—being wired as fuck. The only thing that was able to help me stave off full-blown mania was the fact that I was *abusing* the *fuck* out of weed, particularly edibles. Like if I shared the amount of money I spent feeding that beast, you'd scream.

Anyway that worked for a while . . . until the irritability and anxiousness swung back in the opposite direction. I went from being the Energizer Bunny to being a narcoleptic Eeyore.

Of course, turning into narcoleptic Eeyore meant that my burst of creativity evaporated and now I was faced with a mountain of missed deadlines and work that wasn't even close to being done. There was no motivation to be found anywhere and I was too embarrassed to admit it to anyone—especially to editors waiting on overdue articles. The environment around me suffered too—with the universal telltale sign of depression, water bottles, quickly stacking up in my bedroom.

Guilt due to lack of productivity—and lack of control over my emotional regulation—ate me up from the inside. I felt like a stupid, childish, and crazy piece of shit, and at one point I had to laugh because it all just seemed so silly. Like . . . why was I like this?

And *that's* when the suicidal thoughts kicked open my door like Big Bird.

By the time I registered that my suicide ideation was back and more dangerous than ever, I finally got around to seeing a psychiatrist, Dr. Charlise Wilson. I was still seeing Dr. Siddiq, but my gut just *knew* that I needed additional help. Mainly because after some weeks of finding the energy to take self-diagnostic tests and narrow down specific disorders, I figured the subject of medication was gonna come up soon. But also? Racial bias, however "unconscious," was ironically proving to be a barrier to Dr. Siddiq seeing that I was dealing with something much deeper than simple depression.

This became clear when I first approached Dr. Siddiq in October with the disorder I suspected I was dealing with: bipolar disorder.

"I believe you," she said. I remember sitting across from Dr. Siddiq in one of our routine sessions. "But I just can't . . . put it together in my head? If that makes sense." She tapped her pen against her clipboard. "Are we *sure* that this isn't just anxiety stemming from uncertainty between you and Emiliano?"

"That's just it, though. This is *beyond* him."

Some time passed.

"I just . . . I hesitate to hand down that diagnosis because lesser doctors love to slap it on women of color—"

"And I get that but—"

"And the gaps of time experienced between these symptoms you've described make me think—"

"Dr. Siddiq!" I snapped. "I'm sorry, but if you're not gonna listen to me on this, then I'll just have to end our session early and find someone who will." Woundedness briefly—and I do mean briefly—flashed across her face when I called her out. But rather than instantly reacting as an immature "professional" might have, she took a deep breath before standing up to search for something on her desk. For a second, I wondered what the fuck she was doing . . . until she returned with Dr. Wilson's business card and handed it to me.

"I'm sorry. For being hardheaded," she said.

"Thank you." I grasped the card in my hand.

Weeks later, I was in my fourth meeting with Dr. Wilson. In November. On this particular day, she leaned back in her chair and studied me for the majority of our session. It was kind of funny because leaning back led to her perfectly picked-out Afro being squished by the chair somewhat. But she was so focused that she didn't even notice. I was a little weirded out by it, but I continued to speak because I figured she was doing it for an important reason.

By the time I stopped talking, Dr. Wilson said something that would prove to be a pivotal revelation in my life:

"Alex . . . I *do* think you have bipolar disorder."

My eyes got wide. Did she just . . . *confirm* my hypothesis?

I thought I misheard her. I truly did. And for obvious reasons, like the stigmas associated with bipolar disorder, I was hoping that she was lying through her teeth—even if I *had* heard her right. Even if that *was* something I had expected all along.

"So . . . are you telling me that I have both depression *and* bipolar disorder?

"No," Dr. Wilson continued. "Bipolar disorder is often misdiagnosed as depression in young girls first, and then women much later. This is doubly the case for someone like you and even me. Black women. Because fuck our mental health, right?" She smiled sadly. "I'm gonna have to run some tests to see if it is bipolar I or bipolar II. But I just want you to know that, whatever it is, we're gonna get you the help you need."

"Okay." I smiled weakly at her.

Now that I'm older, I know that I should have been relieved. I should have been grateful that Dr. Wilson finally put a name to the ugly mental space I was in. And perhaps the ugly mental space I had always existed in thanks to a handy-dandy mix of genetics (i.e., my father, the narcissist *and* the schizophrenic) and an environment that still has me waking up in a cold sweat *today*. But . . . I wasn't relieved at the time. To me, it was just another problem that I had to add to my smorgasbord of problems. It was just another issue that I had to deal with. Just more evidence of what was "wrong" with me. Not to mention all the time lost trying to "diagnose" it.

So. If you're counting, I was fat, Black, dark-skinned, queer, physically disabled, and *now* mentally disabled.

And yeah, yeah, yeah, that's a fucked way to look at it considering that the world around me wants me to think these things of myself—that I'm some glitch that happened to make it through the walls of Gaia's creation. But twenty-five years of pain and suffering I had to endure because of every single marginalization I mentioned above meant that ya girl was in a bad place. I was down on myself. There was no upside for me. Especially not with this new revelation.

I ended up crying on the phone to Neal later that week.

Since college, Neal had proudly assumed the role of my big sister. Her own bio sister hadn't been shit either, so we intrinsically understood each other. And because of this built-in understanding, Neal had been worried *sick* about me moving to California with Eve at the time. Mainly because she was hyper-aware of the ridiculous cost of living there.

Now that I was crying into the phone about what a horrendous time I was having in this colorist and fatphobic hellscape after like two years, Neal's big-sister mode kicked in. And she offered a solution.

"You should come here," Neal said.

"What?" I stopped crying.

"You should come here. To Virginia. To where I am."

"But . . . how?"

"If you can get you and your car up here, then we can figure out the rest," she continued. "But we gotta get you up here first."

I hesitated to answer. Or to say anything, really. The thought of moving back in that direction, one that was a little too close to Tennessee for my comfort, was unnerving. And kind of jarring. Though it was appealing because I did need to be back in a state where I was near my brothers Craig and Tommy (they were both going *through* it at the time). But it was scary. And I didn't really know what to say to articulate all of that. Neal chimed back in when the silence became a little too unbearable. "You still there?"

"I'm still here." I nodded as if she could see me. "I just don't . . . know what to say."

"Well, what do you want to say?"

"I get what you're saying about leaving," I thought out loud.

"But . . . I feel so bad for even considering that. Do you know what I mean?"

"You mean . . . that you feel bad for possibly leaving because it would feel like you wasted your time there, right?" Neal said. I nearly gasped. Because I shit you not, it was like she had snuck into my ear, ran straight to my brain, and grabbed my thoughts right before I had a moment to piece everything together. "You'd feel like you failed? Like you lost?"

"Yeah," I whispered.

"I understand. For real," she continued. "But thirty years on this planet have proved to me that we are too fucking obsessed with failure in this country. Like, that's not what it's for. It's merely for learning what to do and what not to do. Learning what works for you and what sure as fuck *doesn't*," she explained. "You can't heal where you were hurt—which is what California is to you right now. And what Tennessee was too. Still. I don't consider California a failure for you. But I know that you do. And that your feelings supersede mine in this situation. But I just want to let you know that you didn't *fail*," Neal reassured me. "Not in the way that you're thinking, at least. You moved to a completely new state that you didn't know shit about. Didn't know anyone in it. And while it has been *shit*, you still managed to accomplish so much and make so many connections—personal and professional ones—in such a short amount of time. I personally don't think that's 'failing,' but what do I know?"

Despite everything, I laughed—no, guffawed!—into the phone, thanking her for her advice. And her loving snark.

And we both decided that I would be moving to Virginia in the new year.

IT TOOK me about two months to pack my shit up for my big move to Virginia—which I figured was a great way to start the year 2020.

Which . . . *well*. We know how that went.

But before I got there in January, I knew I needed to wrap up some loose ends in December and say goodbye to the people I would be leaving behind in LA.

My friends in the city were devastated that I was leaving. But they fully assumed the responsibility of giving me quite the beautiful and memorable send-offs. One of my friends dragged me to several clubs as a way to get all the last-minute partying out of my system. Another friend went on a series of food trips with me, which resulted in us finding the kind of hole-in-the-wall Ethiopian and Nigerian restaurants that I had been searching for the entire time. One friend straight up didn't know how to "properly" send me off, so they just helped me sort through my shit, pack, and plan some of the logistics that came with moving back to the East Coast.

And yes.

She was a Virgo.

Of course, even *after* all of that, I briefly considered leaving the state without saying shit to Emiliano. January was right around the corner, and I *personally* thought this wasn't something that he would want to be bothered with. After all, we were still on break and we hadn't really seen each other in months. We had talked a couple of times, and texted even, but not enough for me to justify reaching out about this so-called development. In short, I figured it would be pointless. Stir up unnecessary trouble and feelings.

But, like the universe always does, it heard me talking shit and saw that I was about to move incredibly *dirty*. So, wouldn't you know, I got a call from Emiliano just about a week before Christmas. He mentioned that Lia would be spending some time with her mom. And that he would love to see me, and do some much-needed catching up if I was available. If I had time.

Considering how much grimier I expected the universe to get if I opted not to acknowledge his reach-out, I ultimately decided to meet up with him in San Francisco and say all that I needed to say in person while I still could.

I REMEMBER arriving at the Airbnb that we had reserved later, and I greeted him at the door. He appeared to be a little *less* put together. Less uptight. But also less *stressed*. He had let fuzz on his face grow out even more and it was starting to form a rather beautiful beard.

"Hi," he said.

"Hi," I replied.

I stepped inside as he closed the door behind me. I had been tempted to say more. You know, compliment the aesthetic of the place that we had picked out together—just because we had such *great* taste. Truly. But before I could form a sentence in my mouth that declared just as much, I felt a hand on my back. I turned to find Emiliano staring at me. I could see that his eyes contained a well of feelings. Of nervousness. Anxiety. Mild regret. And . . . *yearning*.

"I'm sorry it's been so long," he apologized.

"No. No apologies necessary," I said. "We both *needed* that time away." He exhaled slowly, visibly relieved. We were still fairly close though and I looked up at his face. I'm not ashamed to say it. Nor am I ashamed to say that my eyes lingered a bit on his lips. Not because I immediately wanted to jump on him or whatever. But mainly because I liked seeing his face again— lips included. It was comforting. Familiar. And one of the few things that brought me a little bit of joy—despite the complications—while I was in California.

He caught me looking. And while I can't be sure that he was sifting through the same thoughts that I currently was in my head, he cast an equally thoughtful look over me. And before I knew it, our lips were inches apart.

"Emiliano . . ." I put a hand on his chest.

"I—I'm sorry. I don't know why I did tha—" He got flustered. I put a finger to his mouth, stopping him.

"If you would let me finish, I was gonna ask if you had a condom," I said quietly. A slow and genuinely relieved smile started to move across his face and he picked me up as if to respond.

"Yes, yes I do," he replied.

I told him I was moving after the fact. After we had fucked each other senseless.

It was a dirty move. I know. But I figured my departure would be easier to swallow if we both had that final romp. A final memory to hold on to.

We ended up at *the* spot. The one overlooking the city. The one where this whole thing began. Emiliano parked his car and we ended up sitting on its hood together. The moon was big and round tonight, which was a source of solace for me. I closed my eyes, letting her light hit my face.

"I'm gonna ask the thing I'm not supposed to ask," Emiliano finally said after a long silence. "But because I respect you, I want to be hon—"

"I'm not moving because of *you*. If that's what you're thinking." I opened my eyes and looked over at him. "Which is a tad bit narcissistic of you, just so we're clear."

"I know, I know. I'm sorry."

"Thank you."

"So what's gonna happen now?"

"I don't know." I shrugged. "I guess I'll find out in Virginia. When I get there. Either way though? It means I get some sort of clean slate. Away from this fucking place. Thankfully."

"I'm happy to hear that," he added. "It's . . . *exactly* what you need. And I think it's gonna do you a lot of good."

"It's good to hear you say that." I cocked my head to the side. I hadn't expected him to be so receptive, I admit. It was heartwarming. "Thank you. Means a lot."

It looked like he wanted to say more. And I'm sure he was going to say more. He hesitated though, looking down at his hands like he was about to say the most important thing that he had ever said in his life.

"I'm going to miss you," he finally confessed. I probably should have responded with the same kind of vulnerability and quiet sentimentality. But mainly? I was a little shook. He had been *überconservative* about discussing his feelings for the past couple of months. So the thought of him being this frank with them now was very ... *unexpected.* Almost strange.

And I reacted as such.

"Oh God." I fought the urge to roll my eyes. "Em, I'm not dying, okay? We'll still talk or whateve—"

He cut me off. "That's *not* what I mean. We won't be as close. You know. Distance-wise?"

"I'm aware."

"I wish things had been different," he said after a brief pause. "I have such shitty timing, I swear to God." He chuckled sadly. I looked at him. My friend of nearly a decade. My lover too. And decided that I wasn't going to let him take *all* of the responsibility for how both of our lives were just too chaotic to handle a serious relationship right now.

"Well, I have it too, you know." I smirked. "Shitty timing. That's kind of my thing. Can't let you hoard all of the cosmic blame for our collective shitty luck." I nudged one of his shoulders. "I'm gonna miss you too. By the way."

"Took you long enough." He chuckled. "To say it, I mean."

"Mmmhmm. You're not the only one who would rather not acknowledge their feelings."

"Oooooof, I deserve that."

"Yeah, you do." I winked at him.

After trading a couple of more barbs, our conversation melted into this ... serene quietness that was only made sweeter by staring at this cosmic wonder, the moon, together. Hand-in-hand. I felt his thumb move across the back of my hand and I looked over at him—figuring that he was trying to get my attention. He set my hand down gently and proceeded to place one of his hands against my right cheek. I leaned into it, closing my eyes.

"*Alex.* Can I—" He hesitated.

"Kiss me?" I opened my eyes again. "I feel like that would be more than appropriate, *Emiliano.*"

Delighted, Emiliano brought his lips closer, pressing them

to mine. I returned his kiss, relishing the fact that it felt just as needy, *frantic*, and passionate as the first time we had done it. We both lay back on the hood of his car. My hands cradled his face and thumbed through his hair. His hands cradling my face and his lips adorning my neck with kisses. Kissing for God knows how long.

It was a silent prayer. A quiet wish. One that asked the universe if there would ever be a moment on this planet, in this universe, where *this* worked. Where our lives weren't convoluted clusterfucks that proved to be highly *incompatible* clusterfucks in a whole clusterfuck puzzle (at least at this current moment in our lives). Where timing wasn't a troll that was out to beat both of our asses. Or spit in our faces. Or goad us into sabotaging both ourselves and our relationship in ways that we might not be able to recover from.

This prayer didn't receive an instantaneous answer. Because prayers don't work like that. *Obviously.* But . . . it was a prayer nonetheless. One that I was content in letting hang in the air, even as the temperature of San Francisco fell around us and the coldest breeze slid alongside our bodies.

This would be my farewell to this place.

This would be my farewell to the parts of me that were both molded and destroyed by this state. This would be where I bid the uglier parts of myself adieu—the parts that didn't initially want to interrogate why my fatphobic, colorist, biphobic, and ableist internalizations were once again rearing their ugly heads. This would be my *so long* to the audacity of my eating disorders thinking they had *any* right to entrap me once more. This would be my au revoir to the part of me that conflated lack of perfection in all things—in all aspects—with failure.

This would be my farewell.

My unofficial goodbye.

MY GRAND CLOSING

For twenty-seven years, I've been on a journey home. Not in the geographical sense, as one might assume. But rather somewhere between the physical and the metaphorical.

A journey back home to me, Alex, and my body. And a parallel journey from Alex to, proudly, Clarkisha.

And speaking of journeys, I always thought that it was fucking bonkers that it took Odysseus TWENTY fucking years to get home in *The Odyssey*. Forget the fact that the motherfucker was sent off to a TEN-YEAR war, over a basic bitch, that he didn't even want to participate in (and would have very much avoided if it wasn't for resident rat bastard Palamedes). But even after he somehow survived the war, Poseidon then proceeded to send ol' boy and his life into another TEN-YEAR tailspin for *rightfully* blinding his bitch-ass son—Polyphemus—after the latter proudly exercised poor xenia (read: hospitality) by eating a chunk of Ody's crew and trying to prevent the rest of them from leaving.

Homeboy then proceeded to experience cartoonishly outlandish back-to-back calamities that left him with no ship, no crew, and in the extended "care" of Calypso as her prisoner/lover.

I remember reading all that shit and being like, "This man was absolutely set up." Like, the sheer volume of misfortunes that kept slapping this man upside the head was so ridiculous that for a minute there, I truly assumed that Odysseus was just destined to fail. That he wouldn't be making it home at all. That it was a fruitless endeavor to begin with.

Of course, that eventually turned out to not be the case, but I can't help but reflect on the concept of being "set up" where my life is concerned—be it through racism, fatphobia, colorism, texturism, ableism, homophobia—and how I too almost didn't make it back either.

For any young Black girl or seasoned Black woman, the journey back to their body is central both to their origin story and their life story. For them—for us—true self-actualization cannot and will not occur until that journey is complete.

And not a moment sooner.

Much of my enduring love and respect for bell hooks (RIP) lies in the fact that she was steadfast in maintaining that love cannot be fostered in a body that is hated by the woman who occupies it. That hatred of one's body can prove to be a hostile work environment for one's self-esteem.

bell spoke about these ideas at length in *Communion: The Female Search for Love*. Particularly in chapter 8, "grow into a woman's body and love it." But what struck me the most about her observations and cultural analysis here wasn't the more obvious references to the importance of self-love but rather the most insidious force at the center of female self-hatred: fatphobia.

Ironically, bell doesn't explicitly mention the word *fatphobia* in the aforementioned chapter. Not even once. But she very much describes important components of it. She mentions mothers' obsession with their daughters' bodies and the nigh-fascist violence they deploy against them when they fall short—falling short usually means failure to maintain thinness. She mentions fathers who also hyperfixate on their daughters' weight and lack of thinness under the guise of "health" and true "beauty." She even mentions aspiring partners and the fact that thinness, or rather, lack thereof, will be a deciding factor in whether a cis(het) man, in particular, will award them the coveted love that they so desperately crave and most certainly deserve.

She ties this hyperfixation on thinness—and the personal and material value that is attributed to thinness—to the disturbing and tragic prevalence of eating disorders. Sharing her own battle with being "thin anorexically" and experiencing "difficulty eating," she points out the absurdity of modern feminist movements not moving past the "awareness" stage of this pressing issue while claiming to be about self-love in a searing line: "Love your body, but make sure you *starve* it so you can be thin and *beautiful*."

I am quite grateful to bell for railing against thinness as she did in that chapter. And it is important that she is a Black woman doing it—since the origins of fatphobia do not belong to us. Nor is it ours to hold. For it was imposed on us by so-called superior Europeans, who, to racially separate themselves from "gluttonous" and "dim-witted" Africans, found our bodies to be too plump, too corpulent, and too *obscene* upon laying eyes on them.

Word to Sarah "Saartjie" Baartman.

bell taught me a couple of things with that chapter. Most importantly that society-imposed thinness is a form of control when it comes to women and young girls. You are taught to be smaller. You are instructed to stuff all your multitudes into the tiniest frame. And you are forced to take up less space.

The latter is exactly the opposite of what fatness does. And how it functions. Fatness does require space. Demands it. It needs elbow room. And it cannot be easily contained or tamed, nor does it want to be.

If you're someone like me, who has had lifelong struggles with "losing" weight, think of all the times we've been told about pockets of "stubborn fat" on our bodies. Think about how often you cussed those "piece-of-shit" pockets of "stubborn fat" out for occupying precious real estate on your stomach. Think of every flat-tummy recipe and belly-blasting exercise that promised to vaporize lingering fat, only for your fat stomach to stare back at you defiantly. In a "well, that didn't go how you thought that would go, now did it?" kinda way.

Because it's meant to be there. And it was always meant to be there.

Fatness makes a woman and her body a little less controllable. A little less governable. And a little less concerned with chasing whatever body "trend" is being pushed—by the diet industry, by the clothing industry, and by mass media at-large—onto them to suck them into the hamster wheel that is figuring out what is desirable to the common cis(het) man at the moment.

Because it is fatness's demand for space to live, for space to grow, for space to move, for space to expand, for space to prosper, and for space to love openly and *freely* that makes its existence quite, quite radical.

For a long time, I considered fatness to be my adversary, which translated into hatred toward my body. My aversion to fatness made my body my sworn enemy. A nemesis to rival all my nemeses—second only to my enduring loathing of Lena Dunham. But now I'm beginning to understand that my (fat) body was never my opposition. No. She was, in fact, my companion.

She had been with me, in spirit, on this very ghetto and completely unserious path we call life, the entire time. Even during the times that I hated her, couldn't stand her, and couldn't bear to look at her. She remained. Waiting for my triumphant return.

As I am writing this, I've now graduated to the ripe old age of twenty-eight. And my journey back to my fat-ass body is near completion. Now, this doesn't mean that I have achieved full acceptance. I am very much still a big bitch who is human and who will continue to contend with personal and societal messaging that would have me backslide.

Still. No matter where I am on this journey or where I decide to go thereafter, I will honor this body of mine. In all of her glory. Whether she remains fat or not. For she is my protector. My provider. And my shelter.

She is me.

ACKNOWLEDGMENTS

I've never written an acknowledgments section before. Truly. And because I sort of wanted to avoid the awkwardness that surely comes with doing something for the first time, at risk of not doing it *perfectly*, I almost decided against it. However, as my sister told me and as it has already been said, no nigga is an island. Okay, I'm paraphrasing! Still, as I was saying, this journey included countless people. Many people! Some people I can't even name here because I would run out of pages.

That said, I'm going to try.

To Claire Draper. My agent. To think that this all started when you slipped into my DMs! Thanks for trusting yourself enough to take a chance on me. And always advocating for me. It's a pleasure to know you and it's been a pleasure getting to know you. Thank you.

To Jordan. From Facebook friends to family! You are the *best* sister I could ask for! The absolute best. I have learned so much shit from you and, sure, you didn't ask to be a role model, but you're mine anyway (deal with it). I love you very much. And don't you forget it.

To Bria and Alexius. My partners in crime and chaos. What a crazy-ass ride it's been with you all. From sitting in my car during high school and talking about sex bushes and brother-husbands to y'all being the very FIRST people to check on me in person after my house fire, y'all are some real-ass niggas. And I am so grateful to have y'all in my life.

To Vince. Thank you for being part of so many important milestones in my life. And for sticking with me even when I didn't have the spoons to show up as my best self. It's been quite the wild ride with you as well. And I'm so excited to see what the next decade looks like for us.

To Rude Astrology. What a time it's been since we met! Thank you for blessing my life with something as sacred and life-changing as astrology (and your friendship). I honestly don't know or remember how I functioned without it.

To Syd. Thank you for saying what always needs to be said about fatphobia even when it's hard. Even when it's unpopular. Much of the conclusions I come to in this book would not have happened without you.

To Stephanie. Thank you for being fearless and for always being truthful about the reality of dating as a fat, dark-skinned Black woman. You've named my feelings many times over and validated my struggles in so many ways. Thank you.

To Vilissa. My favorite Virgo! I've learned so much from you where ableism is concerned. Your ceaseless work and advocacy for disabled Black people led me to research bipolar disorder and get a diagnosis that had escaped me for a long time. Thank you.

To Tory, Oli, Tor, and Aleezé. Thank you for making my time at UChicago so much easier than it could have been. Your friendship—both together and separately—got me through the last two years of that hellscape post-injury and I don't take that kind of gift, the gift of friendship, lightly.

To Queen. My oldest friend. BITCH! We did it. We made it. I can't believe it. Can you imagine? We did nearly everything we set out to do? Much to the chagrin of our immigrant parents? Ah! I am so glad to still have you in my life. And it has been an honor and a privilege to grow, change, progress, and evolve right next to you.

To Yesha. Thank you for blessing me with my first-ever professional writing job. Nobody wanted to take a chance on my writing until you did and I will never forget that. Thank you.

To Kiku. Thank you for gifting me with your friendship and welcoming me into your home. You arrived in my life at a particularly dark and scary time when I was taking a huge leap in a new (and really tough) city.

To Tika. Thank you for being absolutely fearless when it comes to sticking a middle finger up at colorism. And thank you for helping me confront the ways that I had internalized it. I feel very blessed to know you.

To Jon. One of my favorite Black femmes! Thank you for linking arms with me in the trenches while we were trying to make shit happen as writers in LA. It has been such an honor to know you and watch you grow and succeed.

And to the folks at the Feminist Press. Thank you for taking a chance on *Fat Off, Fat On.*

PHOTO © CHEYENNE EWULU

CLARKISHA KENT is a Nigerian American writer, culture critic, former columnist, and author. Her writing has been featured in outlets like *Entertainment Weekly*, *Essence*, *gal-dem*, *Paper*, BET, HuffPost, MTV News, The Root, and more. She is also the creator of #TheKentTest, a media litmus test designed to evaluate the quality of representation that exists for Black women and women of color in film and other media.

More Nonfiction from the Feminist Press

**Against Memoir: Complaints,
Confessions & Criticisms**
by Michelle Tea

Black Dove: Mamá, Mi'jo, and Me
by Ana Castillo

**But Some of Us Are Brave:
Black Women's Studies (Second Edition)**
edited by Akasha (Gloria T.) Hull, Patricia Bell Scott,
and Barbara Smith

The Crunk Feminist Collection
edited by Brittney C. Cooper, Susana M. Morris,
and Robin M. Boylorn

Enjoy Me among My Ruins
by Juniper Fitzgerald

Grieving: Dispatches from a Wounded Country
by Cristina Rivera Garza,
translated by Sarah Booker

**It Came from the Closet:
Queer Reflections on Horror**
edited by Joe Vallese

**Parenting for Liberation:
A Guide for Raising Black Children**
by Trina Greene Brown

**Radical Reproductive Justice:
Foundations, Theory, Practice, Critique**
edited by Loretta J. Ross, Lynn Roberts, Erika Derkas,
Whitney Peoples, and Pamela Bridgewater Toure

Tastes Like War: A Memoir
by Grace M. Cho

You Have the Right to Remain Fat
by Virgie Tovar

The Feminist Press publishes books that ignite movements and social transformation. Celebrating our legacy, we lift up insurgent and marginalized voices from around the world to build a more just future.

See our complete list of books at
feministpress.org

THE FEMINIST PRESS
AT THE CITY UNIVERSITY OF NEW YORK
FEMINISTPRESS.ORG